The Institute of Chartered Accountants in England and Wales

ASSURANCE

For exams in 2018

Study Manual

ICAEW

www.icaew.com

Assurance
The Institute of Chartered Accountants in England and Wales

ISBN: 978-1-78363-692-1
Previous ISBN: 978-1-78363-454-5

First edition 2007
Eleventh edition 2017

The content of this publication is intended to prepare students for the ICAEW
examinations, and should not be used as professional advice.

British Library Cataloguing-in-Publication Data
A catalogue record for this book is available from the British Library

Originally printed in the United Kingdom on paper obtained from traceable,
sustainable sources.

Welcome to ICAEW

As the future of our profession, I'd like to personally welcome you to ICAEW.

In a constantly changing and volatile environment, the role of the accountancy profession has never been more important to create a world of strong economies, together. ICAEW Chartered Accountants make decisions that will define the future of global business by sharing our knowledge, skills and insight.

Whether you are studying our Certificate in Finance, Accounting and Business (ICAEW CFAB) or our world-leading chartered accountancy qualification, the ACA, you are not only investing in your own future but also gaining the skills and values to meet the challenges of technological change and contribute to future business success.

Joining over 147,000 chartered accountants and over 25,000 fellow students worldwide, you are now part of something special. This unique network of talented and diverse professionals has the knowledge, skills and commitment to maintain the highest professional standards and integrity.

You are all supported by ICAEW as you progress through your studies and career: we will be with you every step of the way to ensure you are ready to face the fast-paced changes of the global economy. Visit page vi to review the key resources available as you study.

It's with our training, guidance and support that our members, and you, will realise career ambitions, develop insights that matter and maintain a competitive edge.

I wish you the best of luck with your studies and look forward to welcoming you to the profession.

Michael Izza
Chief Executive
ICAEW

Contents

Questions within the study manual should be treated as preparation questions, providing you with a firm foundation before you attempt the exam standard questions. The exam standard questions are found in the question bank.

1 Introduction

ACA qualification

The ICAEW chartered accountancy qualification, the ACA, is a world-leading professional qualification in accountancy, finance and business.

The ACA has integrated components that will give you an in-depth understanding across accountancy, finance and business. Combined, they help build the technical knowledge, professional skills and practical experience needed to become an ICAEW Chartered Accountant.

Each component is designed to complement each other, which means that you can put theory into practice and you can understand and apply what you learn to your day-to-day work. Progression through all the elements of the ACA simultaneously will enable you to be more successful in the workplace and exams.

The components are:

- professional development
- ethics and professional scepticism
- three to five years practical work experience
- 15 accountancy, finance and business modules

To find out more on the components of the ACA and what is involved in training, visit your dashboard at icaew.com/dashboard.

ICAEW Certificate in Finance, Accounting and Business

The ICAEW Certificate in Finance, Accounting and Business (ICAEW CFAB) teaches essential skills and knowledge in the three key areas of finance, accounting and business.

ICAEW CFAB consists of the same six modules as the first level of our world-leading qualification, the ACA. This means, it can serve as a stand-alone qualification or as a stepping stone on your journey towards chartered accountancy.

You can find out more about the ICAEW CFAB exams and syllabus at icaew.com/cfabstudents.

To learn more about the ACA qualification and chartered accountancy, visit icaew.com/careers.

Key resources

Whether you're studying the ACA qualification or ICAEW CFAB, we provide a wide range of fantastic resources and services to help you in your studies. They can be found on our website. Depending on the qualification you are studying, be sure to visit the specific area for you.

For dedicated exam resources, guidance and information for the ACA qualification, log in to your dashboard at icaew.com/dashboard.

For everything you need while studying the ICAEW CFAB qualification go to icaew.com/cfabstudents.

If you have a question, our student support team is on hand to help and advise you throughout your studies, don't hesitate to get in touch. Email studentsupport@icaew.com or call +44 (0)1908 248 250 to speak to an adviser.

2 Assurance

The full syllabus and technical knowledge grids can be found within the module study guide.

You can access this guide and more exam resources on our website. If you are studying this exam as part of the ACA qualification go to icaew.com/examresources or if you are studying the ICAEW CFAB qualification go to icaew.com/cfabstudents.

2.1 Module aim

To ensure that students understand the assurance process and fundamental principles of ethics, and are able to contribute to the assessment of internal controls and gathering of evidence on an assurance engagement.

On completion of this module, students will be able to:

- explain the concept of assurance, why assurance is required and the reasons for assurance engagements being carried out by appropriately qualified professionals;

- explain the nature of internal controls and why they are important, document an organisation's internal controls and identify weaknesses in internal control systems;

- select sufficient and appropriate methods of obtaining assurance evidence and recognise when conclusions can be drawn from evidence obtained or where issues need to be referred to a senior colleague; and

- understand the importance of ethical behaviour to a professional and identify issues relating to integrity, objectivity, professional competence and due care, confidentiality, professional behaviour and independence.

2.2 Method of assessment

The Assurance module is assessed by a 1.5 hour computer-based exam. The exam consists of 50 questions worth two marks each, covering the areas of the syllabus in accordance with the weightings set out in the specification grid. The questions are presented in the form of multiple choice, multi-part multiple choice, or multiple response.

2.3 Specification grid

This grid shows the relative weightings of subjects within this module and should guide the relative study time spent on each. Over time the marks available in the assessment will equate to the weightings below, while slight variations may occur in individual assessments to enable suitably rigorous questions to be set.

		Weighting (%)
1	The concept, process and need for assurance	20
2	Internal controls	25
3	Gathering evidence on an assurance engagement	35
4	Professional ethics	20
		100

CHAPTER 1

Concept of and need for assurance

Introduction

Examination context

Topic List

    1   What is assurance?

    2   Why is assurance important?

    3   Why can assurance never be absolute?

    4   The statutory audit

Summary and Self-test

Answers to Interactive questions

Answers to Self-test

Introduction

Learning objectives

- Understand the concept of assurance ☐
- Recognise the criteria which constitute an assurance engagement ☐
- Recognise subject matter suitable to be the subject of an assurance engagement ☐
- Understand the different levels of assurance that can be provided in an assurance engagement, including reasonable assurance ☐
- Understand the need for professional accountants to carry out assurance work in the public interest ☐
- Understand the meaning of 'a true and fair view' ☐
- Understand why users desire assurance reports and recognise examples of the benefits gained from them such as to assure the quality of an entity's published corporate responsibility or sustainability report ☐
- Compare the functions and responsibilities of the different parties involved in an assurance engagement ☐
- Understand the issues which can lead to gaps between the outcomes delivered by the assurance engagement and the expectations of users of the assurance reports ☐
- Identify how these 'expectations gaps' can be overcome ☐

Specific syllabus references for this chapter are: 1a, b, c, d, e, h.

Syllabus links

You have studied the basic books, records and financial statements of a company in the *Accounting* paper. It is in relation to these records that the auditor will seek evidence to be able to give assurance.

As already mentioned, audit is a key form of assurance and you will be able to apply the basic principles learnt in this paper to that form of assurance service both here and in the *Audit and Assurance* paper.

Examination context

It is crucial to the whole syllabus that you understand the concept of assurance, why it is required and the reason for assurance engagements being carried out by appropriately qualified professionals. You can therefore expect to see questions in the exam testing your understanding of the definition of assurance and the different levels of assurance.

In the sample paper, the first five questions relate to the subject matter you will cover in this chapter.

In the assessment, candidates may be required to:

- describe the concept of assurance
- state the benefits of an assurance report
- compare the functions and responsibilities of the different parties involved in an assurance engagement
- describe the levels of assurance obtained from different types of assurance engagement
- describe the concept of the 'expectations gap'

1   What is assurance?

Section overview

- An assurance engagement is one in which a practitioner expresses a conclusion, designed to enhance the degree of confidence of the intended users, other than the responsible party, about the outcome of the evaluation or measurement of a subject matter against criteria.

- Key elements are: three party involvement, subject matter, suitable criteria, sufficient appropriate evidence, written report.

- Assurance engagements can give either a reasonable level of assurance or a limited level of assurance.

- There are various examples of assurance services, the key example in the UK is the audit.

1.1   Definition (parties, subject matter, criteria)

Definition

An **assurance engagement** is one in which a practitioner expresses a conclusion designed to enhance the degree of confidence of the intended users other than the responsible party about the outcome of the evaluation or measurement of a subject matter against criteria.

The key elements of an assurance engagement are as follows:

- Three people or groups of people involved

    - The practitioner (accountant)
    - The intended users
    - The responsible party (the person(s) who prepared the subject matter)

- A subject matter

    As we shall see below, the subject matter of an assurance engagement may vary considerably. However, it is likely to fall into one of three categories:

    - Data (for example, financial statements or business projections)
    - Systems or processes (for example, internal control systems or computer systems)
    - Behaviour (for example, social and environmental performance or corporate governance)

- Suitable criteria

    The person providing the assurance must have something by which to judge whether the information is reliable and can be trusted. So for example, in an assurance engagement relating to financial statements, the criteria might be accounting standards. The practitioner will be able to test whether the financial statements have been put together in accordance with accounting standards, and if they have, then the practitioner can conclude that there is a degree of assurance that they are reliable.

    In the context of company behaviour, suitable criteria to judge whether something is reliable and can be trusted might be the UK Corporate Governance Code, or, if the company has one, its published Code of Practice.

- Sufficient appropriate evidence to support the assurance opinion

    The practitioner must substantiate the opinion that he draws in order that the user can have confidence that it is reliable. The practitioner must obtain evidence as to whether the criteria have been met. We will look at the collection of evidence in detail later in this Study Manual.

- A written report in appropriate form

Lastly, it is required that assurance reports are provided to the intended users in a written form and contain certain specified information. This adds to the assurance that the user is being given, as it ensures that key information is being given and that the assurance given is clear and unequivocal.

Worked example: Assurance engagement

In order to demonstrate these elements of an assurance engagement, the Worked example is that of a house purchase. Imagine you are buying a house. There are certain issues you would want assurance about, particularly whether the house is structurally sound. In this situation, you would be unlikely just to trust the word of the person who was selling the house but would seek the additional assurance of a qualified professional, such as a surveyor.

You should already be able to see the first key element of an assurance engagement, which is the involvement of three people:

- you (the intended user);
- the house owner (the responsible party); and
- the surveyor (the practitioner).

The subject matter of this assurance engagement is the house in question. The surveyor will visit the house to test whether it is sound and will draw a conclusion.

The surveyor will judge whether the house is sound in the context of building regulations, planning rules and best practice in the building industry. These are the criteria by which he will judge whether he can give you assurance that the house is structurally sound.

In order to make a conclusion, the surveyor will obtain evidence from the house (for example, by looking for damp patches and making inspections of key elements of the house).

Lastly, when he has drawn a conclusion, the surveyor will issue a report to you, outlining his opinion as to whether the house is sound or not. This report will contain any limitations to his work, for example, if he was unable to access any of the property or he was unable to lift fitted carpets to inspect the floor underneath them.

Ultimately, when you have read the surveyor's report, you will have more assurance about the state of the property, and correspondingly, more confidence to pay the deposit, take out a mortgage and buy that house.

Interactive question 1: Assurance engagement

You are an accountant who has been approached by Jamal, who wants to invest in Company X. He has asked you for assurance whether the most recent financial statements of Company X are a reliable basis for him to make his investment decision.

Requirement

Identify the key elements of an assurance engagement in this scenario, if you accepted the engagement.

See **Answer** at the end of this chapter.

1.2 Levels of assurance

The definition of an assurance engagement given above is taken from the International Framework for Assurance Engagements, which is issued by the International Federation of Accountants (IFAC), a global organisation for the accountancy profession, which works with its member organisations to protect the public interest by encouraging high quality practices around the world. ICAEW is a member of IFAC.

The Framework identifies two types of assurance engagement:

- reasonable assurance engagement; and
- limited assurance engagement.

Definitions

Reasonable assurance: A high level of assurance, that is less than absolute assurance, that engagement risk has been reduced to an acceptably low level, which then allows a conclusion to be expressed positively.

Limited assurance: A meaningful level of assurance, that is more than inconsequential but is less than reasonable assurance, that engagement risk has been reduced to an acceptable level, which then allows a conclusion to be expressed negatively.

The reason that there are two types of assurance engagement is that the level of assurance that can be given depends on the evidence that can be obtained by the practitioner. Using the surveyor example above, a surveyor can only give assurance that a property is structurally sound if he is allowed to enter the property to inspect it. If he is only given access to part of the building, he can only give limited assurance.

The key differences between the two types of assurance engagement are therefore:

- the evidence obtained
- the type of opinion given

We shall look in detail at obtaining evidence later in this Study Manual. The key point about evidence is that in all assurance engagements, sufficient, appropriate evidence must be obtained. We will look at what constitutes sufficient, appropriate evidence as we go through the course. What determines whether evidence is sufficient and appropriate is the level of assurance that the practitioner is trying to give, so it is tied in with the type of opinion being given, which we shall look at here. In summary, a lower level of evidence will be obtained for a limited assurance engagement.

The opinion given in an assurance engagement therefore depends on what type of engagement it is. As noted above, there are two levels of assurance expressed positively and negatively.

Say, for example, that a practitioner is seeking evidence to conclude whether the report issued by the Chairman of a company in the financial statements is reasonable or not. He could seek evidence, conclude that the statement is reasonable and state in a report something like this:

'In my opinion, the statement by the Chairman regarding X is reasonable'.

This is a positive statement of his conclusion that the statement is reasonable. Alternatively, he could state in a report something like this:

'In the course of my seeking evidence about the statement by the Chairman, nothing has come to my attention indicating that the statement is not reasonable.'

This conclusion is less certain, as it implies that matters could exist which cause the statement to be unreasonable, but that the practitioner has not uncovered any such matters. This is therefore called limited assurance. It is the conclusion that a practitioner gives when he carries out a limited assurance engagement and seeks a lower level of evidence.

Summary of types of engagement		
Type of engagement	Evidence sought	Conclusion given
Reasonable assurance	Sufficient and appropriate	Positive wording
Limited assurance	Sufficient and appropriate (lower level)	Negative wording

1.3 Examples of assurance engagements

The key example of an assurance engagement in the UK is a statutory audit. We shall look at the nature of this engagement later on in this chapter.

Other examples of assurance engagements include other audits, which may be specialised due to the nature of the business, for example:

- Local authority audits (audits of local authorities, with specific reporting requirements which differ from the statutory audit)

- Insurance company audits, bank audits, pension scheme audits (audits of often complex companies in a highly-regulated industry)

- Charity audits (charities may be audited under the Companies Act or the Charities Act)

- Solicitors' audits (audits of firms of solicitors in line with the Solicitors' Accounts Rules)

- Branch audit (where an overseas company trades in the UK through a branch and requires an audit of that branch although an audit is not required by UK law)

There are also many issues users want assurance on, where the terms of the engagement will be agreed between the practitioner and the person commissioning the report, for example:

- Value for money studies (for example, in the public sector where auditors may be asked to conclude on whether a service provides value for money)

- Environmental audits (assurance engagements on information given about an organisation's impact on the natural environment)

- Internal audit

- Circulation reports (for example, for magazines)

- Cost/benefit reports

- Due diligence (where a report is requested on an acquisition target)

- Reviews of specialist business activities

- Reports on website security, such as WebTrust

- Fraud investigations

- Inventories and receivables reports

- Internal control reports

- Reports on business plans or projections

2 Why is assurance important?

Section overview
- Who the users are will depend on the nature of the subject matter.
- Users benefit from receiving an independent, professional opinion on the subject matter.
- Users may also benefit from additional confidence in the subject matter given to others.
- The existence of an assurance service may prevent errors or frauds occurring in the first place.

2.1 Users

In the key assurance service of audit, which we looked at above, the users were the shareholders of a company, to whom the financial statements are addressed. In other cases, the users might be the board of directors of a company or a subsection of them.

2.2 Benefits of assurance

The key benefit of assurance is the **independent, professional verification** being given to the users. This can be seen in the example of the house purchase given above. The importance of independence and objectivity in assurance provision will be looked at in Chapters 14 and 15.

In addition, assurance may have subsidiary benefits.

Although an assurance report may only be addressed to one set of people, it may give additional confidence to other parties in a way that benefits the business. For example, audit reports are addressed to shareholders, but the existence of an unqualified audit report might give the bank more confidence to lend money to that business; in other words, it enhances the credibility of the information.

The existence of an independent check might help prevent errors or frauds being made and reduce the risk of management bias. In other words, the fact that an assurance service will be carried out might make people involved in preparing the subject matter more careful in its preparation and reduce the chance of errors arising. Therefore it can be seen that an assurance service may act as a deterrent.

In addition, where problems exist within information, the existence of an assurance report draws attention to the deficiencies in that information, so that users know what those deficiencies are.

Assurance is also important in more general terms. It helps to ensure that high quality, reliable information exists, leading to effective markets that investors have faith in and trust. It adds to the reputation of organisations and even countries, so that investors are happy to invest in country X because there is a strong culture of assurance provision there.

Businesses are keen to be seen as acting responsibly and are increasingly publishing information such as emissions targets or a pledge not to employ children. There is a growing public perception that this is an important area and stakeholders are unlikely to associate with businesses that could damage their reputation. Corporate responsibility or sustainability reports provide assurance for stakeholders that this published information is reliable and accurate.

3 Why can assurance never be absolute?

Section overview

- Assurance can never be absolute.
- Assurance provision has limitations which may not be understood by users.
- The expectations gap also adds to the lack of guarantee given by assurance.

Assurance can never be absolute. Assurance providers will never give a certification of absolute correctness due to the limitations set out below.

3.1 Limitations of assurance

A key issue for accountants is that there are limitations to assurance services, and therefore there is always a risk involved that the wrong conclusion will be drawn. We shall look in more detail at this issue of assurance engagement risk in Chapter 3.

The limitations of assurance services include:

- the fact that testing is used – the auditors do not oversee the process of building the financial statements from start to finish.

- the fact that the accounting systems on which assurance providers may place a degree of reliance also have inherent limitations (we shall look at control systems and their limitations in Chapter 5).

- the fact that most audit evidence is persuasive rather than conclusive.

- the fact that assurance providers would not test every item in the subject matter (this would be prohibitively expensive for the responsible party, so a sampling approach is used – see Chapter 11).

- the fact that the client's staff members may collude in fraud that can then be deliberately hidden from the auditor or misrepresent matters to them for the same purpose.

- the fact that assurance provision can be subjective and professional judgements have to be made (for example, about what aspects of the subject matter are the most important, how much evidence to obtain etc).

- the fact that assurance providers rely on the responsible party and its staff to provide correct information, which in some cases may be impossible to verify by other means.

- the fact that some items in the subject matter may be estimates and are therefore uncertain. It is impossible to conclude absolutely that judgemental estimates are correct.

- the fact that the nature of the assurance report might itself be limiting, as every judgement and conclusion the assurance provider has drawn cannot be included in it.

3.2 The expectations gap

The problems users may experience in connection with assurance provision also arise from the limitations and restrictions inherent in assurance provision. This is often because users are not aware of the nature of the limitations on assurance provision, or do not understand them and believe that the assurance provider is offering a service (such as a guarantee of correctness) which in fact he is not.

The distinction between reasonable and limited assurance may also be misunderstood by users.

We shall look at the concept of the expectations gap in more detail in Chapter 4, in the context of reporting, but in essence it is this lack of understanding which constitutes the expectations gap – meaning that there is a gap between what the assurance provider understands he is doing and what the user of the information believes he is doing.

Assurance providers need to close this gap as far as possible in order to maintain the value of the assurance provided for the user. This is done in a variety of ways, for example, by issuing an engagement letter spelling out the work that will be carried out and the limitations of that work (which we shall look at in the next chapter) and by regularly reviewing the format and content of reports issued as a result of assurance work.

Interactive question 2: Benefits of assurance

Which **three** of the following are benefits of assurance work?

- [x] An independent, professional opinion
- [x] Additional confidence given to other related parties
- [ ] Testing as a result of sampling is cheaper for the responsible party
- [ ] Judgements on estimates can be conclusive
- [x] Assurance may act as a deterrent to error or fraud

See **Answer** at the end of this chapter.

4 The statutory audit

Section overview

- The statutory audit is the key example of an assurance engagement in the UK.

- Auditors are subject to a variety of legal and professional requirements.

- Audits are composed of five principal stages: obtaining the engagement, planning, procedures, review, and reporting.

- Professional scepticism is an important aspect of the auditor's skillset.

4.1 Statutory audit

An audit is historically the most important type of assurance service in the UK. This is because it is a legal (statutory) requirement that all companies over a certain size have an audit (with small companies being exempt). The statutory external audit is therefore one of the most common forms of assurance engagements.

Definition

The objective of an **audit of financial statements** is to enable the auditor to express an opinion whether the financial statements are prepared, in all material respects, in accordance with an applicable financial reporting framework.

Worked example: Audit

The key criteria of an assurance engagement can be seen in an audit as follows:

- Three party involvement

    - The shareholders (users)
    - The board of directors (the responsible party)
    - The audit firm (the practitioner)

- Subject matter

    - The financial statements

- Relevant criteria

    - Law and accounting standards

- Evidence

    - As has been said earlier, sufficient and appropriate evidence is required to support an assurance opinion. The specific requirements in relation to evidence on assurance engagements will be looked at in Chapters 4 and 11.

- Written report in a suitable form

    - Again, as has been said, an assurance report is a written report issued in a prescribed form. We will look at the specific requirements for an audit report in Chapter 4.

The key outcome of the statutory audit is the audit opinion. In the UK, the auditor will normally express his audit opinion by reference to the 'true and fair view', which is an expression of reasonable assurance. Whilst this term is at the heart of the audit, 'true' and 'fair' are not defined in law or audit guidance. However, for practical purposes the following definitions are generally accepted.

Definitions

True: Information is factual and conforms with reality, not false. In addition the information conforms with required standards and law. The accounts have been correctly extracted from the books and records.

Fair: Information is free from discrimination and bias in compliance with expected standards and rules. The accounts should reflect the commercial substance of the company's underlying transactions.

4.2 Audit exemption in the UK

Small companies are not required to have an audit in the UK (except in some particular situations). How do we tell if a company is small enough? We have the Companies Act 2006 requirements. A company must meet two of three of the following criteria, for both this financial year and the last financial year:

	Periods beginning on or after 1 January 2016
Turnover	< £10.2m
Total assets	< £5.1m
Number of employees	< 50

All companies above these thresholds must have an audit.

4.3 Legal and professional requirements

Auditors in the UK are subject to both legal and professional requirements. The legal requirements are all contained within the Companies Act 2006.

The Companies Act requires that auditors are members of a Recognised Supervisory Body (RSB) and are eligible for appointment under the rules of that body. RSBs are required to have rules to ensure that those eligible for appointment as a company auditor are either:

- individuals holding an appropriate qualification; or
- firms controlled by qualified persons.

ICAEW is an RSB. Professional qualifications are a prerequisite of membership of an RSB, and these are offered by Registered Qualifying Bodies approved by the Secretary of State.

RSBs must also implement procedures for monitoring their registered auditors on a regular basis.

The Companies Act 2006 also sets out factors which make a person ineligible for being a company auditor, for example, if he or she is:

- an officer or employee of the company
- a partner or employee of such a person
- any partner in a partnership in which such a person is a partner
- ineligible by the above for appointment as auditor of any directly connected companies

As you will see later in this course, the professional ethics of the RSBs are usually far stricter in their criteria for ineligibility as an auditor.

In the UK, the Government has delegated the task of independent monitoring of the UK accountancy profession to the Financial Reporting Council (FRC). The FRC is responsible for issuing auditing standards, which it does through its Codes and Standards Committee. The FRC issues the following standards and guidance for auditing:

- Auditing standards
- Ethical standards for Auditors
- Practice notes
- Bulletins
- Standards for reviews of interim financial statements performed by the auditor of the entity

The auditing standards issued by the FRC are the International Standards on Auditing (ISAs), augmented for UK requirements. Note that until July 2012, the FRC's work in this area was done by the Auditing Practices Board (APB). Already existing guidance (eg, ISAs) was issued by the APB and may still be referred to as such, and indeed the FRC has continued to refer to the APB in guidance issued since it ceased to exist.

ISA (UK) 200, *Overall Objectives of the Independent Auditor and the Conduct of an Auditor in Accordance with International Standards on Auditing* states that auditors shall comply with relevant ethical requirements relating to audit engagements. These will be outlined later in this Study Manual. An auditor must conduct an audit in accordance with ISAs. Relevant ISAs will be referred to in this Study Manual.

4.4 International Standards on Auditing (ISAs)

As stated above, statutory audits conducted in the UK must be conducted in accordance with ISAs (UK) as issued by the FRC. ISAs are made up of:

- introductory material and definitions
- objectives
- requirements
- application and other explanatory material (including appendices)

The requirements must be adhered to if an audit is to be conducted 'in accordance with ISAs' (as UK audits must be). That is to say, the basic principles and essential audit procedures required must be **applied** in the circumstances of each audit: this is where the 'application and other explanatory material' comes in. This part of an ISA is more concrete and practical, and sometimes contains examples of what the auditor must think about (and do) in practice.

The application material is an integral part of an ISA. It does not carry the same weight as the requirements because it may not be relevant in every case, but an auditor must make sure that an audit is conducted in the manner set out by the application guidance.

4.5 The value of the statutory audit

The reason why most companies that have audits do so, is that they are legally required to. However, audits can be invaluable to an entity because they may enhance the credibility of the financial statements, among other key benefits discussed in section 2 above.

4.6 Stages of an audit

In common with other assurance engagements, an audit will comprise several stages along the way to its eventual completion and the issuance of the auditor's opinion.

Before the engagement even begins, it must be obtained; there are various requirements that must be adhered to in relation to this which are covered in Chapter 2. It is important at this stage to consider the professional and ethical requirements around accepting audit engagements, and these are covered in Chapters 14, 15 and 16.

Planning is a crucial aspect of the audit, with the importance of proper planning being emphasised greatly by auditing standards (ISAs). This is covered in Chapter 3.

Audit procedures are designed at the planning stage, and are then performed in order to obtain evidence. Coverage of audit procedures pervades this Study Manual, but is concentrated in Chapters 6, 7 and 8.

Audit reporting is covered in Chapter 4, while review and completion are largely outside the scope of the Assurance syllabus and will be covered later on in your studies.

4.7 Overall objectives of the auditor

ISA 200 *Overall objectives of the independent auditor and the conduct of an audit in accordance with international standards on auditing* states that the overall objectives of the auditor are:

(a) to obtain reasonable assurance about whether the financial statements as a whole are free from material misstatement, whether due to fraud or error, thereby enabling the auditor to express an opinion on whether the financial statements are prepared, in all material respects, in accordance with an applicable financial reporting framework; and

(b) to report on the financial statements, and communicate as required by the ISAs, in accordance with the auditor's findings.

In order to do this, the auditor must:

- comply with relevant ethical requirements

- plan and perform the audit with professional scepticism

- exercise professional judgement

- obtain audit evidence that is both sufficient and appropriate, from which reasonable conclusions may be drawn, on which the auditor's opinion is then based

Definitions

Professional scepticism is an attitude that includes a questioning mind, being alert to conditions which may indicate possible misstatement due to error or fraud, and a critical assessment of audit evidence.

Professional judgement is the application of relevant training, knowledge and experience in making informed decisions about the courses of action that are appropriate in the circumstances of the audit engagement.

ISA 200 states that auditors must plan and perform an audit with an attitude of professional scepticism, recognising that circumstances may exist that cause the financial statements to be materially misstated.

This requires the auditor to be alert to:

- audit evidence that contradicts other audit evidence obtained

- information that brings into question the reliability of documents and responses to inquiries to be used as audit evidence

- conditions that may indicate possible fraud

- circumstances that suggest the need for audit procedures in addition to those required by ISAs

Professional scepticism needs to be maintained throughout the audit to reduce the risks of overlooking unusual transactions, over-generalising when drawing conclusions, and using inappropriate assumptions in determining the nature, timing and extent of audit procedures and evaluating the results of them. Professional scepticism is also necessary to the critical assessment of audit evidence. This includes questioning contradictory audit evidence and the reliability of documents and responses from management and those charged with governance.

ISA 200 also requires the auditor to exercise professional judgement in planning and performing an audit of financial statements. Professional judgement is required in the following areas:

- Materiality and audit risk
- Nature, timing and extent of audit procedures
- Evaluation of whether sufficient appropriate audit evidence has been obtained
- Evaluating management's judgements in applying the applicable financial reporting framework
- Drawing conclusions based on the audit evidence obtained

4.8 Bookkeeping recap

The statutory audit is concerned with the truth and fairness of the financial statements. The audit involves a consideration of the accounting processes (systems) that generate the information presented by the financial statements. It may be helpful to recap how this happens in general terms. What follows is a summary of the overall process of bookkeeping. These processes are crucial because it is through them that the figures in the financial statements are generated; a major focus of many audits is on how reliable the bookkeeping process is. Indeed you could think of much of this Assurance paper as being about how the auditor audits different aspects of a company's bookkeeping systems as they work in different contexts, such as revenue, purchases, or payroll.

Every audited entity must record its financial information. It does this first in its books of original entry, eg, the Sales Day Book, the Purchases Day Book, or the Cash Book. Data is then transferred from these books of original entry into the nominal ledger accounts, using the double-entry system.

At the end of the financial reporting period, the ledger accounts are balanced. The balances are extracted to make a trial balance (TB). An extended trial balance (ETB) is then used to make adjustment journals. Adjustments are made for accruals and prepayments together with any other items, and a final TB is produced.

The statement of profit or loss and the statement of financial position are prepared from the final TB. The statement of profit or loss is prepared by transferring all of the income and expense account balances from the TB into a new ledger account, called the profit or loss ledger account. It is from this that the statement of profit or loss will be prepared.

The remaining balances on the TB are for assets, liabilities and capital. These are listed out in the vertical format statement of financial position. The profit/loss for the period is transferred from the profit or loss ledger account into the capital account. Once this is done then the statement of financial position can be prepared.

The following diagram depicts this process in general overview.

Summary and Self-test

Summary

An assurance engagement is one in which a practitioner expresses a conclusion designed to enhance the degree of confidence of the intended users other than the responsible party about the outcome of the evaluation or measurement of a subject matter against criteria

Levels of assurance:
- Limited
- Reasonable (high)

Key elements:
- Three party relationship
- Subject matter
- Suitable criteria
- Sufficient appropriate evidence
- Written report

Key example: audit
Directors, auditors, shareholders
Financial statements
Law and accounting standards
As prescribed by ISA 500
Audit report

Benefits:
- Independent, professional opinion
- Added confidence to other users
- Deterrent to error/fraud

Limitations:
Subjective, sampled, limitations of systems, information from third parties, limitations of reporting, includes estimates

Self-test

Answer the following questions.

1 Assurance services are required by law.

☐ True

☐ False

2 What **five** elements are required for an engagement to be an assurance engagement?

1.....................................

2.....................................

3.....................................

4.....................................

5.....................................

3 Name **four** limitations of an assurance service.

1.....................................

2.....................................

3.....................................

4.....................................

4 Reasonable assurance is a high level of assurance.

☐ True

☐ False

Now, go back to the Learning Objectives in the Introduction. If you are satisfied you have achieved these objectives, please tick them off.

Answers to Interactive questions

Answer to Interactive question 1

1   Three party involvement:

- Jamal (the intended user)
- You (the practitioner)
- The directors of Company X as they produce the financial statements (the responsible party)

2   Subject matter

The most recent financial statements of Company X are the subject matter.

3   Relevant criteria

It is most likely in this instance that the criteria would be accounting standards, so that Jamal was assured that the financial statements were properly prepared and comparable with other companies' financial statements.

4   Evidence

You would have to agree the extent of procedures in relation to this assignment with Jamal so that he knew the level of evidence you were intending to seek. This would depend on several factors, including the degree of secrecy in the proposed transaction and whether the directors of Company X allowed you to inspect the books and documents.

5   Report

Again, the nature of the report would be agreed between you and Jamal, however, it would be a written report containing your opinion on the financial statements.

Answer to Interactive question 2

An independent, professional opinion
Additional confidence given to other related parties
Assurance may act as a deterrent to error or fraud

1 False (an audit may be required by law if the company does not qualify as a small company)

2   1   Three party relationship
    2   Subject matter
    3   Suitable criteria
    4   Sufficient appropriate evidence
    5   Written report

3 From:

    1   Subjective exercise
    2   Sampling
    3   Limitations in systems
    4   Limitations in report
    5   Information from third parties
    6   Estimations

4 True

CHAPTER 2

Process of assurance: obtaining an engagement

Introduction

Examination context

Topic List

1 Obtaining an engagement

2 Accepting an engagement

3 Agreeing terms of an engagement

Summary and Self-test

Technical references

Answers to Interactive questions

Answers to Self-test

Introduction

Learning objectives

Tick off

- Be aware of how assurance firms obtain work ☐

- Understand the key issues practitioners must consider before accepting engagements ☐

- Know what a letter of engagement is and what it does ☐

The specific syllabus reference for this chapter is: 1f.

Syllabus links

The issues of obtaining engagements will be looked at in much greater detail in the *Audit and Assurance* paper at the Application level.

Examination context

This is a fairly minor area for the exam, but you could expect at least one question on the scope of the engagement (there was a question about engagement letters in the sample paper) and possibly another on the considerations of the assurance firm when deciding to accept engagements.

In the assessment, candidates may be required to:

- identify acceptance procedures
- identify sources of information about new clients
- select procedures required by money laundering legislation
- determine the purpose of a letter of engagement

1 Obtaining an engagement

Section overview

- Accountants are permitted to advertise for clients, within certain professional guidelines.
- Accountants may sometimes be invited to tender for an audit.

How assurance firms obtain clients is an important practical question, but it is largely outside the scope of this syllabus. In brief, you should be aware that:

- accountants are permitted to advertise for clients within certain professional guidelines, the details of which you do not need to know.

- accountants are often invited to tender for particular engagements, which means that they offer a quote for services, outlining the benefits of their firm and personnel, usually in competition with other firms which are tendering at the same time.

In this syllabus, if the topics in this chapter are examined, it will be in the context of an accountant being invited by a potential client to accept an engagement. We will go on now to look at the things which an accountant must consider when he is so invited.

2 Accepting an engagement

Section overview

- The **present** and **proposed auditors** should normally **communicate** about the client prior to the audit being accepted.

- The client must be asked to give permission for communication to occur. If the client **refuses** to give **permission**, the proposed auditors should normally decline the appointment.

- The auditors must ensure they have sufficient resources (time and staff, for example) to carry out the appointment.

- The audit firm must have client due diligence procedures in place in order to comply with the Money Laundering Regulations 2007.

This section covers the procedures that the **auditors must** undertake to **ensure that their appointment is valid** and that they are clear to act.

2.1 Appointment considerations

Section 210 of the ICAEW *Code of Ethics* sets out the rules under which accountants should accept new appointments. Before a new audit client is accepted, the auditors must determine whether there are any **independence** or **other ethical issues** likely to cause significant problems with the ethical code (ie, significant threats to complying with the fundamental principles of ethical behaviour – see later in this Study Manual). Furthermore, new auditors should ensure that they have been appointed in a proper and legal manner.

The nominee auditors must carry out the following procedures.

Acceptance procedures	
Ensure **professionally qualified** to act	Consider whether disqualified on legal or ethical grounds, for example if there would be a conflict of interest with another client. We will look in more detail at ethical issues later in this Study Manual.
Ensure **existing resources adequate**	Consider available time, staff and technical expertise.
Obtain references	Make independent enquiries if directors not personally known.
Communicate with present auditors	Enquire whether there are reasons/circumstances behind the change which the new auditors ought to know, also as a matter of courtesy.

Some of the basic factors for consideration are given below.

- The integrity of those managing a company will be of great importance, particularly if the company is controlled by one or a few dominant personalities.

- The audit firm will also consider whether the client is likely to be high or low risk to the firm in terms of being able to draw an appropriate assurance conclusion in relation to that client. The following table contrasts low and high risk clients.

Low risk	High risk
Good long-term prospects	Poor recent or forecast performance
Well-financed	Likely lack of finance
Strong internal controls	Significant control weaknesses
Conservative, prudent accounting policies	Evidence of questionable integrity, doubtful accounting policies
Competent, honest management	Lack of finance director
Few unusual transactions	Significant unexplained transactions or transactions with connected companies

Where the risk level of a company's audit is determined as anything other than low, then the specific risks should be identified and documented. It might be necessary to assign specialists in response to these risks, particularly industry specialists, as independent reviewers. Some audit firms have procedures for closely monitoring audits which have been accepted, but which are considered high risk.

Generally, the expected fees from a new client should reflect the **level of risk** expected. They should also offer the same sort of return expected of clients of this nature and reflect the overall financial strategy of the audit firm. Occasionally, the audit firm will want the work to gain entry into the client's particular industry, or to establish better contacts within that industry. These factors will all contribute to a total expected economic return.

The audit firm will generally want the relationship with a client to be **long term**. This is not only to enjoy receiving fees year after year; it is also to allow the audit work to be enhanced by better knowledge of the client and thereby offer a better service.

Conflict of interest problems can be significant; the firm should establish that no existing clients will cause difficulties as competitors of the new client. Other services to other clients may have an impact here, not just audit.

The audit firm must have the **resources** to perform the work properly, as well as any **specialist knowledge or skills**. The impact on existing engagements must be estimated, in terms of staff time and the timing of the audit.

Sources of information about new clients	
Enquiries of other sources	Bankers, solicitors
Review of **documents**	Most recent annual accounts, listing particulars, credit rating
Previous accountants/auditors	Previous auditors should be invited to disclose fully all relevant information
Review of **rules and standards**	Consider specific laws/standards that relate to industry

Prospective auditors should seek the prospective client's permission to contact the previous auditors. If this permission is not given, the prospective auditors should normally decline the appointment. Normally permission will be given, so the prospective auditors can write to the outgoing auditors.

Worked example: Initial communication

This is an example of an initial communication.

> To: Retiring LLP
>
>   Chartered Accountants
>
> Dear Sir or Madam
>
> Re: New Client Ltd
>
> We have been asked to allow our name to go forward for nomination as auditors of the above company, and we should therefore be grateful if you would please let us know whether there are any professional reasons why we should not accept nomination ....
>
> Acquiring LLP
>
> Chartered Accountants, Registered Auditors

Having negotiated these steps the auditors will be in a position to accept the nomination, or not, as the case may be.

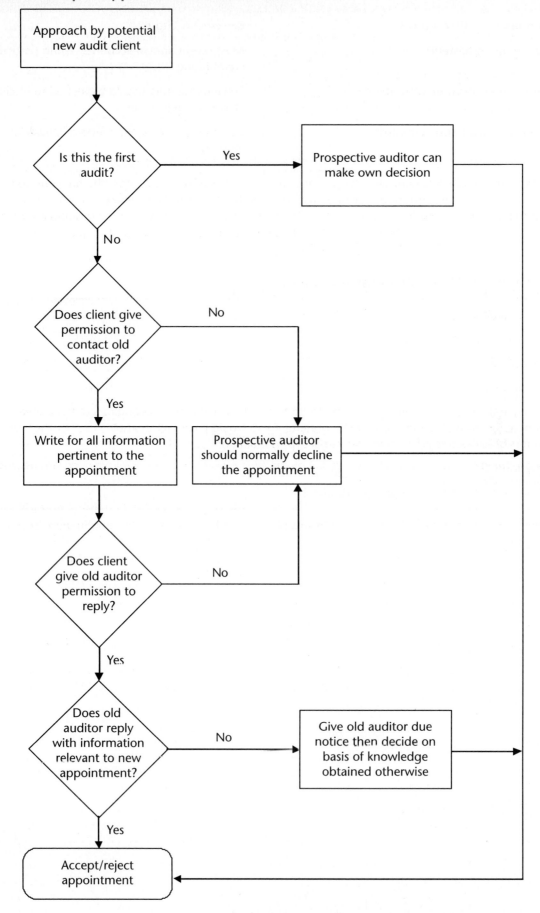

Approach by potential new audit client

Is this the first audit?

Yes → Prospective auditor can make own decision

No

Does client give permission to contact old auditor?

No → Prospective auditor should normally decline the appointment

Yes

Write for all information pertinent to the appointment

Does client give old auditor permission to reply?

No → Prospective auditor should normally decline the appointment

Yes

Does old auditor reply with information relevant to new appointment?

No → Give old auditor due notice then decide on basis of knowledge obtained otherwise

Yes

Accept/reject appointment

Interactive question 1: Accepting appointment

Identify whether the following are true or false. The audit firm should consider the following factors when determining whether to accept an engagement.

	True	False
Whether the firm is ethically barred from acting	✓	
Whether the firm has sufficient resources to carry out the engagement	✓	
Whether the firm can make sufficient profit from the engagement	✓	✗
Whether the client is new to the firm		✓
Whether the client gives permission to contact the outgoing auditors	✓	

See **Answer** at the end of this chapter.

The following procedures should be carried out after accepting nomination.

- **Ensure** that the **outgoing auditors' removal** or **resignation** has been **properly conducted** in accordance with national legislation.

  The new auditors should see a valid notice of the outgoing auditors' resignation, or confirm that the outgoing auditors were properly removed.

- **Ensure** that the **new auditors' appointment is valid**. The new auditors should obtain a copy of the resolution passed at the general meeting appointing them as the company's auditors.

- Set up and **submit a letter of engagement** to the directors of the company.

Where the outgoing auditors have fees still owing by the client, the new auditors need not decline appointment solely for this reason.

Once a new appointment has taken place, the **new auditors should obtain all books and papers which belong to the client from the outgoing auditors**. The outgoing auditors should ensure that all such documents are transferred promptly, **unless** they have a lien (a legal right to hold on to them) because of unpaid fees. An outgoing auditor cannot have a lien over the accounting records of a registered company as the Companies Act requires these to be available for public inspection. The outgoing auditors should also pass any useful information to the new auditors if it will be of help, without charge, unless a lot of work is involved.

2.2 Other assurance engagements

Similar considerations will be required for any assurance engagements. The legal considerations relating to audit will not be relevant to other assurance engagements, but the ethical, risk and practical considerations will be just as valid.

2.3 Money laundering regulations

In order to comply with the Money Laundering Regulations 2007, assurance firms must keep certain records about clients and undertake what is known as client due diligence.

It is mandatory to check the identity of all clients before any work is undertaken when an ongoing relationship is envisaged (this would be the case for certain assurance engagements) or where a one-off transaction or a series of transactions greater than €15,000 will take place.

The identity of clients should be checked by:

- **For individuals**: obtaining official documents including a photograph and identifying the client's full name and permanent address, for example, a passport supported by a number of utilities bills or a driving licence.

- **For companies**: obtaining similar legal information from the Registrar of Companies; for example, a certificate of incorporation, the registered address and a list of shareholders and directors.

Client identification documents must be kept for a minimum of five years and until five years have elapsed since the relationship with the client in question has ceased. It is also necessary to keep a full audit trail of all transactions with the client.

Interactive question 2: Client due diligence

Drew Brothers, chartered accountants, has recently accepted appointment as the auditor of Abysin Ltd. In terms of client due diligence, they should check which **two** of the following documents?

- ☑ Certificate of incorporation
- ☐ Passport
- ☐ Utilities bills
- ☑ Annual return

See **Answer** at the end of this chapter.

3 Agreeing terms of an engagement

Section overview

- An engagement letter should be sent to all clients to clarify the terms of the engagement.

- Agreement of audit engagement terms must be in writing.

- It must include an explanation of the scope of the audit, the limitations of an audit and the responsibilities of auditors and those charged with governance.

- It may contain other information concerning practical details of the audit.

The purpose of an engagement letter is to:

- define clearly the **extent** of the firm's **responsibilities** and so minimise the possibility of any misunderstanding between the client and the firm; and

- provide **written confirmation** of the firm's **acceptance** of the appointment, the scope of the engagement and the form of their report.

If an engagement letter is not sent to clients, both new and existing, there is scope for argument about the precise extent of the respective obligations of the client and its directors and the auditors. The elements of an engagement letter should be discussed and agreed with management before it is sent.

An engagement letter for any type of assurance engagement will contain the same contents as an audit engagement letter (discussed below). Clearly details will be different (for instance, it will cover the **scope** of the engagement, but the scope of an audit and the scope of a review of forecast information, for example, will be different). An engagement letter for an assurance engagement other than audit is likely to refer to specific fees for the engagement. As you will see below, as an audit engagement is often recurring, specific fees are initially not mentioned.

3.1 Audit engagement letters

ISA (UK) 210, *Agreeing the Terms of Audit Engagements* requires that the auditor and the client agree on the terms of the engagement. The agreed terms must be in writing and the usual form would be a **letter of engagement**. Any other form of appropriate contract, however, may be used.

Even in countries where the audit objectives and scope and the auditor's obligations are established by law, an **audit engagement letter** may be informative for clients.

The auditors should send an engagement letter to all new clients soon **after their appointment** as auditors and, in any event, before the commencement of the first audit assignment. They should also consider sending an engagement letter to existing clients to whom no letter has previously been sent as soon as a suitable opportunity presents itself.

The following items shall be included in the engagement letter:

- The **objective** of the **audit** of financial statements

- The **scope** of the audit, which could include reference to applicable legislation, regulations, or pronouncements of professional bodies to which the auditor adheres

- The **auditor's responsibility**

- The **reporting framework** that is applicable for the financial statements being prepared, for example International Financial Reporting Standards

- **Management's responsibility** to prepare the financial statements and to provide the auditor with **unrestricted access** to whatever records, documentation and other information is requested in connection with the audit

- The form of any **reports** of results of the engagement

The form and remaining content of audit engagement letters may vary for each client, but the auditor may wish to include in the letter the following items:

- The form of any **other communication** of the results of the engagement

- The fact that because of the **test nature** and other **inherent limitations** of an audit, together with the inherent limitations of any accounting and internal control system, there is an unavoidable risk that some material misstatements may remain undiscovered

- Arrangements regarding the **planning** of the audit

- Expectation of receiving from management **written confirmation** of **representations** made in connection with the audit

- Agreement of the client to provide the auditor with information in time to allow the auditor to complete the audit in line with the proposed timetable

- Basis on which **fees** are computed and any billing arrangements

- Request for the client to **confirm the terms** of the engagement by acknowledging receipt of the engagement letter

When relevant, the following points could also be made:

- Arrangements concerning the involvement of **other auditors** and **experts** in some aspects of the audit

- Arrangements concerning the involvement of **internal auditors** and other client staff

- Arrangements to be made with the **predecessor auditor**, if any, in the case of an initial audit

- Any **restriction of the auditor's liability** when such possibility exists

- A reference to any **further agreements** between the auditor and the client

- Any obligations to provide audit working papers to **other parties**

Worked example: Audit engagement letter (extract)

To the Board of Directors of ABC Company

ACTING AS AUDITORS UNDER THE COMPANIES ACT 2006

RESPONSIBILITIES AND SCOPE FOR AUDIT SERVICES

Your responsibilities as directors

As directors of the company, you are responsible for preparing financial statements which give a true and fair view and which have been prepared in accordance with the Companies Act 2006 (the Act). As directors you must not approve the financial statements unless you are satisfied that they give a true and fair view of the assets, liabilities, financial position and profit or loss of the company.

In preparing the financial statements, you are required to:

- select suitable accounting policies and then apply them consistently

- make judgements and estimates that are reasonable and prudent

- prepare the financial statements on the going concern basis unless it is inappropriate to presume that the company will continue in business

You are responsible for keeping adequate accounting records that set out with reasonable accuracy at any time the company's financial position, and for ensuring that the financial statements comply with International Financial Reporting Standards (IFRSs) as adopted by the European Union and with the Companies Act 2006 and give a true and fair view.

You are also responsible for such internal control as you determine is necessary to enable the preparation of financial statements that are free from material misstatement whether due to fraud or error.

You are also responsible for safeguarding the assets of the company and hence for taking reasonable steps to prevent and detect fraud and other irregularities.

You are responsible for ensuring that the company complies with laws and regulations that apply to its activities, and for preventing non-compliance and detecting any that occurs.

You have undertaken to make available to us, as and when required, all the company's accounting records and related financial information, including minutes of management and shareholders' meetings, that we need to do our work. You have also undertaken to provide us with unrestricted access to any persons from whom we deem it necessary to obtain audit evidence. Each director is required to take all steps that he ought to take as a director in order to make himself aware of any relevant audit information and to establish that we are aware of that information.

Our responsibilities as auditor

We have a statutory responsibility to report to the members as a body, whether in our opinion the financial statements have been properly prepared in accordance with IFRSs, whether they have been prepared in accordance with the Companies Act 2006 and whether they give a true and fair view. We are also required to report whether the information given in the directors' report is consistent with the financial statements. In arriving at our opinion, we are required to consider the following matters, and report on any that we are not satisfied with:

(a) whether the company has kept adequate accounting records, and whether branches that we have not visited have sent in returns adequate for our audit

(b) whether the company's individual accounts are in agreement with the accounting records and returns

(c) whether we have obtained all the information and explanations which we consider necessary for the purposes of our audit

We may also need to deal with certain other matters in our report. If the company prepares accounts and reports in accordance with the small companies regime when in our opinion it is not entitled to do so we are required to state that fact in our report.

We have a professional responsibility to report if the financial statements do not significantly comply with applicable financial reporting standards, unless we believe there is a good reason for the non-compliance. In deciding whether or not this is the case, we consider:

(a) whether the non-compliance is necessary for the financial statements to give a true and fair view

(b) whether the non-compliance has been clearly disclosed

We also have a professional responsibility to consider whether other information in documents containing audited financial statements is consistent with those financial statements.

Scope of audit

We will carry out our audit in accordance with the International Standards of Auditing (UK) issued by the Financial Reporting Council. Those Standards require that we comply with ethical requirements and plan and perform the audit to obtain reasonable assurance about whether the financial statements are free of material misstatements. An audit involves performing procedures to obtain audit evidence about the amounts and disclosures in the financial statements. The procedures selected depend on the auditors' judgment, including the assessment of the risks of material misstatement of the financial statements, whether due to fraud or error. An audit also includes evaluating the appropriateness of accounting policies used and the reasonableness of accounting estimates made by management, as well as evaluating the overall presentation of the financial statements. Because of the test nature and other inherent limitations of an audit, together with the inherent limitations of any accounting and internal control system, there is an unavoidable risk that even some material misstatements may remain undiscovered.

We shall obtain an understanding of the accounting and internal control systems in order to assess their adequacy as a basis for the preparation of the financial statements and to establish whether adequate accounting records have been maintained by the company. We shall expect to obtain such appropriate evidence as we consider sufficient to enable us to draw reasonable conclusions there from. In addition to our report on the financial statements, we will provide you with a separate letter concerning any significant deficiencies in accounting and internal control systems which come to our notice.

The nature and extent of our audit will vary according to our assessment of the company's accounting system and, where we wish to rely on it the internal control system, and may cover any aspect of the business's operations that we consider appropriate. Our audit is not designed to identify all significant deficiencies in the company's systems and internal controls but, if we detect significant deficiencies we will report them to you in writing.

As part of our normal audit procedures, we may ask you to confirm in writing representations you have made to us during the audit. In particular, where misstatements in the financial statements that we bring to your attention are not adjusted, you must state your reasons. In connection with representations and the supply of information to us generally, we draw your attention to section 501 of the Companies Act 2006, under which it is an offence for anyone to recklessly or knowingly supply information to the auditors that is false or misleading and to fail to promptly provide information requested.

To help us examine your financial statements, we will ask to see all documents or statements that are due to be issued with the financial statements. We are also entitled to receive details of all written resolutions that are to be circulated to members, to attend all the company's general meetings and to receive notice of them all.

You are responsible for safeguarding the company's assets and for preventing and detecting fraud, error and non-compliance with law or regulations. We will plan our audit so that we can reasonably expect to detect significant misstatements in the financial statements or accounting records (including those resulting from fraud, error or non-compliance with law or regulations), but you cannot rely on us finding all such errors.

In respect of the expected form and content of our report, we refer you to the most recent bulletin on auditors' reports published by the Financial Reporting Council. The form and content of our report may need to be amended in the light of our findings.

Once we have issued our report, we have no further responsibility in relation to the financial statements for that financial year. However, we expect that you will inform us of any material event occurring between the date of our report and the date the financial statements are sent out in accordance with section 423 Companies Act 2006, which may affect the financial statements.

We look forward to full cooperation from your staff during our audit.

[Other relevant information]

[Insert other information, such as fee arrangements, billings and other specific terms, as appropriate.]

XYZ & Co.

Acknowledged and agreed on behalf of ABC Company by
(signed)
....
Name and Title

Interactive question 3: Engagement letters

Which **three** of the following may be contained within a letter of engagement?

- ☑ Responsibilities of the auditors
- ☑ Responsibilities of the directors
- ☐ The names of the staff assigned to the engagement
- ☑ The scope of the audit

See **Answer** at the end of this chapter.

Summary and Self-test

Summary

> Auditors may advertise their services, within certain boundaries

> Auditors will often be invited to tender for audits

> When an audit firms is invited to accept an engagement (usually as a result of a successful tender), it must:
> - Consider whether it is ethically barred from acting
> - Consider whether it has the resources available to undertake the engagement
> - Obtain permission to contact the outgoing auditors, and so do

> When an audit firm accepts an engagement it must:
> - Check the outgoing auditors' removal was carried out properly
> - Ensure its appointment is valid
> - Carry out customer due diligence in accordance with Money Laudering Regulations 2007
> - Set up Letter of engagement

Clarifies terms of engagement

Must be sent prior to first audit

Self-test

Answer the following questions.

1 An audit firm must not accept an engagement if the client is not previously known to them.

    ☐ True

    ☑ False

2 If a prospective client declines permission to contact the previous auditors, the audit firm should:

    A   report the client to the Companies Registrar
    B   contact the previous auditors anyway
    C   accept the engagement provisionally and continue to request permission
    Ⓓ   normally decline the appointment

3 Complete the questions that should be in the diagram.

4   In accordance with the money laundering regulations, client identification documents should be
     kept for:

    A   five years
    B   five years after the cessation of the relationship with the client
    C   seven years
    D   seven years after the cessation of the relationship with the client

5   An engagement letter is only ever sent to a client before the first audit.

    ☐   True

    ☑   False

6   An engagement letter defines the scope of the engagement.

    ☑   True

    ☐   False

Now, go back to the Learning Objectives in the Introduction. If you are satisfied you have achieved
these objectives, please tick them off.

Technical references

1 Accepting an engagement

2 Agreeing terms of an engagement

- Agree the terms in writing

- Send letter before first audit

- Contents of engagement letter

Section 210, ICAEW Code of Ethics

ISA (UK) 210.10

ISA (UK) 210.A22

ISA (UK) 210.10, A23

Answer to Interactive question 1

The auditors should consider all these factors except whether the client is new to the firm. This is irrelevant in making the decision, although the firm may have to carry out additional procedures to get to know the client if it is a new client. The auditors must consider if they are ethically qualified to act, whether they have sufficient resources and whether the client gives permission to contact the previous auditors (if this is declined, the auditors must consider carefully the reasons for the refusal). As the audit firm is also a commercial enterprise, it must consider whether taking on the engagement is commercially viable.

Answer to Interactive question 2

They should check the certificate of incorporation and the annual return (which should give details of the registered office and the shareholders and directors). If they are taking on any work for any individuals connected with Abysin (for example, personal tax for the directors) they should also obtain information for them from passports and utilities bills.

Answer to Interactive question 3

Responsibilities of the auditors
Responsibilities of the directors
The scope of the audit.

The specific staff assigned to the engagement will not normally be referred to (as the auditors will reserve the right to change their arrangement and the client should not have influence over assurance staff anyway). The composition of the audit team may be referred to – for example the number of senior and junior staff in the team.

Answers to Self-test

1 False. However, if the client is unknown to the audit firm, they should seek references in respect of key personnel associated with the client, and must carry out customer due diligence (as they must with all clients).

2 D Normally decline the appointment. The auditors must not contact the previous auditors without permission as this would be a breach of confidentiality. The client is legally entitled to refuse this permission so there is no reason to report to the Companies Registrar.

3 • Is this the first audit?
  • Does the client give permission to contact the old auditor?
  • Does the client give old auditor permission to reply?
  • Does the old auditor reply with information relevant to the new appointment?

4 B

5 False. It should be re-issued if there is a change in circumstances.

6 True

CHAPTER 3

Process of assurance: planning the assignment

Introduction

Examination context

Topic List

1 Planning

2 Analytical procedures

3 Materiality

4 Audit risk

5 Fraud

Summary and Self-test

Technical references

Answers to Interactive questions

Answers to Self-test

Introduction

Learning objectives

Tick off

- Define overall audit strategy and audit plan ☐
- Define professional scepticism ☐
- Understand the need to obtain an understanding of the entity and its environment ☐
- Be aware how such an understanding is obtained ☐
- Understand what analytical procedures are ☐
- Understand the use of analytical procedures at the planning stage ☐
- Define materiality ☐
- Understand the concept of planning materiality and how it is set ☐
- Define audit risk and its individual components ☐
- Understand how auditors use the risk model ☐
- Be able to identify and classify risks ☐
- Recognise the characteristics of fraud and distinguish between fraud and error ☐

Specific syllabus references for this chapter are: 1f, g, i.

Syllabus links

Planning is a large part of the *Audit and Assurance* syllabus, so when you reach that paper you will build on the knowledge you have gained in this syllabus and learn to apply that knowledge in a more practical way.

Examination context

Planning and risk are key issues for assurance providers and you should expect this area to come up in your assessment. Ensure that you understand the definitions that are set out in this chapter, since all could be examined. In addition, work through the examples and questions in the chapter identifying risks, as your assessment could include a question in such an area.

In the assessment candidates may be required to:

- identify the content of an audit strategy and an audit plan
- select appropriate procedures used by the auditor in obtaining an understanding of the entity
- describe professional scepticism
- identify how analytical procedures are applied throughout the course of the audit
- describe the concept of materiality
- describe audit risk and its components
- identify the type of risks illustrated in a given set of circumstances

1 Planning

In this chapter, we will look at the major ISAs covering the planning process. Remember that an audit is a high level assurance engagement, and therefore the auditor will carry out more procedures than would be the case on a lower level assurance assignment. However, the general principles discussed in this chapter would be relevant to another assurance assignment such as a review. Remember that in a lower level engagement, less detailed procedures are likely to be carried out.

An effective and efficient audit relies on proper planning procedures. The planning process is covered in general terms by ISA (UK) 300, *Planning an Audit of Financial Statements*. ISA 300 states 'The objective of the auditor is to plan the audit so that it will be performed in an effective manner'.

Definitions

Audit strategy: The formulation of the general strategy for the audit, which sets the scope, timing and direction of the audit and guides the development of the audit plan.

Audit plan: An audit plan is more detailed than the strategy and sets out the nature, timing and extent of audit procedures (including risk assessment procedures) to be performed by engagement team members in order to obtain sufficient appropriate audit evidence.

An **audit plan** shows how the overall audit strategy will be implemented.

Audits are planned to:

- ensure appropriate attention is devoted to important areas of the audit
- identify potential problems and resolve them on a timely basis
- ensure that the audit is properly organised and managed
- assign work to engagement team members properly
- facilitate direction and supervision of engagement team members
- facilitate review of work

Audit procedures may be discussed with the client's management, staff and/or audit committee in order to coordinate audit work, including that of internal audit. However, all audit procedures remain the responsibility of the external auditors.

A structured approach to planning will include:

Step 1

Ensuring that ethical requirements continue to be met

Step 2

Ensuring the terms of the engagement are understood

Step 3

Establishing the overall audit strategy

- Identifying the relevant characteristics of the engagement, such as the reporting framework used as this will set the scope for the engagement

- Discovering key dates for reporting and other communications

- Determining materiality, preliminary risk assessment, whether internal controls are to be tested

- Consideration of when work is to be carried out, for example before or after the year end

- Consideration of 'team members' available, their skills and how and when they are to be used, for example particular skills for high risk areas. In addition, appropriate levels of staff are required to facilitate direction, supervision and review of more junior team members' work

Step 4

Developing an audit plan including risk assessment procedures, audit tests and any other procedures necessary to comply with ISAs

The audit plan and any significant changes to it during the audit must be documented.

Key contents of an overall audit strategy	
Understanding the entity's environment	General economic factors and industry conditions
	Important characteristics of the client: (a) business, (b) principal business strategies, (c) financial performance, (d) reporting requirements, including changes since the previous audit
	The general level of competence of management
Understanding the accounting and internal control systems	The accounting policies adopted by the entity and changes in those policies
	The effect of new accounting or auditing pronouncements
	The auditors' cumulative knowledge of the accounting and internal control systems, and the relative emphasis expected to be placed on different types of test (we shall consider this in Chapter 4)
Risk and materiality	The expected assessments of risks of fraud or error and identification of significant audit areas
	The setting of materiality for audit planning purposes
	The possibility of material misstatements, including the experience of past periods, or fraud
	The identification of complex accounting areas including those involving estimates
Consequent nature, timing and extent of procedures	Possible change of emphasis on specific audit areas
	The effect of information technology on the audit
Coordination, direction, supervision and review	The number of locations
	Staffing requirements
	Need to attend client premises for inventory count or other year-end procedures
Other matters	The possibility that the going concern basis may be subject to question
	Conditions requiring special attention
	The terms of the engagement and any statutory responsibilities
	The nature and timing of reports or other communication with the entity that are expected under the engagement

Worked example: Overall audit strategy for Kwikstore Ltd

Area	Typical comment on the audit strategy/explanation
The terms of engagement	'Normal audit report – we write up the nominal ledger and draft statutory accounts from client records.'
	The letter of engagement should be read carefully to see exactly what the contractual commitments are.
Understanding the company and its business	'Old established confectioners, tobacconists and newsagents with main shop in high street and a branch in Kings Road Estate. Revenue £8m.'
	The auditor will use knowledge of the client to:
	• assess risks and identify procedures • plan and perform the audit effectively and efficiently • evaluate the audit evidence
Special audit problems (risks)	'Review profit margins (profits as a percentage of sales) and directors' salaries to ensure that both appear reasonable in the light of the other evidence, the nature and location of the business and the proprietor's standard of living.'
	Here, it has been identified that in a cash business all earnings might not be reported. The audit team is therefore being alerted that they should see if reported earnings are consistent with other information that is available.
Results of analytical procedures	'No results currently available – we expect gross margins of 26% (newspapers), 10% (tobacco), and 20% (confectionery). Normally sales mix has been approximately 5:3:2.'
	Another influence on how the auditor would perform the audit is the analytical procedures. (We look at this in more detail later in this chapter, but in summary it means looking at ratios and the changes in the accounts to see if anything looks odd.)
Materiality	'Accounting – all posting to be accurate – whenever possible work to be the nearest £ or £10. Audit materiality – £50,000 based on 5% profits.'
	We look at this in more detail later. However, the auditor does not claim to find every misstatement (see the engagement letter), but material misstatements should be discovered.
	This section of the audit strategy gives the audit team some indication as to materiality levels.
Risk evaluation and audit approach	'No reliance can be placed on internal controls or analytical procedures. Generally a substantive approach will be adopted.' (We will see what this means in Chapter 4.)
	'As far as the risk of understatement of sales is concerned, we will check till rolls to cash book, estimate the sales mix and purchase mix and predict gross margins. We will also review cash movements over ten weeks at random and check that they appear reasonable.'
Other matters	'None.'
	This section could contain details of inventory counts and other year-end procedures (which we will look at in Chapter 13).
Budget and fee	'Fee: £15,000.
	Detailed time budget is shown on the current audit file'

Area	Typical comment on the audit strategy/explanation
Timetable	'Accounts to be ready for discussion with client by 30 September 20X4.'
Staffing	'Senior – 2 weeks Junior – 1 week. There will be one audit visit after year-end commencing 11 August 20X4. Manager review: 1 day (23 August 20X4) Partner review: 1 day (30 August 20X4).' This ties in with the fees section. The auditor will set a time budget for each level of staff involved on the audit. The time budget will be analysed over the different parts of the audit.

Interactive question 1: The overall audit strategy

Which **three** of the following would ordinarily be contained in the overall audit strategy?

☐ The contract between the audit firm and the client

☐ The results of audit risk assessment

☐ Calculation of preliminary materiality

☐ Detailed plan of audit procedures to be carried out

☐ List of staff to be involved with the audit

See **Answer** at the end of this chapter.

1.1 Understanding the entity and its environment

ISA (UK) 315, *Identifying and Assessing the Risks of Material Misstatement through Understanding the Entity and its Environment* states that 'the objective of the auditor is to **identify and assess the risks of material misstatement,** whether due to fraud or error, at the financial statement and assertion levels, through **understanding the entity and its environment,** including the entity's internal control, thereby providing a basis for designing and implementing responses to the assessed risks of material misstatement'.

In order to be able to identify problem areas which might cause difficulties in collecting evidence or drawing assurance conclusions, auditors must have an understanding of the nature of the business and the context in which it operates.

Summary	Obtaining an understanding of the entity and its environment
Why?	To identify and assess the risks of material misstatement in the financial statements. To enable the auditor to design and perform further audit procedures. To provide a frame of reference for exercising audit judgement, for example, when setting audit materiality (which we shall look at later in this chapter).
What?	Industry, regulatory and other external factors, including the reporting framework. Nature of the entity, including selection and application of accounting policies. Objectives and strategies and relating business risks that might cause material misstatement in the financial statements. Measurement and review of the entity's financial performance. Internal control (which we shall look at in detail in Chapter 5).

How?   Inquiries of management and others within the entity

Analytical procedures (which we shall look at in the next section of this chapter)

Observation and inspection

Prior period knowledge

Discussion of the susceptibility of the financial statements to material misstatement among the engagement team

As can be seen in the table above, the reasons the auditor is to obtain the understanding of the entity and its environment are very much bound up with assessing risks and exercising audit judgement. We shall look at these aspects further later in this chapter.

1.1.1   What?

The ISA sets out a number of requirements about what the auditors must consider in relation to obtaining an understanding of the business. These were summarised in the table above and are covered in more detail in the diagram on page 44.

1.1.2   How?

ISA 315 *Identifying and assessing the risks of material misstatement through understanding of the entity and its environment* also sets out the methods that the auditor **must** use to obtain the understanding (listed above in the summary). The auditor does not have to use all of these for each area, but a combination of these procedures should be used. These are as follows.

- Inquiries of management and others within the entity. (The auditors will usually obtain most of the information they require from staff in the accounts department, but may also need to make enquiries of other personnel, for example, internal audit, production staff or directors.)

Worked example: Inquiries of management and others

Directors may give insight into the environment in which the financial statements are prepared. In-house legal advisers may help with understanding matters such as outstanding litigation, or compliance with laws and regulations. Sales and marketing personnel may give information about marketing strategies and sales trends.

- Analytical procedures (which we will look at in the next section).

- Observation and inspection (these techniques are likely to confirm the answers made to inquiries made of management. They will include observing the normal operations of a company, reading documents or manuals relating to the client's operations or visiting premises and meeting staff).

- If it is a recurring audit, the auditors may have obtained a great deal of knowledge about the entity and the environment in the course of prior year audits. The auditor is entitled to use this information in the current year audit, but he must make sure that he has determined whether any **changes** in the year have affected the relevance of information obtained in previous years.

- The **audit team** is also required by ISA 315 to **discuss the susceptibility of the financial statements to material misstatement**. Judgement must be exercised in determining which members of the team should be involved in which parts of the discussion, but all team members should be involved in the discussion relevant to the parts of the audit they will be involved in.

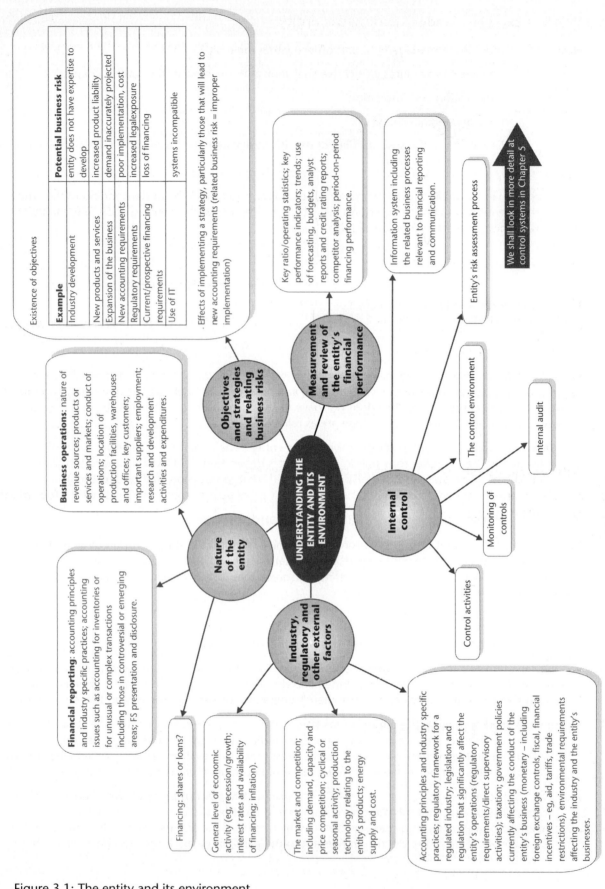

Figure 3.1: The entity and its environment

Existence of objectives

Example	Potential business risk
Industry development	entity does not have expertise to develop
New products and services	increased product liability
Expansion of the business	demand inaccurately projected
New accounting requirements	poor implementation, cost
Regulatory requirements	increased legal exposure
Current/prospective financing requirements	loss of financing
Use of IT	systems incompatible

· Effects of implementing a strategy, particularly those that will lead to new accounting requirements (related business risk = improper implementation)

Objectives and strategies and relating business risks

Measurement and review of the entity's financial performance

Key ratio/operating statistics; key performance indicators; trends; use of forecasting, budgets, analyst reports and credit rating reports; competitor analysis; period-on-period financing performance.

Information system including the related business processes relevant to financial reporting and communication.

Entity's risk assessment process

We shall look in more detail at control systems in Chapter 5

UNDERSTANDING THE ENTITY AND ITS ENVIRONMENT

Business operations: nature of revenue sources; products or services and markets; conduct of operations; location of production facilities, warehouses and offices; key customers; important suppliers; employment; research and development activities and expenditures.

Nature of the entity

Internal control

The control environment

Internal audit

Monitoring of controls

Control activities

Financial reporting: accounting principles and industry specific practices; accounting issues such as accounting for inventories or for unusual or complex transactions including those in controversial or emerging areas; FS presentation and disclosure.

Industry, regulatory and other external factors

Financing: shares or loans?

General level of economic activity (eg, recession/growth; interest rates and availability of financing; inflation).

The market and competition; including demand, capacity and price competition; cyclical or seasonal activity; production technology relating to the entity's products; energy supply and cost.

Accounting principles and industry specific practices; regulatory framework for a regulated industry; legislation and regulation that significantly affect the entity's operations (regulatory requirements/direct supervisory activities); taxation; government policies currently affecting the conduct of the entity's business (monetary – including foreign exchange controls, fiscal, financial incentives – eg, aid, tariffs, trade restrictions), environmental requirements affecting the industry and the entity's businesses.

Worked example: Understanding the entity

The auditors want to build up a profile of the audit client against the background of the general economic climate. Here is an example for a new audit client, Icket Ltd.

Icket Ltd

Shareholders:	Members of Icket family – (Jane, Chris, Annabel and James)
	Other shareholders – (Eddie Stewart, Vikram Sandhu)
Directors:	Chris Icket, Jane Icket, Eddie Stewart
Operations:	Manufactures tableware for high street stores and standard lines for a number of wholesalers
	Activity tends to be seasonal with new lines being brought into shops in October and April
Customers:	Three major high street retailers, 50 wholesalers
Suppliers:	Three key suppliers of fabrics and threads – Fine Fabrics Limited, Sundry Sewing plc and All Sewing Supplies (Manchester) Limited
IT:	The accounting system is completely computerised
Financial performance:	Company formed 20 years ago and has always been profitable. Company is financed by equity capital and has a substantial bank loan from National Bank
Future plans:	No new plans that we are aware of

This is a very basic company profile. In carrying out risk assessment, more detail would be sought in each area, as you will see when this example is continued in section 4.

Interactive question 2: Understanding the entity

In order to obtain an understanding of the entity, auditors must use a combination of which **four** of the following procedures?

- ☐ Inspection
- ☐ Observation
- ☐ Inquiry
- ☐ Analytical procedures
- ☐ Computation

See **Answer** at the end of this chapter.

2 Analytical procedures

Section overview

- Analytical procedures are used at all stages of the audit, but here we consider only their use in planning the audit.

- Analytical procedures consist of the analysis of significant ratios and trends including the resulting investigations of fluctuations and relationships that are inconsistent with other relevant information or which deviate from predictable amounts.

- During **planning**, analytical procedures are used as a means of **understanding the business** and **identifying audit risk**.

Definition

Analytical procedures: Evaluations of financial information through analysis of plausible relationships among both financial and non-financial data. Analytical procedures also encompass such investigation as is necessary of identified fluctuations or relationships that are inconsistent with other relevant information or that differ from expected values by a significant amount.

They include consideration of comparisons of the entity's financial information with other information, and the consideration of relationships among elements of financial information that would be expected to conform to a particular pattern or between financial information and relevant non-financial information.

ISA (UK) 520, *Analytical Procedures* requires auditors to apply analytical procedures in the overall review at the end of the audit and as substantive procedures, to obtain audit evidence directly. ISA (UK) 315, *Identifying and Assessing the Risks of Material Misstatement through Understanding the Entity and its Environment* also requires the auditor to use analytical procedures. Here they are used as risk assessment procedures to obtain an understanding of the entity and its environment. We will look at the uses of analytical procedures for purposes other than planning later in the Study Manual.

The ISA states that analytical procedures include:

- the consideration of comparisons with:

    - **comparable information** for prior periods

    - **anticipated results** of the entity, from budgets or forecasts or expectations of the auditor

    - similar **industry information**, such as a comparison of the client's ratio of sales to trade receivables with industry averages, or with the ratios relating to other entities of comparable size in the same industry

- consideration of relationships between:

    - elements of financial information that are expected to conform to a predicted pattern based on the entity's experience, such as the relationship of gross profit to sales

    - financial information and relevant non-financial information, such as the relationship of payroll costs to number of employees

A variety of methods can be used to perform the procedures discussed above, ranging from **simple comparisons** to **complex analysis** using statistics. The choice of procedures is a matter for the auditor's professional judgement.

2.1 Analytical procedures in planning the audit

As we have discussed, analytical procedures should be used at the risk assessment stage. Possible sources of information about the client include:

- interim financial information
- budgets
- management accounts
- non-financial information
- bank and cash records
- VAT returns
- board minutes
- discussions or correspondence with the client at the year end

Auditors may also use specific industry information or general knowledge of current industry conditions to assess the client's performance.

As well as helping to determine the nature, timing and extent of other audit procedures, such analytical procedures may also indicate aspects of the business of which the auditors were previously unaware. Auditors are looking to see if developments in the client's business have had the expected effects. They will be particularly interested in changes in audit areas where problems have occurred in the past.

Certain accounting ratios may be used as analytical procedures. Here are the key ratios used:

Heading/Ratio	Formula	Purpose
Performance Return on capital employed	$\dfrac{\text{Profit before interest and tax}}{\text{Equity + net debt}}$	Effective use of resources
Return on shareholders' funds	$\dfrac{\text{Net profit for the period}}{\text{Share capital + reserves}}$	Effective use of resources
Gross profit margin	$\dfrac{\text{Gross profit} \times 100}{\text{Revenue}}$	Assess profitability before taking overheads into account
Cost of sales percentage	$\dfrac{\text{Cost of sales} \times 100}{\text{Revenue}}$	Assess relationship of costs to revenue
Operating cost percentage	$\dfrac{\text{Operating costs} \times 100}{\text{Revenue}}$	Assess relationship of costs to revenue
Net margin = operating margin	$\dfrac{\text{Profit before interest and tax} \times 100}{\text{Revenue}}$	Assess profitability after taking overheads into account
Short-term liquidity Current ratio	Current assets : current liabilities	Assess ability to pay current liabilities from reasonably liquid assets
Quick ratio	Receivables + Current investments + Cash : current liabilities	Assess ability to pay current liabilities from reasonably liquid assets
Long-term solvency Gearing ratio	$\dfrac{\text{Net debt}}{\text{Equity}} \times 100$	Assess reliance on external finance
Interest cover	$\dfrac{\text{Profit before interest payable}}{\text{Interest payable}}$	Assess ability to pay interest charges
Efficiency Net asset turnover	$\dfrac{\text{Revenue}}{\text{Capital employed}}$	Assess revenue generated from asset base
Inventory turnover	$\dfrac{\text{Cost of sales}}{\text{Inventories}}$	Assess level of inventory held
Trade receivables collection period	$\dfrac{\text{Trade receivables} \times 365}{\text{Revenue}}$	Assess ability to turn receivables into cash
Trade payables payment period	$\dfrac{\text{Trade payables} \times 365}{\text{Credit purchases}}$	Assess ability to pay suppliers

Worked example: Analytical procedures

Here are some extracts from a statement of profit or loss for a company. The areas which analytical procedures suggest may indicate risks are highlighted in grey.

	20X6	20X5	Comments
	£'000	£'000	
Revenue	1,566,088	950,339	Revenue has risen substantially
Cost of sales	1,237,231	757,700	Cost of sales and gross margin have risen in line with the rise in revenue
Gross profit	328,857	192,639	
Salaries and wages	141,984	185,664	Salaries have fallen despite rise in revenue. If rise is due to increased output, why has related labour cost fallen?
Other administrative costs	10,988	9,939	
Audit fee	5,400	5,350	
Bank charges	64	33	Bank charges have nearly doubled – indicating large loan taken out? Why? Potential problem?
Other finance costs	32	35	
Advertising	276	463	Seems odd that sales appear to have increased when advertising costs have been slashed?

Interactive question 3: Analytical procedures

Here is some budget financial information for Fleming plc, contrasted with the management results for the 12 months under review.

	Budget 20X6 £	Actual 20X6 £
Sales	1,350,000	1,339,588
Cost of sales	850,000	994,663
Gross margin	500,000	344,925
Salaries	245,000	243,873
Repairs and renewals	7,500	24,983
Depreciation	7,500	7,551
Motor expenses	25,750	14,678
Other costs	44,000	43,968

Requirement

Which **three** of the following areas would you be **most likely** to investigate further as a result of carrying out analytical procedures on the above?

- [ ] Sales
- [x] Cost of sales
- [ ] Sales and cost of sales
- [ ] Depreciation
- [x] Repairs and renewals
- [x] Motor expenses

See **Answer** at the end of this chapter.

3 Materiality

Section overview

- Materiality relates to the level of misstatement that affects the decisions of users of the accounts.

- Materiality must be calculated at the planning stages of all audits. The calculation or estimation of materiality is based on experience and judgement.

- Materiality must be reviewed during the audit.

Materiality relates to the level of misstatement that affects the decisions of users of the accounts, where users are taken as a group. The needs of specific individuals are not considered as their needs may vary considerably.

Definitions

Materiality: An expression of the relative significance or importance of a particular matter in the context of financial statements as a whole. The IFRS *Conceptual Framework for Financial Reporting* states that a matter is material if its omission or misstatement could influence the economic decisions of users taken on the basis of the financial statements.

Performance materiality: The amount or amounts set by the auditor at less than materiality for the financial statements as a whole to reduce to an appropriately low level the probability that the aggregate of uncorrected and undetected misstatements exceeds materiality for the financial statements as a whole.

ISA (UK) 320, *Materiality in Planning and Performing an Audit* states that 'materiality and audit risk are considered throughout the audit, in particular, when:

- identifying and assessing the risks of material misstatement;

- determining the nature, timing and extent of further audit procedures; and

- evaluating the effect of uncorrected misstatements, if any, on the financial statements and in forming the opinion in the auditor's report'.

Figure 3.2 shows how materiality is used in the course of an assurance engagement.

Figure 3.2: Audit materiality

Materiality considerations during **audit planning** are extremely important. The assessment of materiality at this stage should be based on the most recent and reliable financial information and will help to determine an effective and efficient audit approach. Materiality assessment will help the auditors to decide:

- how many and what items to examine

- whether to use sampling techniques

- what level of misstatement is likely to lead to an auditor to say the financial statements do not give a true and fair view

The resulting combination of audit procedures should help to reduce audit risk to an appropriately low level. This is how risk and materiality are closely connected. The value of discovered misstatements should be aggregated at the end of the audit to ensure the total is still below tolerable misstatement. **Tolerable misstatement** is the maximum misstatement that an auditor is prepared to accept in a class of transactions or balances in the financial statements. It will be considered in more detail in Chapter 11.

To set the materiality level the auditors need to decide the level of misstatement that would distort the view given by the accounts. Because many users of accounts are primarily interested in the profitability of the company, the level is often expressed as a proportion of its profits.

Materiality can be thought of in terms of the size of the business. Hence, if the company remains a fairly constant size, the materiality level should not change; similarly if the business is growing, the level of materiality will increase from year to year.

The size of a company can be measured in terms of revenue and total assets, both of which tend not to be subject to the fluctuations which may affect profit.

Note that the auditors will often calculate a range of values, such as those shown below, and then take an average or weighted average of all the figures produced as the preliminary materiality level. However, **different firms have different methods** and this is **just one of the available approaches**.

Value	%
Profit before tax	5–10
Revenue	½–1
Total assets	1–2

However, bear in mind that materiality has qualitative, as well as quantitative, aspects. For example, transactions relating to directors are considered material by nature regardless of their value.

You must not simply think of materiality as being a percentage of items in the financial statements.

3.1 Performance materiality

The concept of performance materiality focuses on the difference between the level of tolerable misstatement and the level of actual misstatements detected. For example, if a misstatement were detected that was just below overall materiality, then there is a difficulty for the auditor: the financial statements are not materially misstated, but there is a risk that there may be undetected misstatements which would push over the materiality threshold. The auditor needs to think of materiality not just as a whole, but in relation to the specific areas which have been tested. Thinking in terms of performance materiality means thinking of what the effect of individual misstatements might be on audit risk for the financial statements as a whole. This provides the auditor with a **margin of safety** in relation to any undetected misstatements, which are then less likely to exceed materiality as a whole.

Performance materiality therefore entails a **prudent approach** to materiality, and to determining the procedures that are needed to conclude on whether or not the financial statements are materially misstated. The higher the assessed risk, the lower the performance materiality must be set. This means that the auditor will perform **more audit work** than if the concept of performance materiality did not exist.

As with overall materiality, setting performance materiality involves the use of **professional judgement**. This judgement must take into account **qualitative** aspects, such as the level of risk attached to a particular balance in the financial statements.

Worked example: Performance materiality

An auditor might judge an entity's non-current assets to be a high-risk area. If non-current assets are £10 million and total assets are £25 million, then setting overall materiality at 2% of total assets gives an overall materiality figure of £0.5 million.

Performance materiality for non-current assets could then be set in proportion to their size relative to total assets ie, at £200,000 (= £10m/£25m × £0.5m).

Taking into account the auditor's judgement that non-current assets are higher risk, this could thus be decreased to £150,000 in order to provide a greater margin of safety. Any misstatements above this level would be judged material.

3.2 Review of materiality

The level of materiality must be reviewed constantly as the audit progresses and **changes** may be required because:

- **Draft financial statements** are **altered** (due to material misstatement and so on) and therefore overall materiality changes.

- **External factors may cause changes** in risk estimates.

  Such changes are caused by **misstatements** found during testing.

4 Audit risk

Section overview

- The auditor adopts a **risk-based approach** to auditing and focuses his testing on the riskiest balances and classes of transactions.

- Audit risk has two elements, the **risk that the financial statements contain a material misstatement** and the **risk that the auditors will fail to detect any material misstatements**.

- Risk of material misstatement in the financial statements has two elements, **inherent** and **control** risk.

- The risk that the auditor will fail to detect material misstatements is known as **detection** risk.

- Auditors set an acceptable level for overall audit risk and carry out sufficient tests to ensure this level is met.

- When the auditor has obtained an understanding of the entity, he must assess the risks of material misstatement in the financial statements, also identifying significant risks.

- **Significant risks** are complex or unusual transactions ie, those that may indicate fraud or other special risks.

Auditors follow a **risk-based approach** to auditing. In the risk-based approach, auditors analyse the risks associated with the client's business, transactions and systems which could lead to misstatements in the financial statements, and direct their testing to risky areas. They are therefore not concerned with individual routine transactions, although they will still be concerned with material, non-routine transactions.

Definition

Audit risk: The risk that the auditor expresses an inappropriate audit opinion when the financial statements are materially misstated. Audit risk is a function of the risks of material misstatement and detection risk.

Figure 3.3: Audit risk

As you can see from Figure 3.3, audit risk has two major components. One is dependent on the entity, and is the risk of material misstatement arising in the financial statements. The other is dependent on the auditor, and is the risk that the auditor will not detect material misstatements in the financial statements.

The risk of material misstatement means more than just the risk that the financial statements contain the wrong numbers. ISAs do not conceive of audit as a process of simply checking the financial statements that the entity has prepared. Rather, the financial statements should be seen as more than just a series of figures, but as embodying certain underlying assertions eg, that the figures are not only correct but are complete and do not miss anything out, and ultimately that they give a 'true and fair view' of the entity's financial position and performance. (The financial statement assertions are covered in more detail in Chapter 4.) As a result, ISAs see auditing as the process whereby the auditor performs an assessment of the risk of these financial statement assertions being materially misstated. The starting point for this process is not the draft financial statements (not just checking the numbers), but the auditor's understanding of the entity and its environment as a whole, as it is from this underlying reality that any risks of material misstatement may later arise.

4.1 Risk of material misstatement in the financial statements

Definition

Inherent risk: The susceptibility of an assertion about a class of transaction, account balance or disclosure to a misstatement that could be material, either individually or when aggregated with other misstatements, before consideration of any related controls.

Inherent risk is the risk that items will be misstated due to characteristics of those items. Example of issues that might increase inherent risk are:

* Balance is, or includes, an estimate

* Balance is important in the account

* Financial statements are liable to misstatement because:

    – Company is in trouble

    – Company is seeking to raise finance

    – Other motivation for directors to misstate the figures (such as profit targets or profit related bonuses)

* Financial statements contain balances with complex financial accounting requirements or a choice of treatment

The auditors must use their professional judgement and all available knowledge to assess inherent risk. If no such information or knowledge is available then the inherent risk is **high**.

Inherent risk is affected by the nature of the entity; for example, the industry it is in and the regulations it falls under, and also the nature of the strategies it adopts. These are the kind of things we looked at in Figure 3.1, when obtaining an understanding of the entity.

Definition

Control risk: The risk that a misstatement that could occur in an assertion about a class of transaction, account balance or disclosure and that could be material, either individually or when aggregated with other misstatements, will not be prevented, or detected and corrected, on a timely basis by the entity's internal control.

In other words this is the risk that a material misstatement would not be prevented, detected or corrected by the accounting and internal control systems.

We shall look at controls in more detail in Chapter 5, where you will learn about the sort of controls you might expect to see in a company, and therefore be able to identify weaknesses, which indicate control risk.

4.2 Risk that the auditor will not detect a material misstatement in the financial statements

Definition

Detection risk: The risk that the procedures performed by the auditor to reduce audit risk to an acceptably low level will not detect a misstatement that exists and that could be material, either individually or when aggregated with other misstatements.

This is the component of audit risk that the auditors have a degree of control over, because, if risk is too high to be tolerated, the auditors can carry out more work to reduce this aspect of audit risk, and therefore audit risk as a whole.

ISA 200 *Overall objectives of the independent auditor and the conduct of an audit in accordance with international standards on auditing* states that 'the auditor shall obtain sufficient appropriate audit evidence to reduce audit risk to an acceptably low level and thereby enable the auditor to draw reasonable conclusions on which to base the auditor's opinion'.

Auditors will want their overall audit risk to be at an acceptable level, or it will not be worth them carrying out the audit. In other words, if the chance of them giving an inappropriate opinion and being sued is high, it might be better not to do the audit at all.

The auditors will obviously consider how risky a new audit client is during the acceptance process, and may decide not to go ahead with the relationship. However, they will also consider audit risk for each individual audit, and will seek to manage the risk.

As we have seen above, it is not in the auditors' power to affect inherent or control risk. As they are risks integral to the client, the auditor cannot change the level of these risks.

The auditor therefore manages overall audit risk by manipulating detection risk, the only element of audit risk the auditor has control over. This is because, the more audit work the auditors carry out, the lower detection risk becomes, although it can never be entirely eliminated due to the inherent limitations of an audit.

This audit risk management can be shown crudely in a mathematical equation. The auditor will decide what level of overall risk is acceptable, and then determine a level of audit work so that detection risk makes the equation work.

Worked example: Audit risk 1

Inherent risk	Control risk	Detection risk	Audit risk
High	High	Low	Acceptable

- Is variable
- Is a high level of audit work

In Worked example 1, inherent and control risk were both high. This has the following effects on the audit.

- The auditors are unlikely to rely on tests of controls, but will carry out extended tests of details (we will look at what this means in practice in Chapter 4).

- Detection risk must be rendered low, which will mean carrying out a substantial number of tests of details.

Audits are not all the same, however. A different company could produce the following audit risk calculation.

Worked example: Audit risk 2

Inherent risk	Control risk	Detection risk	Audit risk
Medium	Low	Medium	Acceptable

In Worked example 2, as control risk is low, the auditors are likely to carry out tests of controls and seek to rely on the client's system. As you will see in Chapter 4, this does not mean substantive procedures can be eliminated entirely. Detection risk in this instance would be affected by the amount of tests of controls and tests of details carried out.

It is important to understand that there is not a standard level of audit risk which is considered generally by auditors to be acceptable. This is a matter of audit judgement, and so will vary from firm to firm and audit to audit. Audit firms are likely to charge higher fees for higher risk clients. Regardless of the risk level of the audit, however, it is vital that audit firms always carry out an audit of **sufficient quality**.

Interactive question 4: Audit risk

Audit risk can be split into three components: inherent risk, control risk and detection risk.

For each of the following examples, indicate the type of risk illustrated.

1 The organisation has few employees in the accounts department
2 The organisation is highly connected with the building trade
3 The assurance firm may do insufficient work to detect material misstatements
4 The financial statements contain a number of estimates

See **Answer** at the end of this chapter.

4.3 Identifying and assessing the risks

ISA 315 says that 'the objective of the auditor is to **identify** and **assess the risks of material misstatement**, whether due to fraud or error, at the **financial statement and assertion levels**, through understanding the entity and its environment...'. It requires the auditor to take the following steps:

Step 1
Identify risks throughout the process of obtaining an understanding of the entity and its environment

Step 2
Assess the identified risks and relate them to what can go wrong at the assertion level (this is the assertions made in the financial statements by the directors, for example, that inventory is £X)

Step 3
Consider whether the risks are of a magnitude that could result in a material misstatement

Step 4
Consider the likelihood of the risks causing a material misstatement

Worked example: Understanding the entity and identifying risks

The audit team at Icket Ltd has been carrying out procedures to obtain an understanding of the entity. In the course of making inquiries about the inventory system, they have discovered that Icket Ltd designs and produces tableware to order for a number of high street stores. It also makes a number of standard lines of tableware, which it sells to a number of wholesalers. By the terms of its contracts with the high street stores, it is not entitled to sell uncalled inventory designed for them to wholesalers. Icket Ltd regularly produces 10% more than the high street stores have ordered, in order to ensure that they meet requirements when the stores do their quality control check. Certain stores have more stringent control requirements than others and regularly reject some of the inventory.

The knowledge above suggests two risks, one that the company may have obsolete inventory, and the other that if their production quality standards are insufficiently high, they could run the risk of losing custom.

We shall look at each of these risks in turn and relate them to the assertion level.

Inventory

If certain of the inventories are obsolete due to the fact that they have been produced in excess of the customer's requirement and there is no other available market for the inventory, then there is a risk that inventory as a whole in the financial statements will not be carried at the appropriate value. Given that inventory is likely to be a material balance in the statement of financial position of a manufacturing company, and the misstatement could be up to 10% of the total value, this has the capacity to be a material misstatement.

The factors that will contribute to the likelihood of these risks causing a misstatement are matters such as:

- Whether management regularly review inventory levels and scrap items that are obsolete
- Whether such items are identified and scrapped at the inventory count
- Whether such items can be put back into production and changed so that they are saleable

Losing custom

The long-term risk of losing custom is a risk that in the future the company will not be able to operate. It could have an impact on the financial statements, if disputed sales were attributed to customers, sales and trade receivables could be overstated, that is, not carried at the correct value. However, it appears less likely that this would be a material problem in either area, as the problem is likely to be restricted to a few customers, and only a few number of sales to those customers.

Again, review of the company's controls over the recording of sales and the debt collection procedures of the company would indicate how likely these risks to the financial statements are to materialise.

Interactive question 5: Identifying risks

You are involved with the audit of Tantpro Ltd, a small company. You have been carrying out procedures to gain an understanding of the entity. The following matters have come to your attention.

The company offers standard credit terms to its customers of 60 days from the date of invoice. Statements are sent to customers on a monthly basis. However, Tantpro Ltd does not employ a credit controller, and other than sending the statements on a monthly basis, it does not otherwise communicate with its customers on a systematic basis. On occasion, the receivables ledger clerk may telephone a customer if the company has not received a payment for some time. Some customers pay regularly according to the credit terms offered to them, but others pay on a very haphazard basis and do not provide a remittance advice. Receivables ledger receipts are entered onto the receivables ledger but not matched to invoices remitted. The company does not produce an aged list of balances.

Requirement

Which **one** of the following is the risk most likely to arise out of the above scenario?

☐ Inventory may be overstated	☐ Inventory may be understated
☐ Purchases may be overstated	☐ Purchases may be understated
☐ Trade receivables may be overstated	☐ Trade receivables may be understated

See **Answer** at the end of this chapter.

4.4 Significant risks

Some risks may be **significant risks**, which require **special audit consideration**. When the auditor is identifying and assessing risks, they must consider whether any of the risks identified are significant risks. When the auditor identifies a significant risk, they must evaluate the design and implementation of the entity's **controls** in that area.

ISA 315 sets out the following factors which indicate that a risk may be a significant risk:

- Risk of fraud
- Related to recent significant economic, accounting or other development
- The complexity of the transaction
- It is a significant transaction with a related party
- The degree of subjectivity in the financial information
- It is an unusual transaction

Routine, non-complex transactions are less likely to give rise to significant risk than unusual transactions or matters of director judgement. This is because unusual transactions are likely to have more:

- management intervention
- manual intervention
- complex accounting principles or calculations
- opportunity for control procedures not to be followed

The ISA notes that although it is less likely that the entity will have controls for non-routine risks, there may still be some. After all, management will still need to respond to these risks in some way. The auditor should understand whether there are controls such as:

- review of assumptions by senior management or experts
- documented processes for estimations
- approval by those charged with governance

An example of a control for a non-routine risk might be that where the entity receives notice of a significant lawsuit, it takes advice from legal counsel and considers the effect on the financial statements.

4.4.1 Related party transactions

There is an auditing standard devoted to this area: ISA (UK) 550, *Related Parties*.

Although hard to define precisely, a related party is someone (or a company) who is related to the entity, its owners or its management. Transactions with related parties might take place for reasons other than the entity's normal business.

Consider the example of North Ltd, whose director, Mr Smith, arranges for the company to make a loan to a business owned by his son. This transaction is outside of North Ltd's normal course of business, and it is possible that it has not been conducted on normal market terms and conditions. The fact that the loan was made to the son's business means that it is not immediately clear that the loan is to a related party. But this transaction is clearly something that users of the financial statements need to know about.

Most financial reporting frameworks, including IFRS, therefore require companies to disclose related party transactions, and this is usually done in the notes to the financial statements. Auditors therefore need to verify these disclosures.

From the auditor's point of view, related party transactions are inherently **risky** because the auditor may not be aware that a party is related. A company might conduct thousands of transactions during the year, and it would be very difficult for the auditor to tell if any of these were with related parties. The matter is made even riskier by the fact that management might not even be aware of reporting requirements in relation to these transactions.

In addition, ISA 550 notes that auditors need to understand related party relationships and transactions in order to ensure that the economic reality of a transaction is reflected in the financial statements.

4.4.2 Risks for which substantive procedures alone are not sufficient

For some of the most significant risks identified, the ISA notes that substantive procedures may not be enough. In many audits there will be a risk that routine transactions are not recorded accurately. There will, by definition, be lots of these transactions, so if the auditor used only substantive procedures then they would have to do a very large amount of work in order to obtain sufficient evidence. Indeed, performing these substantive procedures may not really help to identify problems anyway, especially where processes are highly automated, because errors are less likely to occur as a result of a fault in the routine processing than because of a failure of control to begin with.

5 Fraud

Section overview

- Fraud is an **intentional act** which may result in the financial statements being misstated.

- Errors are **unintentional**.

- **Management** is primarily **responsible** for preventing and detecting fraud.

- The **auditor** is responsible for detecting **material misstatements**, whether as a result of fraud or error.

ISA (UK) 240, *The Auditor's Responsibilities Relating to Fraud in an Audit of Financial Statements* provides guidance to auditors in this area.

5.1 Fraud and error

Definitions

Fraud: An intentional act by one or more individuals among management, those charged with governance, employees, or third parties, involving the use of deception to obtain an unjust or illegal advantage.

Error: An unintentional misstatement in financial statements, including the omission of an amount or a disclosure.

The financial statements can fail to give a true and fair view (ie, be misstated) as a result of either **fraud** or **error**. Fraud is a wide legal concept, but the auditor's main concern is with fraud that causes a material misstatement in the financial statements. It is distinguished from error, which is when a material misstatement is caused by mistake; for example, in the misapplication of an accounting policy.

An example of a fraud might be if a management accountant submits false invoices that she pretends are from a supplier, and then approves them for payment, knowing the payment will actually go into a bank account belonging to her. An example of an error might be if she enters the wrong amount when entering the invoice onto the accounting system, misstating the amount of the expense.

5.2 Characteristics of fraud

There are two types of fraud causing material misstatement in financial statements:

- Fraudulent financial reporting
- Misappropriation of assets

Fraudulent financial reporting involves **intentional misstatements**, including omissions of amounts or disclosures in financial statements, to deceive financial statement users.

Misappropriation of assets involves the **theft of an entity's assets** and is often perpetrated by employees in relatively small and immaterial amounts. However, it can also involve management who are usually more capable of disguising or concealing misappropriations in ways that are difficult to detect.

5.3   Responsibilities in relation to fraud

The company's management is responsible for preventing and detecting both fraud and error. They do this by putting in place a system of internal control over the company's transactions and exercising oversight over this system, and by creating a culture of honesty and ethical behaviour.

The auditor is responsible for obtaining reasonable assurance that the financial statements are free from material misstatement, whether caused by fraud or error. Material misstatements from fraud are at greater risk of not being detected than material misstatements from error. This is because:

- fraud may involve sophisticated schemes designed to conceal it

- fraud may be perpetrated by individuals in collusion

- management fraud is harder to detect because management is in a position to manipulate accounting records or override control procedures

The auditor is responsible for maintaining professional scepticism throughout the audit, considering the possibility of management override of controls, and recognising that audit procedures effective for detecting errors may not be effective for detecting fraud.

5.4   Auditor's objectives

The auditor's objectives in relation to fraud are:

(a)   to identify and assess the risks of material misstatement due to fraud

(b)   to obtain evidence regarding these risks by designing and implementing appropriate responses

(c)   to respond appropriately to any actual or suspected fraud identified during the audit

ISA 315 requires there to be a discussion among the engagement team about where fraud might take place at the entity, which is usually done during the planning phase.

Summary and Self-test

Summary

Planning is necessary to ensure work is carried out efficiently and effectively

Key elements of an overall audit strategy:
- Undestanding the entity and its environment
- Risk and materiality
- Practical matters

In order to identify risks:
- Inquiry
- Analytical procedures
- Inspection and observation

Need professional scepticism

Analysis of significant fluctuations from expected results

The concept of significance to readers. A matter is generally considered to be material if it would affect the decision of a user of financial statements

Audit risk =
inherent risk ×
control risk ×
detection risk ×

→ The risk that a material misstatement exists in the financial statements

→ The risk that auditors do not uncover material misstatements

Self-test

Answer the following questions.

1 Complete the definitions:

An .... is the formulation of a general strategy for the audit.

An .... is a set of instructions to the audit team that sets out the further audit procedures to be carried out.

2 Name **four** sources of information which could be used at the planning stage of the audit.

1 ....

2 ....

3 ....

4 ....

3 Which of the following procedures might an auditor use in gaining an understanding of the entity?

(a) Inquiry
(b) Recalculation
(c) Analytical procedures
(d) Reperformance of a control
(e) Observation and inspection

4 The audit team is required to discuss the susceptibility of the financial statements to material misstatements.

☐ True

☐ False

5 Match the percentages to the values for a typical calculation of materiality.

	%
Profit before tax	5–10
Revenue	1–2
Total assets	½–1

6 Complete the definitions.

.... risk is the risk that.. expresses an.. opinion when the financial statements are materially misstated.

.... risk is the .... of an assertion about a ...., account balance or disclosure to a .... that could be material, either individually or when aggregated with other misstatements, before consideration of any related controls.

7 If control and inherent risk are assessed as sufficiently low, substantive procedures can be abandoned completely.

☐ True

☐ False

8 Name **four** factors which might indicate a significant risk.

1 ....

2 ....

3 ....

4 ....

9   The main difference between fraud and error is that fraud involves a material loss of assets.

☐   True

☐   False

Now, go back to the Learning Objectives in the Introduction. If you are satisfied you have achieved these objectives, please tick them off.

Technical references

1 Planning

- The role and timing of planning | ISA (UK) 300.2
- Objective | ISA (UK) 300.4
- Requirements | ISA (UK) 300.5 – 13
- Risk assessment procedures | ISA (UK) 315.5 – 10
- Understanding the entity | ISA (UK) 315.11 – 24
- Professional scepticism | ISA (UK) 200.15

2 Analytical procedures

- Definition | ISA (UK) 520.4, A1, A2
- Analytical procedures in planning | ISA (UK) 315.6

3 Materiality

- Definition | ISA (UK) 320.9
- Use in auditing | ISA (UK) 320.A1
- Revision | ISA (UK) 320.12

4 Audit risk

- Definitions | ISA (UK) 200.13
- Identifying and assessing the risks | ISA (UK) 315.3
- Significant risks | ISA (UK) 315.28 – 30

5 Fraud

- Definitions | ISA (UK) 240.11 / IAASB Glossary of Terms
- Fraud and error | ISA (UK) 240.2
- Characteristics | ISA (UK) 240.3
- Responsibilities | ISA (UK) 240.4 – 8
- Objectives | ISA (UK) 240.10

Answer to Interactive question 1

The results of audit risk assessment

Calculation of preliminary materiality

List of staff to be involved with the audit

The contract between the firm and client is generally found in the engagement letter which is a separate document. Detailed plan of audit procedures to be carried out would be contained in the audit plan.

Answer to Interactive question 2

Inspection
Observation
Inquiry
Analytical procedures

Although the auditor may use computation, particularly when carrying out analytical procedures, it is not a required tool, whereas a combination of the procedures outlined above is required by the ISA.

Answer to Interactive question 3

Sales and cost of sales

Repairs and renewals

Motor expenses

On the face of it, sales do not appear to have fallen much below what was anticipated for the year, but the fact that the gross margin has changed so much (from 37% to 26%) indicates that there may be a problem somewhere in sales and cost of sales, hence rather than focus on one or the other (you might have selected cost of sales only, due to the fact that the major difference from budget is here) it would be best to look at the whole issue together. Gross margin may look wrong because sales are understated in error – and sales were actually much better for the year than anticipated.

Depreciation, as you might expect, appears to have been predicted accurately and is low risk. Problems with depreciation if they existed would probably be uncovered by an analysis of the statement of financial position.

Repairs and renewals and motor expenses vary substantially from budget, so are worth further investigation.

Answer to Interactive question 4

1   Control – the fact that there are few employees in the accounts department means that segregation of duties will be limited (see Chapter 5 for more details in this area)

2   Inherent – this is a naturally risky industry

3   Detection – this is in essence the definition of detection risk

4   Inherent – there is a risk that estimates may be inappropriate

Answer to Interactive question 5

The key risk arising from the above information is that trade receivables will not be carried at the appropriate **value** in the financial statements, as some may be irrecoverable. Where receipts are not matched against invoices in the ledger, the balance on the ledger may include old invoices that the customer has no intention of paying.

It is difficult to assess at this stage whether this is likely to be material. Trade receivables is likely to be a material balance in the financial statements, but the number of irrecoverable balances may not be material. Analytical procedures, for example, to see if the level of accounts receivable has risen year on year, in a manner that is not explained by price rises or levels of production, might help to assess this.

A key factor that affects the likelihood of the material misstatement arising is the poor controls over the receivables ledger. The fact that invoices are not matched against receipts increases the chance of old invoices not having been paid and not noticed by Tantpro Ltd. It appears reasonably likely that the trade receivables balance is overstated in this instance.

Answers to Self-test

1　Overall audit strategy, audit plan

2　Four from:

- Interim financial information
- Budgets
- Management accounts
- Non-financial information
- Bank and cash records
- Sales tax returns
- Board minutes
- Discussions or correspondence with the client at the year-end

3　(a), (c), (e)

4　True

5

	%
Profit before tax	5–10
Revenue	½–1
Total assets	1–2

6　Audit, the auditor, inappropriate audit

　Inherent, susceptibility, class of transactions, misstatement

7　False

8　Any of:

- Risk of fraud
- Relationship with recent developments
- Degree of subjectivity in the financial information
- The fact that it is an unusual transaction
- Transaction with a related party
- Complexity of the transaction

9　False. Both fraud and error could result in the loss of assets. The main difference between fraud and error is intent.

CHAPTER 4

Process of assurance: evidence and reporting

Introduction
Examination context
Topic List
    1 Evidence
    2 Reporting
Summary and Self-test
Technical references
Answers to Interactive questions
Answers to Self-test

Learning objectives

Tick off

- Define the assurance process, including obtaining evidence ☐
- Identify when tests of controls and substantive procedures will be used ☐
- Understand that assurance may be positive or negative ☐
- Know the contents of the audit report ☐
- Be aware of the other types of report that may be issued after an assurance engagement ☐

This topic will be covered in more detail in subsequent chapters.

Specific syllabus references for this chapter are: 1, f, g, 3b.

Syllabus links

The issue of drawing conclusions and reporting will be looked at in more detail in *Audit and Assurance*. Clearly the basic evidence collection that you learn at this level will feed into the drawing of conclusions at the Application level.

Examination context

Evidence is a very important topic for the exam, and half of this Study Manual is dedicated to the collection of evidence. Gathering evidence on an assurance engagement represents 35% of the syllabus. In contrast, reporting is a minor area of the syllabus, so you should expect no more than one or two questions in this area.

In the assessment, candidates may be required to:

- identify the different methods of obtaining evidence including tests of control, substantive procedures including analytical procedures and data analytics
- evaluate the quality of different types of audit evidence
- identify the financial statement assertions
- determine the level of assurance provided by audit reports and other assurance reports

1 Evidence

Section overview

- Auditors must obtain sufficient, appropriate audit evidence.
- Evidence can be in the form of tests of controls or substantive procedures.
- The reliability of audit evidence is influenced by its source and by its nature.
- Audit tests are designed to obtain evidence about the financial statement assertions.

1.1 Evidence

The objective of an assurance engagement is to enable practitioners to express an opinion on whether the subject of the assurance engagement is in accordance with the identified criteria. There is an ISA on audit evidence (ISA 500), which we shall look at here.

Remember that audit requires a reasonable level of assurance to be given, and correspondingly detailed audit evidence needs to be obtained. In a lower level assurance engagement, less evidence will be required to support the conclusion. We shall look at the sufficiency of evidence obtained in more detail in a later chapter.

In this section, we shall introduce the **audit evidence** auditors gather, to **enable** them to express an opinion of reasonable assurance on financial statements. We shall look at the process of gathering evidence in more detail later in this study manual, particularly in Chapters 5–8 and 11–13.

Definition

Audit evidence: Information used by the auditor in arriving at the conclusions on which the auditor's opinion is based.

Audit evidence includes both the information contained within the accounting records underlying the financial statements, and other information gathered by the auditors, such as confirmations from third parties. Auditors are **not expected to look at all the information** that might exist. They will often perform their testing on a sample basis, as we shall see in Chapter 11.

In order to reach a position in which they can express a professional opinion, the auditors need to gather evidence from various sources. There are potentially two types of test which they will carry out: tests of controls and substantive procedures.

Definitions

Tests of controls: Audit procedures designed to evaluate the operating effectiveness of controls in preventing, or detecting and correcting material misstatements at the assertion level.

Substantive procedures: Audit procedures designed to detect material misstatements at the assertion level. Substantive procedures comprise:

- Tests of detail (of classes of transactions, account balances and disclosures)
- Substantive analytical procedures

We shall look in detail at financial statement assertions later in this chapter.

When the auditors carry out tests of controls, they are seeking to rely on the good operation of the control system that the company has in place to draw a conclusion that the financial statements give a true and fair view. The logic is as follows.

- The directors set up systems of internal controls to ensure they report correctly to the shareholders (we shall look at internal controls in more detail in the next chapter).

- The auditors are required to conclude whether the financial statements give a true and fair view.

- The auditors evaluate the control system put in place to assess whether it is capable of producing financial statements which give a true and fair view.

- The auditors test the control system to assess whether it has operated as it was intended to, therefore giving assurance that the financial statements give a true and fair view.

When the auditors carry out substantive procedures, they are testing whether specific items within balances or transactions in the financial statements are stated correctly.

ISAs require that auditors must always carry out some substantive procedures, because the limitations in internal control systems (which we will look at in the next chapter) mean that the control system can never be fully relied on. However, there may also be instances of cases where it is more appropriate to test controls than to test specific balances or transactions (this will be discussed more later).

1.2 Sufficient appropriate audit evidence

ISA (UK) 500, *Audit Evidence* requires auditors to 'obtain **sufficient appropriate** audit evidence to be able to draw **reasonable conclusions** on which to base the auditor's opinion'. 'Sufficiency' and 'appropriateness' are interrelated and apply to both tests of controls and substantive procedures.

- **Sufficiency** is the measure of the **quantity** of audit evidence.
- **Appropriateness** is the measure of the **quality** or relevance and **reliability** of the audit evidence.

How much evidence is required will depend on the level of assurance being offered in an engagement.

The **quantity** of audit evidence required is affected by the **level of risk** in the area being audited. It is also affected by the **quality** of evidence obtained. If the evidence is high quality, the auditor may need less than if it were poor quality. However, obtaining a high quantity of poor quality evidence will not cancel out its poor quality. The following generalisations may help in assessing the **reliability** of audit evidence.

Quality of evidence	
External	Audit evidence from **external sources** is more reliable than that obtained from the entity's records
Auditor	Evidence obtained **directly by auditors** is more reliable than that obtained indirectly or by inference
Entity	Evidence obtained from the entity's records is more reliable when related **control systems operate effectively**
Written	Evidence in the form of **documents (paper or electronic)** or **written representations** are more reliable than oral representations
Originals	Original documents are more reliable than photocopies, or facsimiles

Auditors will often use information produced by the entity when obtaining audit evidence, although this will not always be a strong form of audit evidence. When doing so, the ISA requires that the auditor ensures it is sufficiently reliable, including 'obtaining audit evidence about the **accuracy and completeness** of the information and evaluating whether the information is sufficiently precise and detailed for the auditor's purposes'. This may be achieved by testing controls in the related area.

1.3 Financial statement assertions

Definition

Financial statement assertions: Representations by management, explicit or otherwise, that are embodied in the financial statements, as used by the auditor to consider the different types of potential misstatements that may occur.

By approving the financial statements, the directors are making representations about the information therein. These representations or assertions may be described in general terms in a number of ways.

ISA (UK) 315, *Identifying and Assessing the Risks of Material Misstatement through Understanding the Entity and its Environment* states that 'The objective of the auditor is to identify and assess the risks of material misstatement, whether due to fraud or error, **at the financial statement and assertion levels,** through understanding the entity and its environment, including the entity's internal control, thereby providing a basis for designing and implementing responses to the assessed risks of material misstatement'. The auditor must therefore identify risks both for the specific assertions (classes of transactions etc) and for the financial statements as a whole.

ISA 315 gives the following examples of financial statement assertions.

Assertions used by the auditor	
Assertions about **classes of transactions** and events, and **related disclosures**, for the period under audit	**Occurrence:** transactions and events that have been recorded or disclosed, have occurred, and such transactions and events pertain to the entity
	Completeness: all transactions and events that should have been recorded have been recorded, and all related disclosures that should have been included in the financial statements have been included
	Accuracy: amounts and other data relating to recorded transactions and events have been recorded appropriately, and related disclosures have been appropriately measured and described
	Cut-off: transactions and events have been recorded in the correct accounting period
	Classification: transactions and events have been recorded in the proper accounts
	Presentation: transactions and events are appropriately aggregated or disaggregated and clearly described, and related disclosures are relevant and understandable in the context of the requirements of the applicable financial reporting framework
Assertions about **account balances**, and **related disclosures**, at the period end	**Existence:** assets, liabilities and equity interests exist
	Rights and obligations: the entity holds or controls the rights to assets, and liabilities are the obligations of the entity
	Completeness: all assets, liabilities and equity interests that should have been recorded have been recorded and all related disclosures that should have been included in the financial statements have been included
	Accuracy, valuation and allocation: assets, liabilities, and equity interests have been included in the financial statements at appropriate amounts and any resulting valuation or allocation adjustments have been appropriately recorded, and related disclosures have been appropriately measured and described
	Classification: assets, liabilities, and equity interests have been recorded in the proper accounts
	Presentation: assets, liabilities, and equity interests are appropriately aggregated or disaggregated and clearly described, and related disclosures are relevant and understandable in the context of the requirements of the applicable financial reporting framework

Interactive question 1: Financial statement assertions

The senior financial controller of the audited entity has been off work with illness for six months. Her temporary replacement has not worked in a role at this level before and appears to be struggling to keep up with her workload.

Requirement

At which **one** of the following levels does this situation present an audit risk?

☐ Financial statement level

☐ Assertion level

See **Answer** at the end of this chapter.

1.4 Tests of controls or tests of detail?

ISA (UK) 330, *The Auditor's Responses to Assessed Risks* follows on from ISA 315. Both ISAs are of particular use at the planning stage of the audit. ISA 315 required auditors to assess the risks of material misstatement. ISA 330 then simply requires auditors to respond to the risks of misstatement that they have found ie, to determine how to they are going to obtain evidence about the risks of misstatement. This involves designing and performing audit procedures in order to detect material misstatements – to manage detection risk, as we saw in Chapter 3.

The auditor must choose what kind of procedures to perform. In most cases this will be a mixture of tests of controls and substantive procedures. The auditor must always perform **some** substantive procedures, no matter how reliable an entity's internal controls are.

What that means is that the auditors must carry out tests to reduce the risk of there being a material misstatement that they do not know about, and the audit opinion therefore being incorrect. What tests the auditors will carry out is largely a matter of judgement for the auditors and depends on the nature of the risk.

Worked example: What type of test?

SuperRetail plc is a large retailing operation which has sophisticated point of sale technology and a revenue from sales of £5 billion annually. This represents millions of point of sale transactions.

In order to test the **completeness of revenue** in the financial statements, rather than sample millions of individual transactions and verify them to individual sales receipts, it is going to be significantly more efficient and cost effective for the auditors to test whether the revenue system, with regard to sales recording, operates effectively overall. In this case, the auditors would choose to test controls over revenue recording to establish whether they can rely on the fact that the system worked as it was supposed to and material mistakes in the recording of sales have not occurred.

During the year, SuperRetail plc also invested in new premises for stores. This involved the purchase of three pieces of land. In one case, building work on the new store has started, but in the other two it has not.

In order to test the **valuation** of these **additions to non-current assets** in the financial statements, rather than look in detail at the systems surrounding land purchase and building, it will be more efficient and cost effective for the auditors to verify the cost of the land to purchase documentation and the cost of the building to date to the surveyor's reports. This will be a substantive procedure.

In the first instance, the auditors had to consider a vast number of transactions which were all carried out in a normal, routine fashion through a sophisticated system, in the second, a small number of large transactions, which, although they were probably carried out in line with an established company policy, were easily verified by available, third party evidence. Thus the auditors made a judgement about the best way to collect evidence concerning those different assertions.

We will look in more detail at obtaining evidence in the following chapters of this study manual. First we shall look at obtaining evidence by testing controls, then in more detail at obtaining evidence by substantive procedures.

When the auditor believes controls are operating effectively, the auditor shall perform tests of controls to obtain sufficient appropriate audit evidence that the controls were operating effectively at relevant times during the period under audit. So, for example, if controls over revenue and receivables were expected to operate effectively, auditors need to test controls in that area.

It is also necessary to undertake tests of controls when it will not be possible to obtain sufficient appropriate audit evidence simply from substantive procedures. This might be the case if the entity conducts its business using IT systems which do not produce documentation of transactions.

In carrying out tests of control, auditors must use **inquiry**, but must not only use inquiry. Other procedures must also be used. In testing controls, **reperformance** by the auditor will often be a helpful procedure, as will **observation**.

When considering timing in relation to tests of controls, the purpose of the test will be important. For example, if the company carries out a year-end inventory count, controls over the inventory count can only be tested at the year end. Other controls will operate all year, and the auditor will need to test that controls have been effective all year.

Some controls may have been tested in prior audits and the auditor may choose to rely on that evidence of their effectiveness. If this is the case, the auditor must obtain evidence about any changes since the controls were last tested and must test the controls if they have changed. In any case, controls should be tested for effectiveness at least once in every three audits.

If the related risk has been designated a significant risk, the auditor cannot rely on testing carried out in prior years, but shall carry out testing in the current year.

The auditor must always carry out substantive procedures on material items.

In addition, the auditor **must** carry out the following substantive procedures:

- agreeing the financial statements to the underlying accounting records
- examining material journal entries
- examining other adjustments made in preparing the financial statements

As you know, substantive procedures fall into two categories: analytical procedures and other procedures. The auditor must determine when it is appropriate to use which type of substantive procedure.

Analytical procedures tend to be appropriate for large volumes of predictable transactions (for example, wages and salaries). **Other procedures (tests of detail)** may be appropriate to gain information about account balances (for example, inventories or trade receivables), particularly verifying the assertions of existence and valuation.

Tests of detail rather than analytical procedures are likely to be more appropriate with regard to matters which have been identified as **significant risks**, but the auditor must determine procedures that are specifically responsive to that risk, which may include analytical procedures. Significant risks are likely to be the most difficult to obtain sufficient appropriate evidence about.

1.4.1 Effect of data analytics

The rise of data analytics in recent years has led some to think again about how and why auditors test internal controls.

Data analytics is the examination of data to try to identify patterns, trends or correlations. Recent advances in IT make it increasingly possible for auditors to examine a complete data set – 100% of the transactions – and to represent trends graphically, almost instantly. Some have claimed that these techniques may bring about a long-term revolution in audit approaches, since they enable auditors to focus on 100% of the transactions rather than just a sample (as auditing standards assume).

This raises a question not only about sampling, but about the whole approach of placing reliance on an entity's internal controls. It is a basic assumption of the concept of an audit contained in ISAs that it is impractical to test 100% of transactions. It is because of this that the audit is conceived of as a risk-management exercise, in which the auditor obtains evidence of the effectiveness of the entity's own internal controls, as a way of assessing the risk of there being a material misstatement. But if the auditor can now test 100% of the transactions, why worry about controls at all?

Even if nothing else, the auditor relying on data analytics would still have to understand the system which produced the data being analysed. The auditor would also need to understand and test how data got into the system in the first place: for example, a data set might show that a certain amount of cash has been received by an entity, but the only way you can really tell whether this is reliable is by testing the actual cash receipts. Data analytics is unlikely to help here.

It appears likely that, even if it does not eliminate controls testing *in toto*, data analytics will lead to a reconsideration of how controls are tested, particularly controls in an IT environment.

Interactive question 2: Types of procedure

For each of the following statements, indicate whether they are true or false.

Tests of controls are tests designed to give evidence of whether the controls in a company are operating effectively or not.

☐ True

☐ False

Analytical procedures are a type of substantive procedure.

☐ True

☐ False

A lack of credit control activities would affect the valuation assertion for trade receivables.

☐ True

☐ False

See **Answer** at the end of this chapter.

2 Reporting

Section overview

- Reasonable or limited assurance can be given.

- The auditor's report contains a number of elements required by law and by ISAs.

- The auditor's report gives a high level of assurance, but concerns remain about the gap between what users think it means and what it actually means.

- The purpose of gathering evidence is to be able to express an opinion on the subject matter of the assurance engagement.

2.1 Types of opinion

We have already mentioned in Chapter 1 the different levels of assurance that can be offered in an assurance engagement (reasonable and limited). The difference between these types of assurance can be seen by comparing the reports produced at the end of an audit and at the end of a review (lower level engagement).

Worked example: Opinion

Auditor's opinion

In our opinion, the financial statements:

- give a true and fair view of the state of the company's affairs as at _ and of its profit (loss) for the year then ended;

- have been properly prepared in accordance with IFRSs as adopted by the European Union; and

- have been prepared in accordance with the requirements of the Companies Act 2006.

In this text we refer to the auditor's report as given in FRC Bulletin *Compendium of illustrative auditor's reports on United Kingdom private sector financial statements for periods commencing on or after 17 June 2016* (October 2016). This document provides illustrative examples of standard UK auditor's reports which include references to the Companies Act 2006 and UK GAAP, and to UK auditing standards.

2.2 Content of the auditor's report

In this syllabus, you are only concerned with cases where the auditor finds that he **can** conclude that the financial statements give a true and fair view. Such an auditor's report is referred to as an 'unmodified' auditor's report.

Explicit opinions

In respect of the **state of the company's affairs** at the end of the financial year.

In respect of the **company's profit or loss** for the financial year.

In relation to the **financial reporting framework** (IFRSs or UK GAAP).

In respect of other legal requirements of the **Companies Act 2006**.

The **information** given in the **strategic report and the directors' report** is **consistent** with the **financial statements**.

In addition, certain requirements are reported on **by exception**. What this means is that the auditor only has to report on them if they have not been met (if there is a problem). Another way of saying this is that they are 'implied opinions', because the unmodified auditor's report does not explicitly state an opinion on them, but merely implies that no problems have been found.

Items included only by exception

Adequate accounting records have been kept.

Returns adequate for the audit have been received from branches not visited.

The **financial statements** are in **agreement** with the **accounting records** and returns.

All information and **explanations** have been **received** as the auditors think necessary and they have had access at all times to the company's books, accounts and vouchers.

Details of directors' **emoluments** and other benefits have been correctly **disclosed** in the financial statements.

Particulars of loans and other **transactions** in favour of **directors** and others have been correctly disclosed in the financial statements.

The auditor's report should include the following basic elements, usually in the following layout.

- **Title**

- **Addressee**

- **Auditor's opinion** section comes first, with the heading 'Opinion', expressing an opinion on the financial statements

- **Basis for opinion** section

- **Going concern** section, where applicable
- **Key audit matters** section, for audits of listed companies
- **Other information** section
- **Responsibilities of management for the financial statements** section
- **Auditor's responsibilities for the audit of the financial statements** section
- **Opinion on other matters** such as specific statutory requirements eg, on whether the Directors' Report and the Strategic Report are consistent with the financial statements
- Matters on which the auditor is required to report on **by exception**
- **Name** of engagement partner
- **Signature** of engagement partner
- Auditor's **address**
- **Date** of the report

The Companies Act 2006 states that where the auditor is a firm, the auditor's report must be signed by the **senior statutory auditor** in his own name, for and on behalf of the audit firm. Under ISAs, senior statutory auditor has the same meaning as the term 'engagement partner'.

A measure of uniformity in the form and content of the auditor's report is desirable because it helps to promote the reader's understanding and to identify unusual circumstances when they occur. However the standard unmodified auditor's report for listed entities does include a section on Key Audit Matters, which must be tailored to each audit. This allows auditors to provide more information in their reports but without expressing a modified opinion.

The FRC had been the first standard setter in the world to develop this new style of auditor reporting in relation to key audit matters, and for some time its ISA (UK) 700 differed from the IAASB's ISA 700. Things changed, however, in 2015 when the IAASB's project on auditor reporting was completed and key audit matters were included in the standard IAASB auditor's report. As a result, the FRC adopted the IAASB's version of ISA 700 in 2016, and the two are now substantially similar.

ISA (UK) 701, *Communicating Key Audit Matters in the Independent Auditor's Report* is a totally new standard. As its name suggests, this standard gives guidance on determining which key audit matters to include in the auditor's report, and on what information should be given in respect of them. Key audit matters are 'matters of most significance' to the audit. ISA (UK) 701 largely follows the IAASB's ISA 701, but requires the auditor to provide further information about how it applied materiality in the audit. Many of these requirements were already in place in the previous version of ISA (UK) 700.

ISA (UK) 701 requires the auditor to choose which matters are key matters. Broadly speaking, these are the areas of the audit that were risky, and which needed the most audit work/attention. More precisely, ISA (UK) 701: para. 9 states that the auditor takes into account: areas of high risk; areas of significant auditor and management judgment (eg, accounting estimates); significant transactions or events.

An example of a complete UK auditor's report is given below, adapted from Appendix 3 of the FRC Bulletin referred to in section 2.1 above.

Worked example: UK auditor's report (FRC Bulletin (2016))

Independent Auditor's Report to the Members of XYZ Ltd

Opinion

We have audited the financial statements of [XYZ Limited] (the 'company') for the year ended [date] which comprise [specify the titles of the primary statements] and notes to the financial statements, including a summary of significant accounting policies. The financial reporting framework that has been applied in their preparation is applicable law and International Financial Reporting Standards (IFRSs) as adopted by the European Union.

In our opinion, the financial statements:

- give a true and fair view of the state of the company's affairs as at [date] and of its [profit/loss] for the year then ended;

- have been properly prepared in accordance with IFRSs as adopted by the European Union; and

- have been prepared in accordance with the requirements of the Companies Act 2006.

Basis for opinion

We conducted our audit in accordance with International Standards on Auditing (UK) (ISAs (UK)) and applicable law. Our responsibilities under those standards are further described in the Auditor's responsibilities for the audit of the financial statements section of our report. We are independent of the company in accordance with the ethical requirements that are relevant to our audit of the financial statements in the UK, including the FRC's Ethical Standard as applied to listed entities, and we have fulfilled our other ethical responsibilities in accordance with these requirements. We believe that the audit evidence we have obtained is sufficient and appropriate to provide a basis for our opinion.

Conclusions relating to going concern

We have nothing to report in respect of the following matters in relation to which the ISAs (UK) require us to report to you where:

- the directors' use of the going concern basis of accounting in the preparation of the financial statements is not appropriate; or

- the directors have not disclosed in the financial statements any identified material uncertainties that may cast significant doubt about the company's ability to continue to adopt the going concern basis of accounting for a period of at least twelve months from the date when the financial statements are authorised for issue.

Key audit matters

Key audit matters are those matters that, in our professional judgment, were of most significance in our audit of the financial statements of the current period and include the most significant assessed risks of material misstatement (whether or not due to fraud) we identified, including those which had the greatest effect on: the overall audit strategy, the allocation of resources in the audit; and directing the efforts of the engagement team. These matters were addressed in the context of our audit of the financial statements as a whole, and in forming our opinion thereon, and we do not provide a separate opinion on these matters.

[Description of each key audit matter in accordance with ISA (UK) 701.]

Our application of materiality

[Explanation of how the auditor applied the concept of materiality in planning and performing the audit. This is required to include the threshold used by the auditor as being materiality for the financial statements as a whole but may include other relevant disclosures.]

An overview of the scope of our audit

[Overview of the scope of the audit, including an explanation of how the scope addressed each key audit matter and was influenced by the auditor's application of materiality.]

Other information

The directors are responsible for the other information. The other information comprises the information included in the annual report, other than the financial statements and our auditor's report thereon. Our opinion on the financial statements does not cover the other information and, except to the extent otherwise explicitly stated in our report, we do not express any form of assurance conclusion thereon.

In connection with our audit of the financial statements, our responsibility is to read the other information and, in doing so, consider whether the other information is materially inconsistent with the financial statements or our knowledge obtained in the audit or otherwise appears to be materially misstated. If we identify such material inconsistencies or apparent material misstatements, we are required to determine whether there is a material misstatement in the financial statements or a material misstatement of the other information. If, based on the work we have performed, we conclude that there is a material misstatement of this other information, we are required to report that fact.

We have nothing to report in this regard.

Opinion on other matters prescribed by the Companies Act 2006

In our opinion, based on the work undertaken in the course of the audit:

- the information given in the strategic report and the directors' report for the financial year for which the financial statements are prepared is consistent with the financial statements; and

- the strategic report and the directors' report has been prepared in accordance with applicable legal requirements.

Matters on which we are required to report by exception

In the light of the knowledge and understanding of the company and its environment obtained in the course of the audit, we have not identified material misstatements in the strategic report and the directors' report.

We have nothing to report in respect of the following matters in relation to which the Companies Act 2006 requires us to report to you if, in our opinion:

- adequate accounting records have not been kept, or returns adequate for our audit have not been received from branches not visited by us;

- the financial statements are not in agreement with the accounting records and returns;

- certain disclosures of directors' remuneration specified by law are not made; or

- we have not received all the information and explanations we require for our audit.

Responsibilities of directors

As explained more fully in the directors' responsibilities statement [set out on page ...], the directors are responsible for the preparation of the financial statements and for being satisfied that they give a true and fair view, and for such internal control as the directors determine is necessary to enable the preparation of financial statements that are free from material misstatement, whether due to fraud or error.

In preparing the financial statements, the directors are responsible for assessing the company's ability to continue as a going concern, disclosing, as applicable, matters related to going concern and using the going concern basis of accounting unless the directors either intend to liquidate the company or to cease operations, or have no realistic alternative but to do so.

Auditor's responsibilities for the audit of the financial statements

Our objectives are to obtain reasonable assurance about whether the financial statements as a whole are free from material misstatement, whether due to fraud or error, and to issue an auditor's report that includes our opinion. Reasonable assurance is a high level of assurance, but is not a guarantee that an audit conducted in accordance with ISAs (UK) will always detect a material misstatement when it exists. Misstatements can arise from fraud or error and are considered material if, individually or in the aggregate, they could reasonably be expected to influence the economic decisions of users taken on the basis of these financial statements.

A further description of our responsibilities for the audit of the financial statements is located on the Financial Reporting Council's website at: [website link]. This description forms part of our auditor's report.

[Signature]   Address

John Smith (Senior statutory auditor)   Date

for and on behalf of ABC LLP, Statutory Auditor

The FRC is clear that auditors' reports must not simply use the same standard wording, but should be tailored to the circumstances of each engagement. We have therefore reproduced below extracts from two real auditor's reports in order to help illustrate this. The extracts focus on the sections of the reports dealing with the key audit matters.

Please note that at this stage in your studies you are not expected to understand all of the technical audit and accounting terminology used in these reports. Furthermore, at the time these materials went to print, auditors had not yet begun to use the Bulletin on which your exam is based, so no real-world examples of auditors' reports based on this guidance were available. Some of the technical detail in these reports therefore differs from what will be in your exam.

Worked example: Extracts from auditor's report on Lloyds Banking Group plc, 2017

Independent auditors' report to the members of Lloyds Banking Group plc

REPORT ON THE FINANCIAL STATEMENTS

Our opinion

In our opinion:

– Lloyds Banking Group plc's consolidated financial statements and parent company financial statements (the 'financial statements') give a true and fair view of the state of the Group's and of the parent company's affairs as at 31 December 2016 and of the Group's profit and the Group's and the parent company's cash flows for the year then ended;

– the consolidated financial statements have been properly prepared in accordance with International Financial Reporting Standards ('IFRSs') as adopted by the European Union;

– the parent company financial statements have been properly prepared in accordance with IFRSs as adopted by the European Union and as applied in accordance with the provisions of the Companies Act 2006; and

– the financial statements have been prepared in accordance with the requirements of the Companies Act 2006 and, as regards the consolidated financial statements, Article 4 of the IAS Regulation.

[…]

Our audit approach

Overview

– Overall Group materiality: £325 million which represents 5 per cent of the 3 year average of adjusted profit before tax. Statutory profits were adjusted to remove the effects of certain items which are exceptional and/or one-off in nature.

– The scope of our audit and the nature, timing and extent of audit procedures performed were determined by our risk assessment, the financial significance of reporting units and other qualitative factors (including history of misstatement through fraud or error).

– We performed audit procedures over reporting units we considered financially significant in the context of the Group (full scope audit) or in the context of individual primary statement account balances (audit of specific account balances). We also performed other procedures including testing entity level controls and analytical review procedures to mitigate the risk of material misstatement in the residual reporting units.

The areas of focus for our audit which involved the greatest allocation of our resources and effort were:

– Loan loss impairment provisions
– Conduct risk and provisions
– Insurance actuarial assumptions
– Defined benefit obligations
– Hedge accounting

– Deferred tax asset
– Uncertain tax positions
– Significant transactions
– Privileged access to IT systems

These items were initially discussed with the Audit Committee as part of our audit plan. There were no modifications to this initial assessment and these were the key matters for discussion at the conclusion of our audit.

[…]

Areas of focus

We conducted our audit in accordance with International Standards on Auditing (UK and Ireland) ('ISAs (UK & Ireland)').

We designed our audit by applying materiality and assessing the risks of material misstatement in the financial statements. In particular, we looked at where the directors made subjective judgements, for example in respect of significant accounting estimates that involved making assumptions and considering future events that are inherently uncertain. We also addressed the risk of management override of internal controls, including evaluating whether there was evidence of bias by the directors or management that represented a risk of material misstatement due to fraud.

The risks of material misstatement that had the greatest effect on our audit, including the allocation of our resources and effort, are identified as 'areas of focus' in the table below. We have also set out how we tailored our audit to address these specific areas in order to provide an opinion on the financial statements as a whole, and any comments we make on the results of our procedures should be read in this context. This is not a complete list of all risks identified by our audit.

Privileged access to IT systems

The Group's financial reporting processes are heavily reliant on automated processes and controls performed by IT systems. As part of the audit, we validate the design and operating effectiveness of in-scope automated and IT dependent controls at a point in time as well as review the supporting IT General Computer Controls (ITGCs) that provide assurance over the continued integrity of these controls for the full financial reporting period.

In our 2015 audit, we identified control matters in relation to the management of IT privileged access to IT systems and therefore relied on compensating controls and performed additional procedures.

While there is an ongoing programme of activities to address such control matters, their exercise during 2016 meant there was an increased risk that the data and reports from the affected systems were not reliable.

We understood and tested key controls surrounding Group IT's central process for the periodic recertification of user access entitlements across in-scope systems as well as reviewed the processes for managing privileged access to IT systems.

We have observed significant progress in terms of remediating the control matters, however several of the controls did not operate effectively for the full financial reporting period.

Where these control matters affected applications and supporting IT systems within the scope of our audit, we performed a combination of additional controls testing, including compensating controls where relevant and substantive audit procedures.

On the basis of our additional audit testing we were able to place reliance on the data and reports from in-scope applications.

[Source: www.lloydsbankinggroup.com/globalassets/documents/investors/2016/2016_lbg_annual_report_v2.pdf]

Compare the extracts from the Lloyd's auditor's report above with those from the report on BP below.

Worked example: Extracts from auditor's report on BP group, 2016

Consolidated financial statements of the BP group

Independent auditor's report on the Annual Report and Accounts to the members of BP p.l.c.

Opinion on financial statements
In our opinion:

* the financial statements give a true and fair view of the state of the group's and of the parent company's affairs as at 31 December 2016 and of the group's profit for the year then ended;
* the group financial statements have been properly prepared in accordance with IFRS as adopted by the European Union;
* the parent company financial statements have been properly prepared in accordance with United Kingdom generally accepted accounting practice including FRS 101 'Reduced Disclosure Framework'; and
* the financial statements have been prepared in accordance with the requirements of the Companies Act 2006 and, as regards the group financial statements, Article 4 of the IAS Regulation.

Separate opinion in relation to IFRS as issued by the International Accounting Standards Board
As explained in Note 1 to the consolidated financial statements, the group in addition to applying IFRS as adopted by the European Union, has also applied IFRS as issued by the International Accounting Standards Board (IASB). In our opinion the consolidated financial statements comply with IFRS as issued by the IASB.

[...]

Our assessment of the risks of material misstatement
We identified the risks of material misstatement described below as those that had the greatest effect on our overall audit strategy, the allocation of resources in the audit and the direction of the efforts of the audit team. In addressing these risks, we designed and performed the procedures below for the purpose of expressing an audit opinion on the financial statements as a whole. We do not express any opinion on these individual risks. Other than as described, these matters are unchanged from those we reported in our 2015 audit opinion.

Risk	Our response to the risk	What we concluded to the Audit Committee

The determination of the liabilities, contingent liabilities and disclosures arising from the significant uncertainties related to the Gulf of Mexico oil spill (as described on page 71 of the report of the audit committee and Note 2 of the financial statements).
 	
Following significant progress in 2016 in resolving outstanding claims, management concluded they were able to reliably estimate the remaining material liabilities arising from the 2010 Deepwater Horizon incident.
 	
There is uncertainty around estimating and valuing the remaining outstanding business economic loss claims. The determination of the liability is subject to judgement as to the amount that each remaining claim will be settled at.
	For the liabilities and contingent liabilities related to the Gulf of Mexico oil spill the primary audit engagement team performed the following audit procedures.
	
	* We walked through and tested the controls designed and operated by the group relating to the provisions and payables for the Gulf of Mexico oil spill.
	* We met with the group's legal team to understand developments across key remaining Gulf of Mexico oil spill matters and their status. We discussed legal developments with the group's external lawyers, reviewed audit enquiry response letters from external legal counsel and read determinations and judgments made by the courts.
	* In respect of the provision for the outstanding business economic loss claims:
	  * We compared the key assumptions that have been used in the determination of the year end provision, to historical experience. These assumptions are the proportion of outstanding claims that will receive a monetary award and the average monetary claim value.
	  * We reconciled the number of undetermined claims to third party claims management data.
		We are satisfied that management is able to determine a reliable estimate for the remaining business economic loss claims and that the disclosures presented in relation to contingent liabilities are appropriate.
		
		Based on our procedures we are satisfied that the amounts provided in the financial statements, as disclosed in Note 2 of the financial statements, are supported by claims experience.

[...]

We apply the concept of materiality in planning and performing the audit, in evaluating the effect of identified misstatements on the audit and in forming our audit opinion.

The magnitude of an omission or misstatement that, individually or in the aggregate, could reasonably be expected to influence the economic decisions of the users of the financial statements. Materiality provides a basis for determining the nature and extent of our audit procedures.

We determined materiality for the group to be $0.5 billion (2014 $1 billion), which is 5.7% (2014 5%) of underlying replacement cost profit (as defined on page 258) before interest and taxation. We believe that underlying replacement cost profit before interest and taxation is the most appropriate measure upon which to calculate materiality, due to the fact it excludes the impact of both changes in crude oil and product prices and items disclosed as non-operating items that can significantly distort the group's results.

During the course of our audit, we re-assessed initial materiality in the context of the group's performance and this resulted in no change from our original assessment of materiality.

The application of materiality at the individual account or balance level. It is set at an amount to reduce to an appropriately low level the probability that the aggregate of uncorrected and undetected misstatements exceeds materiality.

On the basis of our risk assessments, together with our assessment of the group's overall control environment, our judgement was that performance materiality was 75% (2014 75%) of our materiality, namely $375 million (2014 $750 million). We have set performance materiality at this percentage to reduce to an appropriately low level the probability that the aggregate of uncorrected and undetected misstatements exceeds materiality.

Audit work at component locations for the purpose of obtaining audit coverage over significant financial statement accounts is undertaken based on a percentage of total performance materiality. The performance materiality set for each component is based on the relative scale and risk of the component to the group as a whole and our assessment of the risk of misstatement at that component. In the current year, the range of performance materiality allocated to components was $75 million to $300 million (2014 $150 million to $640 million).

An amount below which identified misstatements are considered as being clearly trivial.

We agreed with the audit committee that we would report to them all uncorrected audit differences in excess of $25 million (2014 $50 million), which is set at 5% of materiality, as well as differences below that threshold that, in our view, warranted reporting on qualitative grounds.

We evaluate any uncorrected misstatements against both the quantitative measures of materiality discussed above and in light of other relevant qualitative considerations in forming our opinion.

[…]

In our opinion:

- the part of the Directors' remuneration report to be audited has been properly prepared in accordance with the Companies Act 2006; and
- the information given in the Strategic report and the Directors' report for the financial year for which the financial statements are prepared is consistent with the financial statements.

[…]

[Source: www.bp.com/content/dam/bp/en/corporate/pdf/investors/bp-annual-report-and-form-20f-2016.pdf]

2.3 Level of assurance and the expectations gap

The above report is designed to give a reasonable (high) level of assurance. However, critics argue that it can fail to do so due to what is known as the 'expectations gap'.

The **'expectations gap'** is defined as the difference between the apparent public perceptions of the responsibilities of auditors on the one hand (and hence the assurance that their involvement provides) and the legal and professional reality on the other. The question remains: how can we make the **meaning** of an unmodified auditor's report clear to the user?

The above definition of the expectations gap is not definitive and it is not a 'static phenomenon'. However, we can highlight some specific issues.

- **Misunderstanding of the nature of audited financial statements,** for example that:

    - the statement of financial position provides a fair valuation of the reporting entity

    - the amounts in the financial statements are stated precisely

    - the audited financial statements will guarantee that the entity concerned will continue to exist

- **Misunderstanding as to the type and extent of work undertaken by auditors,** for example that:

    - all items in financial statements are tested
    - auditors will uncover all errors
    - auditors should detect all fraud

- **Misunderstanding about the level of assurance provided by auditors**, for example that:

  - the auditors provide absolute assurance that the figures in the financial statements are correct (ignoring the concept of materiality and the problems of estimation)

2.4 Other reports

The main assurance report is addressed to users of the assurance material. The international standard on assurance engagements requires that an assurance report must have the following components:

- A title that clearly indicates the report is an independent assurance report

- An addressee

- An identification and description of the subject matter information and, when appropriate, the subject matter

- Identification of the criteria

- Where appropriate, a description of any significant inherent limitations associated with the evaluation or measurement of the subject matter against the criteria

- When the criteria used to evaluate or measure the subject matter are available only to specific intended users, or are relevant only to a specific purpose, a statement restricting the use of the assurance report to those intended users or that purpose

- A statement to identify the responsible party and to describe the responsibilities of the responsible party and the practitioner

- A statement that the engagement was performed in accordance with International Standards on Assurance Engagements (ISAEs)

- A summary of the work performed (usually limited, particularly where a negative conclusion is being given)

- The practitioner's conclusion (positive or negative, depending on the level of assurance being given and the work carried out)

- The assurance report date

- The name of the firm or practitioner, and a specific location, which ordinarily is the city where the practitioner maintains the office that has responsibility for the engagement

To illustrate some of these points, here is an extract from a sample report on prospective financial information, from the ISAE 3400, *The Examination of Prospective Financial Information*.

Worked example: Extract from a report on prospective financial information

We have examined the forecast in accordance with the International Standard on Assurance Engagements applicable to the examination of prospective financial information. Management is responsible for the forecast including the assumptions set out in Note X on which it is based.

Based on our examination of the evidence supporting the assumptions, nothing has come to our attention which causes us to believe that these assumptions do not provide a reasonable basis for the forecast. Further, in our opinion the forecast is properly prepared on the basis of the assumptions and is presented in accordance with.....

Actual results are likely to be different from the forecast since anticipated events frequently do not occur as expected and the variation may be material.

The assurance provider also may sometimes issue reports to the party that has engaged them as well as the main report to users of the assurance material. So for example, in an audit, the auditors will sometimes issue a report to the directors or management as a by-product of the audit. One major issue that such a report might cover is internal control deficiencies, and this is looked at in the next chapter.

Interactive question 3: Auditor's report

Which **three** of the following are reported by exception in the auditor's report?

	All information and explanations required for the audit have been received
	Adequate accounting records have been kept
	The directors' report is consistent with the financial statements
	The financial statements have been prepared in accordance with the Companies Act 2006
	Details of directors' emoluments have been properly disclosed in the financial statements

See **Answer** at the end of this chapter.

Summary

Auditors must obtain **sufficient, appropriate** audit evidence

Evidence can be in the form of **tests of control** or **substantive procedures**

The **reliability** of audit evidence is influenced by its **source** and by its **nature**

Audit tests are designed to obtain evidence about the financial statement assertions

Evidence allows the practitioner to draw a conclusion on the assurance engagement

An assurance conclusion can be positive or negative (limited)

An audit opinion is always a positive opinion and gives a reasonable level of assurance. There are implied and explicit opinions

However, the expectations gap can serve to limit the amount of assurance

Less testing will be carried out on lower level assignments

Self-test

Answer the following questions.

1   Name **seven** financial statement assertions.

2   Fill in the **blanks**.

Audit evidence from external sources is .... than that obtained from the entity's records.

Evidence obtained directly .... is more .... than that obtained indirectly or by inference.

3   Complete the standard opinion paragraph.

In our opinion the financial statements:

- give a .... of the state of the company's affairs as at _ and of its .... for the year then ended;

- have been ....in accordance with IFRSs as adopted by the European Union;

- have been .... in accordance with the requirements of the Companies Act 2006.

4   Give **three** examples of misunderstandings which contribute to the expectations gap.

1   ....

2   ....

3   ....

Now, go back to the Learning Objectives in the Introduction. If you are satisfied you have achieved these objectives, please tick them off.

CHAPTER

4

Technical references

1 Evidence

• Definition	ISA (UK) 500.5
• Types of test	ISA (UK) 330.4
• Sufficient appropriate evidence	ISA (UK) 500.4
• Quality of evidence	ISA (UK) 500.A31
• Use of entity information	ISA (UK) 500.9
• Financial statement assertions	ISA (UK) 315.25, ISA (UK) 315.A124
• Tests of controls or tests of detail	ISA (UK) 330.8 – 23

2 Reporting

• Content of the auditor's report	FRC Bulletin (Oct 2016)
	ISA (UK) 700

Answer to Interactive question 1

Financial statements level, as this would affect all controls and therefore potentially any area of the financial statements

Answer to Interactive question 2

True

True

True

Answer to Interactive question 3

All information and explanations required for the audit have been received

Adequate accounting records have been kept

Details of directors' emoluments have been properly disclosed in the financial statements

Answers to Self-test

1   Any of:

   Existence, rights and obligations, occurrence, completeness, valuation, accuracy, classification, cut-off, allocation

2   More reliable

   By auditors, reliable

3   True and fair view, profit (loss), properly prepared

4   1   The nature of the financial statements
     2   The type and extent of work undertaken by auditors
     3   The level of assurance given by auditors

CHAPTER 5

Introduction to internal control

Introduction

Examination context

Topic List

Summary and Self-test

Technical references

Answers to Interactive questions

Answers to Self-test

Learning objectives

- Understand the role of internal control within a business ☐
- Understand the limitations of internal control ☐
- Identify the components of internal control ☐
- Understand how the auditor obtains and records information about internal controls ☐

Specific syllabus references for this chapter are: 2a, b, c, d, e, f, i.

Syllabus links

You will have studied the basic components of an information system when studying for your Accounting paper and should therefore know the basic set up of initial documents, books of prime entry, ledgers, journals, trial balances and financial statements.

You will learn more about a business's risk management and control in your Business and Finance paper.

Examination context

Internal control is an important practical area in auditing. It is therefore 25% of the syllabus and you should expect that to be reflected in your assessment. In the sample paper there were 15 questions on internal control related issues. This is the first chapter of four in this area.

In the assessment candidates may be required to:

- state the reasons for organisations having effective systems of controls
- identify factors which contribute to an effective control environment
- identify the components of internal control in both manual and IT environments
- identify types of control activity
- distinguish between general controls and application controls
- identify inherent limitations of a system of internal controls
- specify the composition of an audit committee

1 What is internal control?

Section overview

- Internal control is the process designed to mitigate risks to the business and ensure that the business operates efficiently and effectively.

- Key limitations to internal controls include the fact that they may be expensive, the fact that they generally rely on humans to operate them and the fact that they are generally only designed for routine, normal transactions.

- Small companies in particular may have difficulties implementing effective internal control systems due to employing fewer staff to implement internal controls than larger companies.

1.1 Definition

ISA (UK) 315, *Identifying and Assessing the Risks of Material Misstatement through Understanding the Entity and its Environment* contains the following definition of internal control.

Definition

Internal control: The process designed, implemented and maintained by those charged with governance, management, and other personnel to provide reasonable assurance about the achievement of an entity's objectives with regard to reliability of financial reporting, effectiveness and efficiency of operations and compliance with applicable laws and regulations. The term 'controls' refers to any aspects of one or more of the components of internal control.

'Those charged with governance', a phrase used in the definition above, is a technical term used by ISAs. It means the people responsible for the 'strategic oversight' of the entity. This is distinguished from 'management', which refers to the people responsible for the 'conduct of the entity's operations'. In the UK, those charged with governance and management are often one and the same people – the company directors – acting in slightly different roles.

Worked example: Company objectives

A company has various objectives:

- to ensure it reports its financial position correctly to shareholders
- to ensure that it operates effectively and efficiently
- to ensure that it complies with relevant laws and regulations

In order to meet these objectives, the directors will take the following steps:

Step 1

Identify risks to these objectives not being fulfilled, for example, in terms of reporting financial position, the directors might identify that a risk of not being able to report correctly is computer failure and consequent destruction of the financial records.

Step 2

Implement internal controls to mitigate this risk. The controls to mitigate the above risk could be many and varied, for example, ensuring that all users have passwords to limit unauthorised access to the computer and therefore the risk of it being infected, or, at the other end of the scale, detailed back up and emergency procedures, including a reconstruction plan, to kick into action in the event of computer failure.

C
H
A
P
T
E
R

5

1.2 Reasons for internal controls

The reasons for internal controls can be seen in the example. They include:

- minimising the company's business risks
- ensuring the continuing effective functioning of the company
- ensuring the company complies with relevant laws and regulations

Most of these reasons funnel back to the ultimate objective that the company continues to operate. For example, if the company failed to comply with relevant laws and regulations, it might be forced to stop operations.

Worked example: Fairfood Co

Fairfood Co is a food manufacturer. It is subject to a great number of health and safety regulations and therefore must have significant internal controls surrounding the food preparation areas. If these controls were seriously breached, Fairfood Co would be forced to cease operations. The primary objective of each internal control might focus on a particular operation, for example, that all personnel must wear protective clothing when operating machinery however, the ultimate objective is to ensure the operation of the company continues. If the protective clothing wasn't worn and hair or other items, such as jewellery from staff, fell into the food, the company might be forced to stop operating.

1.3 Limitations of internal controls

Internal controls have some limitations. In other words, the risk to the business of operating cannot be eliminated entirely.

Limitation	Explanation
Human element	Another important limitation of controls is the **human element**. Most controls can only function as well as the people that are implementing them. Controls are not necessarily foolproof. If a human being makes a mistake implementing a control, then that control might be ineffective. Another problem for companies associated with the human element of controls is that of the intention of the people using them. Controls, such as keeping your computer password secret, rely on the integrity of the people being asked to implement them. If people do not understand the importance or relevance of the control they may be less inclined to adhere to it.
Collusion	Staff members may want to override or avoid controls in order to defraud the company. Controls may be bypassed very effectively and secretly by two or more people working together, that is, colluding in fraud.
Unusual transactions	Finally, a limitation of internal controls is that they are generally designed to deal with **what normally or routinely happens** in a business. However, it may be the case that an unusual transaction may occur which does not fit into the normal routines, in which case standard controls may not be relevant to the unusual transaction, and hence mistakes may be made in relation to that unusual transaction.

Small companies may have particular problems in implementing effective internal control systems. This is largely because of the **human element** discussed above. Small companies generally have **fewer employees** than larger companies, meaning that there are fewer people to involve in the internal control system.

Involving a large number of people in internal control systems helps to limit the risk of the human element in internal control systems because if a lot of people are involved, there is a greater chance that people's errors or, worse, frauds, will be uncovered by the next person in the control chain. The control of using a number of people in a single system is called **segregation of duties**, and we will look at it in more detail later. In a small company, if its staff capacity is not such to ensure that lots of people are involved in the internal control system, then the control system will be weaker.

Worked example: Large Co and Small Co

Contrast the following examples.

Large Co is a large company with sophisticated controls systems. In respect of purchase ordering, an order is raised by a member of the purchase team (who all have pre-set limits of the price they are allowed to order up to) on the basis of a requisition note from the relevant department, signed by the department manager. Before the order is despatched to the approved supplier, the purchase manager approves the order. If the order is in excess of £30 million, the purchasing director approves the order.

Small Co is a small company with limited controls systems. When the stores manager needs the stores replacing he rings the approved supplier and orders the goods. The annual cost of purchases is £7 million.

You can see that in the second scenario there are far fewer people, indeed just one, compared with a minimum of four at Large Co, involved in the transaction. If one of the people at Large Co made a mistake with the order, then another member of the team might pick it up. If the stores manager makes a mistake at Small Co, there is not another team member to correct the mistake. Small Co has a control, in that it uses an approved supplier, who might query an unusual order, but the internal control in relation to purchasing is weak due to lack of staff members.

Bear in mind also that although the sums of money discussed in the two scenarios are very different, the materiality of those sums to the businesses themselves might be comparable. A mistake in a £30,000 order may not seem as important as a mistake in a £30 million order, but it might be enough to put Small Co into financial difficulties.

2 Components of internal control

Section overview

- Internal control comprises five components.

- The control environment is the context of the internal control system, influenced by management.

- The entity's risk assessment process is the process by which the company determines what control policies and procedures to implement.

- The information system is the system which captures information about transactions and events for financial reporting purposes.

- Control activities are the heart of the internal control system, comprising policies and procedures which may prevent, or detect and correct errors.

- All control systems should be monitored.

ISA 315 sets out that there are five components of internal control, each of which may impact on the audit process differently. We shall look at each of them in more detail below. An internal control may fall into a particular category.

Each particular control activity may also prevent an error occurring (**preventative control**), or may identify that an error has occurred and correct it (**detective control**). It is an important part of understanding internal controls to be able to identify what it is that each specific control actually does.

Some controls may be relevant to audit while others are not. The auditor will not waste time looking at company controls that are not relevant to whether the financial statements are true and fair, however important those controls might be to the overall operating of the business; for example, control processes over asset utilisation.

The extent of reliance on internal control in an assurance engagement will depend on the nature of the engagement and the assurance provider's expectation of the effectiveness of controls. In some engagements, very few controls will be relied on and the assurance provider will carry out more tests of detail instead.

2.1 The control environment

Definition

Control environment: The control environment includes the governance and management functions and the attitudes, awareness and actions of those charged with governance and management concerning the entity's internal control and its importance in the entity. The control environment sets the tone of an organisation, influencing the control consciousness of its people.

Where directors feel that internal control is important, staff members are likely to be better educated about what the controls are and why they are important, so the human element of risk associated with internal controls is reduced. Also, if directors set the tone by taking controls seriously and rigorously applying them, even when they seem silly or unnecessary, then other staff members will be encouraged to do the same.

In a strong control environment, management will ensure that individuals have the competence to perform their roles. Authority and responsibility will be assigned to appropriate levels and staff will be made aware of their specific responsibilities and how these affect the organisation as a whole. Policies will be in place to promote best practice in recruitment, training, promotion and compensation so that employees feel valued. Overall, a strong control environment is a foundation for effective internal control.

The control environment is therefore very important to the auditors and they will evaluate it as part of their risk assessment process. If the control environment is strong, then auditors will be more inclined to rely on the controls system in the entity than if it is weak.

However, it is important to understand that the control environment is only one component of the overall internal control system. Equally important are the other aspects of controls, because if other control components are weak, it will not matter as much to the auditors that the directors think that controls are important, because the auditor will not be happy to rely on well-intentioned, but weak, control systems.

2.1.1 Audit committees

The audit committee is an important aspect of the control environment of the company. It is a sub-committee of the board of directors responsible for overseeing an entity's internal control structure, financial reporting and compliance with relevant laws and regulations.

The audit committee is comprised of non-executive directors. It is a requirement in UK listed companies under the rules of the UK Corporate Governance Code. The Code requires the committee to have written terms of reference which are likely to include the following:

- To review the integrity of the financial statements of the company and formal announcements relating to the company's performance.

- To review the company's internal financial controls and the company's risk management systems (unless there is a separate risk management committee).

- To monitor and review the effectiveness of the company's internal audit function (if relevant).

- To make recommendations to the board in relation to the external auditor.

- To monitor the independence of the external auditor.

- To implement policy on the provision of non-audit services by the external auditor.

The key issue for the audit committee is the financial statements, so the audit committee itself can be seen as a control in relation to the **information system** and the way in which the company produces its financial statements. Note that the committee also has responsibilities with regard to supervising the **identification of risks** and **monitoring controls** (these are all discussed later in this chapter).

2.2 Business risk and the entity's risk assessment process

Definitions

Entity's risk assessment process: A component of internal control that is the entity's process for identifying business risks relevant to financial reporting objectives and deciding about actions to address those risks, and the results thereof.

Business risk: A risk resulting from significant conditions, events, circumstances, actions or inactions that could adversely affect an entity's ability to achieve its objectives and execute its strategies, or from the setting of inappropriate objectives and strategies.

Internal controls are implemented to minimise business risk.

Assurance providers, particularly auditors focusing on the financial statements, are interested in business risk because issues which pose threats to the business may in some cases also be a risk of the financial statements being misstated. For example, if a particular division of a business was threatened with closure, the valuation of all the assets associated with that division would be affected. In more general terms, if an economic downturn puts pressure on a company to meet the expectations of providers of finance, management might be tempted to manipulate the financial statements.

Not all business risks have a direct impact on the financial statements – for example, the risk that production does not meet quality control requirements of customers does not directly impact upon financial statements; the risk that credit notes are not recorded properly does. However, if an assurance provider is aware of the general business risk that there is a stringent quality control process to be met, he will be aware that there is likely to be a correlation with sales and sales returns if the process is not working adequately.

You can see that if the risk assessment process is weak, then the resulting internal controls may not be effective. The process will involve the following elements:

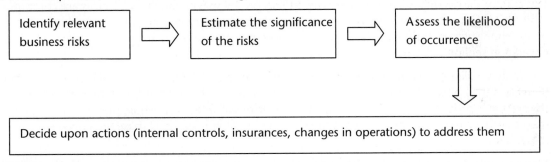

Figure 5.1: Entity's risk assessment process

Assessing the risk assessment process will also take place during audit risk assessment, as identifying business risks that management have identified will assist auditors in identifying audit risks as well. In terms of internal control, the auditors will have to evaluate each aspect of this process. If, during the audit, the auditors identify a risk that the entity did not identify, the auditors will evaluate what this means for the effectiveness of the entity's risk assessment process. ?

2.3 The information system relevant to financial reporting

An information system consists of infrastructure (physical and hardware components), software, people, procedures and data.

Definition

Information system relevant to financial reporting: A component of internal control that includes the financial reporting system, and consists of the procedures and records established to initiate, record, process and report entity transactions (as well as events and conditions) and to maintain accountability for the related assets, liabilities and equity.

The auditors will be interested in:

- the classes of transactions that are significant to the entity's financial statements

- the procedures by which transactions are initiated, recorded, processed, corrected and reported

- the related accounting records and supporting information

- how the information system captures events other than transactions that are significant to the financial statements

- the process of preparing the financial statements

This will typically involve the financial controller and/or director and the use of journals, which the auditors will be interested in.

The auditors will be interested in how this process links in with other internal controls and whether it is at this point that controls are overridden or ignored (by use of journals for example).

2.4 Control activities

Definition

Control activities are the policies and procedures that help ensure that management directives are carried out.

Control activities are the most tangible internal controls that the auditor will concentrate on to a large degree. The auditor will be concerned with understanding whether a control is able to prevent an error, or to detect and correct an error. Control activities may be manual or, if relevant, where processes are computerised, then there may also be computer-specific control activities.

The auditor's approach is likely to differ depending on the extent to which controls are computerised. Systems of internal control will usually involve a mixture of manual and computerised activities. Smaller or less sophisticated entities are likely to place more reliance on manual control systems, which are covered in section 2.4.1 below.

Generally speaking, IT controls come with both benefits and drawbacks. For instance, one of their benefits is their ability to consistently process large volumes of data; but the drawback of this is that if the system is processing data incorrectly then the error will affect the whole population. It is important then that IT systems are designed with their own controls in mind, and these are covered in section 2.4.2 below.

Manual control systems may be more appropriate where judgement is required eg, for large or unusual transactions. They are, however, likely to be error-prone where a large number of similar transactions is being processed; in this situation, well-designed and implemented IT systems are likely to be more effective.

2.4.1 Types of control activity

ISA 315 gives examples of five types of control activities: authorisation, performance reviews, information processing, physical controls and segregation of duties.

Type of control activity	Examples	Explanation
Authorisation	Approval of transactions/documents	Transactions/documents should be approved by an appropriate person. For example, overtime should be approved by departmental managers, purchase orders by the purchasing manager.
Performance reviews	Review and analysis of actual performance versus budgets, forecasts and prior period performance	A review highlights and explains any unexpected variances. This reduces the likelihood of errors or deliberate misstatement.
	Relating different sets of data (operating or financial) to one another	For example, comparing sales reports by units sold to sales in the statement of profit or loss.
	Comparing internal data with external sources of information	For example, comparison of key performance indicators (KPIs) with industry sector KPIs.
	Review of functional or activity performance	For example, a review of sales by branch, region, and product type.
Information processing	Controls to check the accuracy, completeness and authorisation of transactions	The two broad groupings of information systems control activities are **application controls** and **general IT controls** (see later section).
Physical controls	Physical security of assets	Only authorised personnel should have access to certain assets (particularly valuable or portable ones). For example, ensuring that the inventories store is only open when the store personnel are there and is otherwise locked.
	Authorisation for access to computer programs and data files	Passwords over computer programs and data files will ensure only authorised personnel can access them. For example, a password over the payroll system prevents unauthorised changes such as creating a fictitious employee.
	Periodic counting and comparison with amount shown on control accounts	For example, a physical count of petty cash. The balance shown in the cash book should be the same amount as is in the petty cash box.
Segregation of duties	Assigning different individuals the responsibilities of authorising transactions, recording transactions and maintaining custody of assets	Segregation makes it more difficult for fraudulent errors to be processed (since a number of people would have to collude in the fraud) and also for accidental errors to be processed (since the more people that are involved, the more checking there can be). For example, the same staff should not record transactions and carry out the related reconciliations at the period-end.

2.4.2   Information processing controls

The internal controls in a computerised environment include both manual procedures and procedures designed into computer programs. Such manual and computer control procedures comprise two types of control.

Definitions

Application controls: Manual or automated procedures that typically operate at a business process level. Application controls can be preventative or detective in nature and are designed to ensure the integrity of the accounting records. Accordingly, application controls relate to procedures used to initiate, record, process and report transactions or other financial data.

General controls: Policies and procedures that relate to many applications and support the effective function of application controls by helping to ensure the continued proper operation of information systems.

Examples of general controls	
Development of computer applications	Standards over **systems design, programming and documentation**
	Full **testing procedures** using test data (see Chapter 11)
	Approval by **computer users** and **management**
	Segregation of duties so that those responsible for design are not responsible for testing
	Installation procedures so that data is not corrupted in transition
	Training of staff in new procedures and availability of adequate documentation
Prevention or detection of unauthorised changes to programs	**Segregation of duties**
	Full records of program **changes**
	Password protection of programs so that access is limited to computer operations staff
	Restricted access to **central computer** by locked doors, keypads
	Maintenance of program logs
	Virus checks on software: use of anti-virus software and policy prohibiting use of non-authorised programs or files
	Back-up copies of programs being taken and stored in other locations
	Control copies of programs being preserved and regularly **compared** with **actual programs**
	Stricter controls over certain programs (utility programs) by use of **read only memory**
Testing and documentation of program changes	Complete **testing procedures**
	Documentation standards
	Approval of changes by computer users and management
	Training of staff using programs
Controls to prevent wrong programs or files being used	**Operation controls** over programs
	Libraries of programs
	Proper job scheduling

Controls to prevent unauthorised amendments to data files	Such as passwords to prevent unauthorised entry, built in controls to permit changes
Controls to ensure continuity of operations	**Storing extra copies** of programs and data files off-site
	Protection of equipment against fire and other hazards
	Back-up power sources
	Emergency procedures
	Disaster recovery procedures eg, availability of back-up computer facilities
	Maintenance agreements and **insurance**

The auditors will wish to test some or all of the above general controls, having considered how they affect the computer applications significant to the audit.

General controls that relate to some or all applications are usually interdependent controls ie, their operation is often essential to the effectiveness of application controls. As application controls may be useless when general controls are ineffective, it will be more efficient to review the design of **general controls first**, before reviewing the application controls.

The purpose of application controls is to establish **specific control activities** over the accounting applications in order to provide reasonable assurance that all transactions are authorised and recorded, and are processed completely, accurately and on a timely basis. Application controls include the following.

Controls over **input: completeness**	Manual or programmed agreement of control totals
	Document counts
	One-for-one checking of processed output to source documents
	Programmed matching of input to an expected input control file
	Procedures over resubmission of rejected data
Controls over **input: accuracy**	Programs to check data fields (for example value, reference number, date) on input transactions for plausibility:
	• Digit verification (eg, reference numbers are as expected)
	• Reasonableness test (eg, VAT to total value)
	• Existence checks (eg, customer name)
	• Character checks (no unexpected characters used in reference)
	• Necessary information (no transaction passed with missing information)
	• Permitted range (no transaction processed over a certain value)
	Manual scrutiny of output and reconciliation to source
	Agreement of control totals (manual/programmed)
Controls over **input: authorisation**	Manual checks to ensure information input was:
	• authorised
	• input by authorised personnel
Controls over **processing**	Similar controls to input must be completed when input is completed, for example, batch reconciliations
	Screen warnings can prevent people logging out before processing is complete

Controls over **master files and standing data**	One to one checking of master files to source documents (such as payroll master files to individual employee personal files)
	Cyclical reviews of all master files and standing data
	Record counts (number of documents processed) and hash totals (for example, the total of all the payroll numbers) used when master files are used to ensure no deletions
	Controls over the deletion of accounts that have no current balance

Control over input, processing, data files and output may be carried out by IT personnel, users of the system, a separate control group and may be programmed into application software. The auditors may wish to test the following application controls.

Manual controls exercised by the user	If manual controls exercised by the user of the application system are capable of providing reasonable assurance that the system's output is complete, accurate and authorised, the auditors may decide to limit tests of control to these manual controls.
Controls over system output	If, in addition to manual controls exercised by the user, the controls to be tested use information produced by the computer or are contained within computer programs, such controls may be tested by examining the system's output using either manual procedures or computer assisted audit techniques (CAATs) which will be described in more detail in Chapter 11. Such output may be in the form of magnetic media, microfilm or printouts. Alternatively, the auditor may test the control by performing it with the use of CAATs.
Programmed control procedures	In the case of certain computer systems, the auditor may find that it is not possible or, in some cases, not practical to test controls by examining only user controls or the system's output. The auditor may consider performing tests of control by using CAATs, such as test data, reprocessing transaction data or, in unusual situations, examining the coding of the application program.

As we have already noted, general IT controls may have a pervasive effect on the processing of transactions in application systems. If these general controls are not effective, there may be a risk that misstatements occur and go undetected in the application systems. Although weaknesses in general IT controls may preclude testing certain IT application controls, it is possible that manual procedures exercised by users may provide effective control at the **application level**.

Bear in mind that most companies have computerised accounting systems so these controls are important in practice as well as in your assessment.

2.5 Monitoring of controls

An entity should review its overall control system to ensure that it still meets its objectives, still operates effectively and efficiently, and that necessary corrections to the system are made on a timely basis. If it does not, then the control system may not be operating optimally. This is often a role undertaken by a company's internal audit department, as we shall see in Chapter 9. For this reason, it is important to discuss controls with the internal auditors at the planning phase. The internal auditors may, as part of their monitoring of controls, have found control weaknesses that the external auditor should be aware of.

In smaller companies that do not have an internal audit function, the company may make use of auditor feedback to ensure that controls continue to operate efficiently. Auditors will often produce a management report at the end of an audit, outlining any weaknesses they have observed in internal controls. Auditors are also required by ISAs to identify control weaknesses observed to those charged with governance. However, this does not remove the onus from the company itself to monitor its own internal controls.

3 Information about controls

Section overview

- Auditors will obtain information about internal controls from a variety of sources, including company internal control manuals and observing controls in operation.

- Auditors will record information about internal controls in a variety of ways in their files, including notes, flowcharts and questionnaires.

3.1 Information about internal controls

Auditors will obtain information about internal controls from a variety of sources.

The company may have manuals of control activities and copies of internal controls policies, or minutes of meetings of the risk assessment group. These will be useful documents for the auditors to read. In addition, in recurring audits, the auditors should have a record of what the controls were in previous years and therefore will only be looking for new policies in the current year.

The auditors will also obtain knowledge by talking to the people involved with internal control at all stages and asking them what the controls are and why they have been implemented. Again, where auditors have a record of what the controls were last year, inquiry will be useful in updating the picture to what they are now.

Lastly, an important tool for auditors in determining what internal controls exist in an organisation or whether controls in use in an operation are the same as those stated to be in operation is observation. The auditor will watch operations at a company to identify the control activities being put into action.

3.2 Recording of controls

Auditors shall record the control activities that they see.

There are broadly three types of document which are used for recording the understanding of the business:

- narrative notes
- questionnaires/checklists; and
- diagrams.

Narrative notes

These are good for things like:

- short notes on simple systems
- background information

They are less good when things get more complex when diagrams tend to take over.

Questionnaires and checklists

These are:

- good as aide memoires to ensure you have all the bases covered

but

- can lead to a mechanical approach so that an important extra question is never asked
- tick boxes often get ticked whether the brain is engaged or not

Diagrams

These include:

- flowcharts
- organisation charts
- family trees
- records of related parties

Organisation charts and family trees are without doubt the best way of recording relationships, reporting lines, etc.

Flow charts of systems are an excellent and comprehensive way of recording systems, but they are time consuming to construct and can be difficult for the reader to assimilate.

Once the auditors have documented the internal controls that are present, they should check that their understanding of these controls is correct by performing walk-through procedures.

Definition

Walk-through procedure: A procedure that involves tracing a few transactions through the financial reporting system.

Walk-through procedures would normally be performed near the start of the field-work stage of the audit. They involve tracing transactions from the very beginning to the very end, in order to confirm that the auditor has correctly understood how the controls are supposed to operate. Walkthrough procedures aim to test the auditor's understanding, and are not tests of controls.

Interactive question 1: Internal control

Which **one** of the following is a reason that organisations have effective systems of control?

To assist the organisation in:

A   Maximising profitability
B   Maximising operating efficiency
C   Reducing time required for the statutory audit
D   Minimising audit risk

See **Answer** at the end of this chapter.

Interactive question 2: Control activities

The following are examples of internal controls which operate at Searson plc.

For each example, select the **one** type of control activity which it illustrates.

	Authorisation	Performance review	Information processing	Physical
1 The receivables ledger clerk checks the manually calculated batch total for a batch of sales invoices entered to the sales day book to the computer generated batch total	☐	☐	☐	☐
2 The sales director compares monthly budgeted sales figures to actual	☐	☐	☐	☐

See **Answer** at the end of this chapter.

Interactive question 3: IT controls

Most entities use IT systems for financial reporting and operational purposes. Controls operating in an IT environment can be split into general controls and application controls.

Requirement

Which **two** of the following are application controls?

	Document counts
	Digit verification
	Passwords
	Virus checks

See **Answer** at the end of this chapter.

Summary and Self-test

Summary

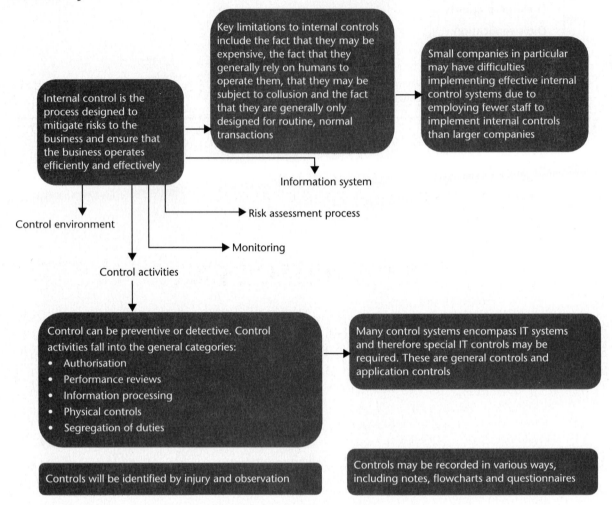

Internal control is the process designed to mitigate risks to the business and ensure that the business operates efficiently and effectively

Key limitations to internal controls include the fact that they may be expensive, the fact that they generally rely on humans to operate them, that they may be subject to collusion and the fact that they are generally only designed for routine, normal transactions

Small companies in particular may have difficulties implementing effective internal control systems due to employing fewer staff to implement internal controls than larger companies

Information system

Risk assessment process

Control environment

Monitoring

Control activities

Control can be preventive or detective. Control activities fall into the general categories:
- Authorisation
- Performance reviews
- Information processing
- Physical controls
- Segregation of duties

Many control systems encompass IT systems and therefore special IT controls may be required. These are general controls and application controls

Controls will be identified by injury and observation

Controls may be recorded in various ways, including notes, flowcharts and questionnaires

Self-test

Answer the following questions.

1 Complete the definition taking the words given below.

The .... includes the governance and management functions and the ...., ... and .... of those charged with ....and management concerning the entity's internal .... and its importance in the entity. It sets the .... of an organisation, influencing the control .... of its people.

attitudes   consciousness   awareness   governance   actions   control

control   environment   tone

2 Name **two key** inherent limitations of an internal control system.

1 ....

2 ....

3 For each of the following controls, state whether they are general or application:

Control		General		Application
One-to-one checking	☐	General	☐	Application
Segregation of duties	☐	General	☐	Application
Review of master files	☐	General	☐	Application
Back-up copies	☐	General	☐	Application
Virus checks	☐	General	☐	Application
Passwords	☐	General	☐	Application
Training	☐	General	☐	Application
Record counts	☐	General	☐	Application
Hash totals	☐	General	☐	Application
Program libraries	☐	General	☐	Application
Controls over account deletions	☐	General	☐	Application
Back-up power source	☐	General	☐	Application

Now go back to the Learning Objectives in the Introduction. If you are satisfied you have achieved these objectives, please tick them off.

Technical references

1 What is internal control?

- Definition of internal control   ISA (UK) 315.4

- Limitations of internal controls   ISA (UK) 315.A46 – A48

2 Components of internal control

- Control environment   ISA (UK) 315.14, A69 – A78

- The entity's risk assessment process   ISA (UK) 315.15, A79

- Information system   ISA (UK) 315.18, A81

- Control activities   ISA (UK) 315.20, A88 – 97, Appendix 1, 9 – 10

- Monitoring of controls   ISA (UK) 315.22 – 24

Answers to Interactive questions

Answer to Interactive question 1

B

Answer to Interactive question 2

1   Information processing
2   Performance review

Answer to Interactive question 3

Document counts and digit verification

Answers to Self-test

1   Control, environment, attitudes, awareness, actions, governance, control, tone, consciousness

2   Two from:

Human error

Possibility of staff colluding in fraud

Only designed for routine, normal transactions

May be expensive to implement

3

Application controls	General controls
One-to-one checking	Virus checks
Hash totals	Program libraries
Review of master files	Segregation of duties
Record counts	Passwords
	Controls over account deletions
	Training
	Back-up power source
	Back-up copies

CHAPTER 6

Revenue system

Introduction

Examination context

Topic List

    1   Ordering

    2   Despatch and invoicing

    3   Recording

    4   Cash collection

    5   Deficiencies

Summary and Self-test

Answers to Interactive questions

Answers to Self-test

Introduction

Learning objectives

- Identify relevant controls to mitigate risk

- Identify tests of those controls

- Identify risks in a sales system

- Recognise weaknesses in a sales system

Specific syllabus references for this chapter are: 2f, g, h, 3f.

Syllabus links

You will have learnt about the various books of record in the sales system in Accounting.

Examination context

As the sales system is an important practical area, your assessment might well include a scenario internal controls question in this area. The sample paper contained one question looking at strengths and weaknesses in a given sales system.

In the assessment, candidates may be required to:

- Show how specific internal controls in a revenue system mitigate risk and state their limitations
- Identify internal controls for an organisation in a given scenario
- Identify internal control strengths and weaknesses in a given scenario
- Determine the extent to which tests of controls should be used in a given set of circumstances

1 Ordering

Section overview

- Key risks include accepting customers who are a poor credit risk and not fulfilling orders.

- Key controls include authorising credit terms to customers and ensuring orders are matched with production orders and despatch notes.

1.1 Risks and control objectives

When considering sales orders, a company might recognise all or some of the following risks:

- Orders may be taken from customers who are not able to pay.
- Orders may be taken from customers who are unlikely to pay for a long time.
- Orders may not be recorded properly and therefore not fulfilled and customers might be lost.

The controls put into place will be designed to mitigate these risks. Hence the objectives of the controls will be to prevent these risks from occurring. Here are the control objectives which might arise from the risks noted above:

- **Goods** and **services** are **only supplied** to **customers** with **good credit ratings.**
- **Customers** are encouraged to **pay promptly.**
- **Orders** are **recorded correctly.**
- **Orders** are **fulfilled.**

1.2 Controls

Once the company has identified the risks which exist in the sales system, it will try and create controls which mitigate those risks (that is, meet the control objectives outlined above). What controls will be put into place depend on the nature of the company and the specific risks associated with the way it operates, but the following controls can be used as examples of how the above risks can be mitigated.

- **Segregation** of duties; credit control, invoicing and inventory despatch

- **Authorisation** of **credit terms** to customers

    - References/credit checks obtained
    - Authorisation by senior staff
    - Regular review

- **Authorisation** for changes in **other customer data**

    - Change of address supported by letterhead
    - Deletion requests supported by evidence of balances cleared/customer in liquidation

- **Orders** only **accepted** from **customers** who have no credit problems

- **Sequential numbering** of blank pre-printed order documents and subsequent checking of sequence for completeness

- **Correct prices quoted** to **customers**

- **Matching** of **customer orders** with production orders and despatch notes and querying of orders not matched

- **Dealing** with **customer queries**

Worked example: Controls over ordering

Manufacturing Company Ltd (MCL) is a large manufacturing company selling a unique product. It has an established customer base, but as its product is unique, it also receives regular inquiries from potential customers that have not bought products from MCL before. In respect of such new customers, MCL has a significant risk of taking orders from customers who might not be able to pay.

In order to mitigate this risk, MCL should put the following controls into place:

- MCL should have a policy of obtaining credit checks on all new customers from a reputable credit agency, such as Dun and Bradstreet.

- MCL should ensure that it sets limited credit terms for new customers, such as a low credit limit or a short credit period, although these terms could be reviewed once the relationship is established.

- A senior member of staff should sign off on all new customers before orders are accepted. This member of staff should check that appropriate credit references have been obtained and that the credit terms extended are reasonable.

- New customer accounts should be reviewed and followed up for prompt payment until a relationship is established.

MCL is in a strong position to set limited credit terms to new customers as it is the sole source of a product. Other companies might have to balance the risk of customers not paying with the need to encourage new customers to use them rather than their competitors. In this case, companies would concentrate on the credit checks and the authorisation by senior staff.

1.3   Tests of controls

The tests that the assurance providers carry out over such controls will obviously also depend on the exact nature of the control and the business. However, again, some general ideas can be generated.

- **Check** that **references** are being **obtained** for **all new customers.**

- **Check** that all **new accounts** on the receivables ledger have been **authorised** by senior staff.

- **Check** that **orders** are only **accepted** from customers who are **within** their **credit terms** and **credit limits.**

- **Check** that **customer orders** are being **matched** with **production orders** and **despatch notes.**

Worked example: Tests of controls over ordering

The audit senior at MCL has been asked to test controls over sales, particularly with reference to new customers. There are three controls in particular that he should check – obtaining credit references, setting credit terms and authorisation.

The senior would select a sample of new customers by comparing the current year receivables ledger with the prior year one. He would then ask a member of the sales team for the customer files. These files should contain the details of the credit check, terms and evidence that the customer has been authorised by the sales director and when.

Interactive question 1: Ordering

MC plc is a company that has had a number of inquiries from potential new customers in recent months. The sales director is excited at this potential sales growth, but the financial controller is concerned that the company could be exposed to the risk of increased irrecoverable receivables.

Requirement

Which **two** of the following internal controls will mitigate the risk of irrecoverable receivables arising from new customers?

- [ ] Obtaining a credit reference for new customers
- [ ] Matching of customer orders with **despatch** notes
- [ ] Quoting the correct prices to customers making orders
- [ ] Authorisation of new customers by a senior staff member
- [ ] Authorisation for changes in customer data

See **Answer** at the end of this chapter.

2 Despatch and invoicing

Section overview

- A key risk is despatching goods to a customer but not invoicing for them.
- A control to mitigate that risk is matching despatch notes to invoices.

2.1 Risks and control objectives

When considering despatch and invoicing, a company might recognise all or some of the following risks:

- Goods may be despatched but not recorded so they are lost to the business.
- Goods may be despatched but not invoiced for.
- Invoices may be raised in error with resulting customer dissatisfaction.
- Invoices may be wrongly cancelled by credit notes resulting in loss to the business.

These risks lead to the following control objectives:

- All **despatches** of goods are **recorded.**
- All **goods and services** sold are **correctly invoiced.**
- All **invoices** raised **relate to goods and services supplied** by the business.
- **Credit notes** are only given for **valid reasons.**

2.2 Controls

The following are types of controls which could be put in place to fulfil the above objectives.

- Authorisation of **despatch** of goods

  - Despatch only on sales order
  - Despatch only to authorised customers
  - Special authorisation of despatches of goods free of charge or on special terms

- Examination of goods outwards as to quantity, quality and condition

- Recording of all goods outwards on a despatch note

- Agreement of despatch notes to customer orders and invoices

- Pre-numbering of despatch notes and regular checks on sequence

- Condition of returns checked

- Recording of goods returned on goods returned notes

- Signature of despatch notes by customers

- Preparation of invoices and credit notes

    - Authorisation of selling prices/use of price lists
    - Authorisation of credit notes
    - Checks on prices, quantities, extensions and totals on invoices and credit notes
    - Sequential numbering of blank invoices/credit notes and regular sequence checks

- Inventory records updated

- Matching of sales invoices with despatch notes and sales orders

- Regular review for despatch notes not matched by invoices

Worked example: Controls over despatch

MCL has experienced a number of requests for credit notes recently as a result of the alleged poor condition of goods when they arrive with customers.

In order to ensure that credits are not being wrongly issued, MCL needs to ensure that it has sufficient control over the despatch of its goods and their receipt by the customer.

MCL should ensure that goods are checked before they leave MCL's premises to ensure that the goods are packaged appropriately and are not damaged when they leave. Evidence of this check could be made by the checker signing a despatch note to accompany the goods to the customer. MCL could try to ensure that goods are not left with the customer until a similar quality check has been carried out by a member of the customer's staff, and similarly evidenced on the despatch note, a copy of which can be left with the customer.

These steps would mean that MCL had more control over the quality of the goods that arrived at the customer and more knowledge about the condition of the goods and whether a credit note was required. If the customer has signed that the condition appeared fine when the goods arrived, customers will have to give further justification to obtain a credit.

2.3 Tests of controls

The following tests could be used in relation to the controls noted above.

- Verify details of trade sales or goods despatch notes with sales invoices checking:

    - quantities
    - prices charged with official price lists
    - trade discounts have been properly dealt with
    - calculations and additions
    - entries in sales day book are correctly analysed
    - VAT, where chargeable, has been properly dealt with
    - postings to receivables ledger

- Verify details of trade sales with entries in inventory records

- Verify non-routine sales (scrap, non-current assets etc) with:

    - appropriate supporting evidence
    - approval by authorised officials
    - entries in plant register

- Verify credit notes with:

    - correspondence or other supporting evidence
    - approval by authorised officials
    - entries in inventory records

- entries in goods returned records
- calculations and additions
- entries in day book, checking these are correctly analysed
- postings to receivables ledger

- Test numerical sequence of despatch notes and enquire into missing numbers

- Test numerical sequence of invoices and credit notes, enquire into missing numbers and inspect copies of those cancelled

- Test numerical sequence of order forms and enquire into missing numbers

- Check that despatches of goods free of charge or on special terms have been authorised by management

Worked example: Tests of controls over invoicing

MCL have recently been the subject of an HMRC enquiry into errors in their invoicing impacting on VAT declared. MCL have asked an assurance provider to review the controls in place over invoicing to see what can be improved in the system.

As a minimum, the assurance providers would expect to see the following controls over invoice preparation:

- Evidence that the sales invoice has been agreed to the goods despatch note to confirm quantities of goods sold.

- Evidence that the sales invoice has been agreed to the order to confirm the price of the goods sold.

- Evidence that the calculations on the invoice, including the VAT calculation, have been checked.

In a large computerised function, these checks are likely to be carried out by a computer program, so could be checked by processing 'dummy' invoices through the system, some of which contain errors, to ensure that the appropriate checks are being made.

In a less complex system, these checks might be made manually by a member of staff. In this case, the checks might be evidenced by signature or initials by that staff member. This is sometimes done by using a pre-printed stamp on the copy of the invoice, such as the following:

Quantity agreed to despatch note?	NM
Price agreed to price list?	NM
Calculations checked?	NM

Interactive question 2: Despatch and invoicing

Which **three** of the following controls will help to mitigate the risk of goods being despatched but not invoiced?

- [ ] Pre-numbering of goods despatched notes and regular checks on sequence
- [ ] Pre-numbering of invoices and regular checks on sequence
- [ ] Matching of goods despatched notes with orders and invoices
- [ ] Regular review of despatch notes not matched with invoices

See **Answer** at the end of this chapter.

3 Recording

Section overview

- A key risk is failure to record sales so that payment is not prompted.

- Controls include various methods of prompting payment, such as statements sent out to customers.

3.1 Risks and control objectives

The following risks arise at this stage:

- Invoiced sales might not be properly recorded.
- Credit notes might not be properly recorded.
- Sales might be recorded in the wrong customer accounts.
- Debts might be included on the receivables ledger that are not collectable.

These risks lead to the following objectives:

- All sales that have been **invoiced** are **recorded** in the nominal and receivables ledgers.
- All **credit notes** that have been **issued** are **recorded** in the nominal and receivables ledgers.
- All **entries** in the receivables ledger are **made** to the **correct** receivables ledger **accounts**.
- **Cut-off** is applied correctly to the receivables ledger.
- Potential **irrecoverable receivables** are **identified**.

3.2 Controls

The following controls might be used to fulfil the objectives outlined above:

- **Segregation of duties:** recording sales, maintaining customer accounts and preparing statements

- **Recording** of **sales invoices** sequence and **control** over **spoilt invoices**

- **Matching** of **cash receipts** with **invoices**

- **Retention** of **customer remittance advices**

- **Separate recording** of **sales returns, price adjustments** etc

- **Cut-off procedures** to ensure goods despatched and not invoiced (or *vice versa*) are properly dealt with in the correct period

- Regular **preparation** of **trade receivables statements**

- **Checking** of **trade receivables statements**

- **Safeguarding** of **trade receivables statements** so that they cannot be altered before despatch

- **Review** and **follow-up** of **overdue accounts**

- **Authorisation** of **writing off** for **irrecoverable receivables**

- **Reconciliation** of **receivables ledger control account**

- **Analytical review** for receivables ledger and profit margins

Worked example: Controls over recording of sales

In the course of the audit of Perkins Limited, a small family owned company, it becomes clear from other testing that invoices which do not appear in the receivables ledger have been paid by customers. This has been caused by a failure in controls over recording of invoices and payments.

Further inquiry has revealed that since the previous receivables ledger clerk left half-way through the accounting year, customers have not been sent statements of their account on a monthly basis as the new clerk has not had time. She has also not matched receipts with particular invoices, but has simply allocated receipts to the customer accounts on the ledger when they have arrived. Some customers are in credit at the end of the year as a result of the problems arising.

Matching receipts with specific invoices on the ledger would have highlighted immediately if there were invoices missing from the ledger. Had statements been sent it is possible that an honest customer might have queried why invoices he had been sent had not been included on the statement.

(It emerges that a batch of invoices raised on the receivables ledger clerk's last day were not posted to the ledger but were instead lost in a pile of papers which the new receivables ledger clerk had put in a drawer.)

3.3 Tests of controls

The following tests of control might be appropriate.

Sales day book

- **Check entries** with **invoices** and **credit notes** respectively.
- **Check additions** and **cross casts.**
- **Check postings** to **receivables ledger control account.**
- **Check postings** to **receivables ledger.**

Receivables ledger

- **Check** entries in a **sample of accounts** to sales day book.

- **Check additions** and **balances** carried down.

- **Note** and **enquire** into **contra entries.**

- Check that **control accounts** have been **regularly reconciled** to total of receivables ledger balances.

- **Scrutinise accounts** to see if credit limits have been observed.

- **Check** that **trade receivables statements** are **prepared** and **sent out regularly.**

- **Check** that **overdue accounts** have been **followed up.**

- **Check** that **all irrecoverable receivables written off** have been **authorised** by management.

Worked example: Tests of controls over recording of sales

The audit senior wants to ensure that the above error in invoice recording at Perkins Ltd was isolated. He selects a sample of invoices from each month following the incident and traces them through the receivables ledger. The error appears to be isolated.

However, the fact that the error was not picked up indicates that other controls, such as reconciliations between the receivables ledger and receivables ledger control account have not been carried out. As such, it is unlikely that reliance can be placed on the sales recording system, and alternative substantive procedures should be carried out.

Interactive question 3: Recording of sales

The auditor at Icy Limited, a wholesaler of frozen goods, has discovered that the receivables ledger clerk has not matched receipts with invoices when processing receipts onto the ledger.

Requirement

Which **two** of the following are potential risks arising from this failure?

☐ The clerk could be siphoning off individual receipts and defrauding the company

☐ Old outstanding invoices could be left unpaid

☐ Sales might be recorded in the wrong supplier's accounts

☐ Sales may not be recorded properly in the sales account

See **Answer** at the end of this chapter.

4 Cash collection

Section overview

- A risk is that cash is misappropriated before recording and/or banking.
- Segregation of duties is very important.

4.1 Risks and control objectives

The key risks are that money might be received at the business premises but not be recorded or banked (generally due to fraud but also by simply losing cheques received). This leads to two key objectives:

- All monies received are recorded.
- All monies received are banked.

4.2 Controls

As there is a particular risk of fraud in relation to cash receipts, segregation of duties (the involvement of various people in the process) is particularly important. The following controls may be relevant:

Controls: Cash at bank and in hand – receipts

Segregation of duties between the various functions listed below is particularly important.

Recording of receipts received by post	- **Safeguards** to **prevent interception of mail** between receipt and opening - Appointment of **responsible person** to supervise mail - **Protection** of **cash and cheques** (restrictive crossing) - **Amounts received listed** when post opened - **Post stamped** with date of receipt

Recording of cash sales and collections	- **Restrictions** on **receipt of cash** (by cashiers only, or by sales representatives)
	
	- **Evidencing** of receipt of cash
	
	   – Serially numbered receipt forms
	   – Cash registers incorporating sealed till rolls
	
	- **Emptying** of cash offices and registers
	
	- **Agreement of cash collections with till rolls**
	
	- **Agreement of cash collections with bankings and** cash and sales **records**
	
	- **Investigation** of cash shortages and surpluses

Controls: Cash at bank and in hand – receipts

General controls over recording	• Prompt maintenance of records (cash book, ledger accounts)
	
	• Limitation of duties of receiving cashiers
	
	• Ensuring that the person who records cash takes holidays (so they do not have absolute control over cash recording) and controls are continued in their absence
	
	• Giving and recording of receipts
	
	   – Retained copies
	   – Serially numbered receipts books
	   – Custody of receipt books
	   – Comparisons with cash records and bank paying in slips

Banking	• **Daily bankings** • **Make-up** and **comparison** of **paying-in** slips against initial receipt records and cash book • **Banking** of receipts **intact**/control of payments

Safeguarding of cash and bank accounts	• **Restrictions** on **opening new bank accounts**
	
	• **Limitations** on **cash floats** held
	
	• **Restrictions** on **payments** out of **cash received**
	
	• **Restrictions** on **access** to cash registers and offices
	
	• **Independent checks** on cash floats
	
	• **Surprise cash counts**
	
	• **Custody** of **cash** outside **office hours**
	
	• **Custody** over **supply** and issue of cheques
	
	• **Preparation** of **cheques** restricted
	
	• **Safeguards** over **mechanically signed cheques**/cheques carrying printed signatures
	
	• **Restrictions** on issue of **blank** or **bearer** cheques
	
	• **Safeguarding** of **IOUs**, cash in transit
	
	• **Insurance arrangements**
	
	• **Bank reconciliations**
	
	   – Issue of bank statements
	   – Frequency of reconciliations by independent person
	   – Reconciliation procedures
	   – Treatment of longstanding unpresented cheques
	   – Sequence of cheque numbers
	   – Comparison with cash books

Worked example: Controls over cash receipts

Hampton Hotels plc (HH) owns a number of exclusive hotels in England and Wales. The majority of sales are cash sales made on the day guests check out of the hotel. HH take customer credit card details on arrival and reserve the right to extract full payment in the event of non-payment. Only cashiers are allowed to process cash transactions. Till receipts are maintained and reconciled to daily takings (cash and credit card slips) by the cashier in the presence of a member of staff who is not a cashier. This reduces the chance that cash will be misappropriated. Daily takings are entered in the cashbook after the daily reconciliation. Credit card slips are reconciled to statements from the card companies on a monthly basis. Cash transactions are sufficiently slight on a hotel basis to necessitate banking only on a weekly basis. Cash is kept in locked tills in the reception area. The financial controller reconciles the bank statements for each hotel on a monthly basis.

4.3 Tests of controls

The following tests of control may be used:

Area	Tests of control

Receipts received by post	• **Observe procedures** for **post opening** are being followed
	• **Observe** that **cheques** received by post are immediately **crossed** in the company's favour
	• For items entered in the rough cash book (or other record of cash, cheques etc received by post), **trace entries** to:
	  – **cash book**
	  – **paying-in book**
	  – **counterfoil** or carbon copy receipts
	• **Verify amounts entered** as **received** with remittance advices or other supporting evidence

Cash sales, branch takings	• For a sample of cash sales summaries/branch summaries from different locations:
	  – **Verify with till rolls** or copy cash sale notes
	  – **Check to paying-in slip** date-stamped and initialled by the bank
	  – **Verify that takings** are banked intact daily
	  – **Vouch expenditure** out of takings

Collections	• For a sample of items from the original collection records:
	  – **Trace amounts** to **cash book** via collectors' cash sheets or other collection records
	  – **Check entries** on **cash sheets** or collection records with collectors' receipt books
	  – **Verify** that **goods delivered** to travellers/salesmen have been regularly **reconciled** with sales and inventories in hand
	  – **Check numerical sequence** of collection records

Cash receipts cash book	• For cash receipts for several days throughout the period:
	  – **Check to entries in rough cash book**, receipts, branch returns or other records
	  – **Check to paying-in slips** obtained direct from the bank (rather than looking only at client copy of the slip which might have been tampered with), observing that there is no delay in banking monies received
	  – **Check additions of paying-in slips**
	  – **Check additions of cash book**
	  – **Check postings to the receivables ledger**
	  – **Check postings** to the **general ledger**, including control accounts
	• **Scrutinise the cash book** and **investigate items** of a **special** or **unusual nature**

Worked example: Tests of controls over cash receipts

You are a member of the assurance team at Happy Manufacturers Ltd (HM). All of their sales are made on credit terms and they receive cheques daily in the post. In order to ensure that the security over cheques is adequate, you will be observing the post opening, cheque listing and storing procedures. As a minimum, you would expect to see:

- Two people present at post opening (to prevent misappropriation of cheques)

- Cheques received being listed (to prevent misappropriation of cheques after initial receipt but before cheques are passed to accounts department)

- Cheques being put into a safe until banking (to prevent misappropriation of cheques before they are banked – for example, these cheques could be stolen and later cheques allocated to the relevant invoices in the customer account to hide the fraud)

Interactive question 4: Cash receipts

An effective system of internal control requires segregation of basic functions. Which **three** of the following functions should ideally be segregated?

☐	Authorisation of orders	☐	Recording cash receipts on receivables ledger
☐	Invoicing	☐	Credit control
☐	Reconciliation of receivables ledger with receivables ledger control account		

See **Answer** at the end of this chapter.

5 Deficiencies

Section overview

- Identifying the deficiencies of a system is a key exam technique.

Once you can identify control risks in a scenario and are aware of the types of control that will mitigate those risks, you should also be able to identify deficiencies in systems. This is an important area in practice, as auditors must be able to determine whether the control system is capable of operating well and therefore is capable of being relied on by them, and it is also an important exam technique.

Interactive question 5: Sales system deficiencies

The following describes the sales system in operation at Jinbob Company. For each process indicate whether the process indicates a strength or a deficiency of the system.

Written orders are received in the sales office. Orders are processed into the sales system with no further action being taken.	☐ Strength	☐ Deficiency	
The order generates a production note which is forwarded to the production department on the basis of which they fulfil the order. Completed goods are despatched with a delivery note, a copy of which is matched with the production note and sent to the invoicing department.	☐ Strength	☐ Deficiency	
Unfulfilled production notes are placed in a pending file which is reviewed weekly and completed as soon as possible.	☐ Strength	☐ Deficiency	

See **Answer** at the end of this chapter.

Summary

Controls in the sales system are focused on the following keypoints of the cycle

Ordering

Despatch & invoicing

Recording

Cash receipts

Risks:
- Customers cannot pay
- Orders may not be fulfilled

Risks:
- Goods are despatched but not invoiced
- Invoices/credits raised in error

Risks:
- Invoices are not recorded
- Invoices are processed to wrong account

Risks:
- Money received but not recorded
- Money received but not banked

Self-test

Answer the following questions.

1 For each of the following, state whether it is an objective relating to ordering, despatch and invoicing or recording:

(a)	All sales that have been invoiced have been put in the general ledger	☐	Ordering	☐	Despatch/invoice	☐	Recording
(b)	Orders are fulfilled	☐	Ordering	☐	Despatch/invoice	☐	Recording
(c)	Cut-off is correct	☐	Ordering	☐	Despatch/invoice	☐	Recording
(d)	Goods are only supplied to good credit risks	☐	Ordering	☐	Despatch/invoice	☐	Recording
(e)	Goods are correctly invoiced	☐	Ordering	☐	Despatch/invoice	☐	Recording
(f)	Customers are encouraged to pay promptly	☐	Ordering	☐	Despatch/invoice	☐	Recording

2 List **five** controls relating to the ordering and granting of credit process.

1 ....

2 ....

3 ....

4 ....

5 ....

Now, go back to the Learning Objectives in the Introduction. If you are satisfied you have achieved these objectives, please tick them off.

Answers to Interactive questions

Answer to Interactive question 1

Obtaining a credit reference for new customers
Authorisation of new customers by a senior staff member

Answer to Interactive question 2

Pre-numbering of invoices helps to ensure that invoices are not sent out and not recorded, but does not necessarily ensure that all goods despatched are invoiced. The other controls all contribute to ensuring that all despatched goods are invoiced.

Answer to Interactive question 3

The clerk could be siphoning off individual receipts and defrauding the company. (This is a fraud called 'teeming and lading' which can be successful if the outstanding balance on the account does not look unusual and the actions of the receivables ledger clerk are not checked.)

Old outstanding invoices could be left unpaid. This is because if the invoices are not matched then it is not clear which invoices are outstanding, and yet the overall balance outstanding looks reasonable, thus older invoices, which should be being chased up by the company may not be paid and ultimately may be forgotten about.

Answer to Interactive question 4

Authorisation of orders, invoicing and recording cash receipts. If one person was in charge of all these functions, that person would have control over the whole process of making an order and fulfilling it, so that it could make fictitious orders and not invoice for them or invoice for goods but transfer other people's payments to make it look as though the fictitious sale had been paid for.

Answer to Interactive question 5

Deficiency (because the customer's credit status is not checked before the order is processed)

Strength (because the invoices are generated from goods despatched information)

Strength (because production is kept up to date by weekly review of outstanding orders)

1

(a)	All sales that have been invoiced have been put in the general ledger	☐	Ordering	☐	Despatch/invoice	✓	Recording
(b)	Orders are fulfilled	✓	Ordering	☐	Despatch/invoice	☐	Recording
(c)	Cut-off is correct	☐	Ordering	☐	Despatch/invoice	✓	Recording
(d)	Goods are only supplied to good credit risks	✓	Ordering	☐	Despatch/invoice	☐	Recording
(e)	Goods are correctly invoiced	☐	Ordering	✓	Despatch/invoice	☐	Recording
(f)	Customers are encouraged to pay promptly	✓	Ordering	☐	Despatch/invoice	☐	Recording

2   Any of:

- **Segregation** of duties; credit control, invoicing and inventory despatch

- Authorisation of credit terms to customers

  - References/credit checks obtained
  - Authorisation by senior staff
  - Regular review

- Authorisation for changes in other customer data

  - Change of address supported by letterhead
  - Deletion requests supported by evidence of balances cleared/customer in liquidation

- **Orders** only **accepted** from **customers** who have no credit problems

- **Sequential numbering** of blank pre-printed order documents

- **Correct prices quoted** to **customers**

- **Matching** of **customer orders** with production orders and despatch notes and querying of orders not matched

- Dealing with customer queries

CHAPTER 7

Purchases system

Introduction

Examination context

Topic List

1 Ordering

2 Goods inward and recording of invoices

3 Payment

4 Deficiencies

Summary and Self-test

Answers to Interactive questions

Answers to Self-test

Introduction

Learning objectives

- Identify risks in a purchases system

- Identify relevant controls to mitigate risk

- Identify tests of those controls

- Recognise weaknesses in a purchases system

Specific syllabus references for this chapter are: 2f, g, h, 3f.

Syllabus links

You will have learnt about the various books of record in the purchases system in Accounting.

Examination context

As purchases is another important practical area, your assessment might well include scenario internal controls questions in this area. The sample paper contained one such scenario question looking at consequences of given weaknesses in a purchases system.

In the assessment, candidates may be required to:

- Show how specific internal controls in a purchases system mitigate risk and state their limitations
- Identify internal controls for an organisation in a given scenario
- Identify internal control strengths and weaknesses in a given scenario
- Determine the extent to which tests of controls should be used in a given set of circumstances

1 Ordering

1.1 Risks and control objectives

When considering purchase orders, a company might recognise one or both of the following risks:

- Unauthorised purchases may be made for personal use.
- Goods and services might not be obtained on the most advantageous terms.

The controls put into place will be designed to mitigate these risks. Hence the objectives of the controls will be to prevent these risks from occurring. Here are the control objectives which might arise from the risks noted above:

- All **orders for goods and services** are properly **authorised** and duly processed. All orders are for **goods and services** actually **required by** the company.

- Orders are only made with **authorised suppliers.**

- Orders are made at **competitive prices.**

1.2 Controls

Once the company has identified the risks which exist in the purchases system, it will try and create controls which mitigate those risks (that is, meet the control objectives outlined above). What controls will be put into place depend on the nature of the company and the specific risks associated with the way it operates, but the following controls can be used as examples of how the above risks can be mitigated.

- **Segregation** of duties; requisition and ordering

- **Central policy** for choice of suppliers

- Evidence required of **requirements** for purchase before purchase authorised (pre-set re-order quantities and re-order levels)

- **Order forms** prepared only when a **pre-numbered purchase requisition** has been **received**

- **Authorisation** of order forms

- **Pre-numbered order forms**

- **Safeguarding** of **blank order forms**

- **Review** for outstanding **orders**

- **Monitoring** of **supplier terms** and taking advantage of favourable conditions (bulk order and prompt payment discounts)

Worked example: Controls over ordering

Truman Limited buys 'Drox' frequently. Drox is highly marketable and easily portable and the company has a history of theft of inventories of Drox. In order to make sure that only Drox required for business use is purchased in the first place, the directors have decided to put the following controls into operation:

- Simon Radinski, the stores manager, will be in charge of purchase requisitions, which will be made when inventories of Drox have fallen to a pre-set level.

- Orders will only be raised in respect of purchase requisitions made by Simon Radinski, except in periods of Simon's absence, when requisitions may be made by his deputy Cathy Lewis.

- Orders will be authorised by Linda Fairburn, the purchases director.

- Random, occasional spot checks will be carried out by Linda Fairburn on the level of Drox when the requisition is raised.

- Purchase orders will be kept in a locked office in the purchase department.

In addition, in order to control inventories, Drox will only be kept in a locked cupboard in the warehouse.

1.3 Tests of controls

The tests that the assurance providers carry out over such controls will obviously also depend on the exact nature of the control and the business. However, again, some general ideas can be generated.

- Review list of suppliers and check a sample to orders made
- Check sequence of pre-numbered order forms
- Check orders are supported by a purchase requisition
- Review security arrangements over blank orders

Worked example: Tests of controls over orders

The directors of Truman Limited have requested that the auditors review that the new controls over the purchase of Drox are operating effectively. The audit senior has therefore drafted the following plan:

- Spot check on security arrangements over purchase orders.

- Request Linda Fairburn notifies the audit team of requisitions for Drox during the audit and attend spot check on re-order level.

- Observation of premises for evidence of Drox being stored elsewhere than the locked cupboard.

- Review of sample of orders for Drox to ensure that purchase requisition exists and orders were made only by Simon Radinski and were authorised by Linda Fairburn.

- If sampled requisitions were made by Cathy Lewis, check absence records for Simon Radinski.

Interactive question 1: Ordering

The directors of Lyton Limited (LL) have just uncovered a fraud being perpetrated by the stores manager. He was in charge of ordering, had raised a number of false orders to non-existent suppliers, raised goods received notes in respect of non-existent deliveries and forwarded an invoice to the accounts department, which was then paid.

Requirement

Which **two** of the following controls could have prevented this fraud?

- [ ] Approved list of suppliers
- [ ] Check of goods inward by person other than orderer
- [ ] Pre-numbered order forms
- [ ] Blank order forms locked in a safe

See **Answer** at the end of this chapter.

2 Goods inward and recording of invoices

> **Section overview**
>
> - Risks are of accepting goods not ordered or for accepting invoices for poor quality goods.
> - Controls include matching goods received with orders.

2.1 Risks and control objectives

When considering goods inward and recording of invoices, a company might recognise all or some of the following risks:

- Goods may be misappropriated for private use.
- Goods may be accepted that have not been ordered.
- Invoices may not be recorded resulting in non-payment.
- The company may not take advantage of the full period of credit extended.
- The company may not record credit notes resulting in paying invoices unnecessarily.

These risks lead to the following control objectives:

- All goods and services received are used for the **company's purposes**, and not private purposes.

- Goods and services are **only accepted if** they have been **ordered**, and the **order** has been **authorised.**

- All **goods** and **services received** are accurately **recorded.**

- **Liabilities** are **recognised** for all **goods and services** that have been **received.**

- All **credits** to which the company is entitled are **claimed** and **received.**

- **Receipt** of **goods** and **services** is **necessary** for a **liability to be recorded.**

- All **credit notes** that are received are **recorded** in the nominal and payables ledgers.

- All **entries** in the **payables ledger** are **made** to the **correct payables ledger accounts.**

- **Cut-off** is **applied correctly** to the **payables ledger.**

2.2 Controls

The following are types of controls which could be put in place to fulfil the above objectives.

- **Examination** of goods inwards

  - Quality
  - Quantity
  - Condition

- **Recording arrival** and **acceptance** of goods (pre-numbered goods received notes)

- **Comparison** of **goods received notes** with **purchase orders**

- **Referencing** of supplier invoices; numerical sequence and supplier reference

- **Checking** of **suppliers' invoices**

  - Prices, quantities, accuracy of calculation
  - Comparison with order and goods received note

- **Recording return of goods** (pre-numbered goods returned notes)

- Procedures for **obtaining credit notes** from suppliers

- **Segregation** of **duties:** accounting and checking functions

- Prompt **recording of purchases** and **purchase returns** in day books and ledgers

- **Regular maintenance** of **payables ledger**

- **Comparison** of **monthly statements** of account balance from suppliers with **payables ledger balances**

- **Review** of **classification** of expenditure

- **Reconciliation** of **payables ledger** control account to total of **payables ledger** balances

- Create a **cut-off** accrual of goods received notes not matched by invoices at year-end

Worked example: Controls over goods inward

The production department at Manufacturing Company Limited (MCL) works on a just-in-time basis. Orders for necessary materials are dispatched by computer according to pre-set re-order levels. Deliveries are made within 12 hours by the suppliers, who invoice electronically when goods are dispatched. Items are put into production within hours of arriving at MCL's premises.

In this example, it is crucial that controls over goods inward operate effectively. In the first case, it is necessary that the quality of goods being put into production immediately are of appropriate quality or production will be held up. Therefore it is vital that goods inward are checked for quality and quantity on arrival at MCL's premises.

It is also important that goods inwards are recorded, as with the goods being used so quickly it would be more difficult to verify purchase invoices to goods being held in a warehouse.

Therefore MCL have a pre-printed, numbered goods received note (GRN) which contains a number of checks in respect of quality and quantity and on which the warehouse staff note the relevant order number, the time of delivery, and the quantity of goods delivered. A copy of this GRN is forwarded to the accounts department to be matched with the supplier's electronic invoice.

Worked example: Controls over purchase recording

Stibbe Limited have recently discovered that they have been paying invoices that had been credited because the goods had been returned by the production quality controller due to poor quality.

In order to prevent this occurring, Stibbe Limited should have put the following controls in place:

- Raising purchase return notes
- Copy purchase return notes sent to accounts department by production department
- Review of credit notes before payment run authorised
- Regular comparison of supplier statements with payables ledger accounts

2.3 Tests of controls

The following tests could be used in relation to the controls noted above.

- Check invoices for goods are:

    - supported by goods received notes

    - entered in inventory records

    - priced correctly by checking to quotations, price lists to see the price is in order

    - properly referenced with a number and supplier code

    - correctly coded by type of expenditure

    - trace entry in record of goods returned etc and see credit note duly received from the supplier, for invoices not passed due to defects or discrepancy

- For invoices of all types:
    - check calculations and additions
    - check entries in purchase day book and verify that they are correctly analysed
    - check posting to **payables ledger**

- For credit notes:
    - verify the correctness of credit received with correspondence
    - check entries in inventory records
    - check entries in record of returns
    - check entries in purchase day book and verify that they are correctly analysed
    - check posting to **payables ledger**

- Check for returns that credit notes are duly received from the suppliers

- Test numerical sequence and enquire into missing numbers of:
    - purchase requisitions
    - goods received notes
    - suppliers' invoices
    - purchase orders
    - goods returned notes

- Obtain explanations for items which have been outstanding for a long time:
    - unmatched purchase requisitions
    - unmatched purchase orders
    - unmatched goods received notes
    - unrecorded invoices

- Verify that invoices and credit notes recorded in the purchase day book are:
    - initialled for prices, calculations and extensions
    - cross-referenced to purchase orders, goods received notes etc
    - authorised for payment

- Check additions

- Check postings to nominal ledger accounts and control account

- Check postings of entries to payables ledger

Payables ledger

- For a sample of accounts recorded in the payables ledger:
    - test check entries back into books of prime entry
    - test check additions and carried forward balances
    - note and enquire into all contra entries

- Confirm control account reconciliation has been regularly carried out during the year

- Examine control account for unusual entries

Worked example: Tests of controls over goods inward and invoices

The auditor is verifying the controls over goods inward at MCL. He selects a sample of goods received notes and checks that they are in sequence, enquiring into any missing numbers (spoilt copies should be retained) and seeking evidence (initials of relevant staff) that the quality checks have been carried out. These goods received notes would then be checked to purchase invoices to ensure that all invoices had an associated goods received note and also to purchase orders to ensure that the goods were ordered properly.

Interactive question 2: Goods inward and invoices

Weezy plc is a company that has a large number of deliveries daily.

Which **one** of the following internal controls is most likely to prevent Weezy plc paying for goods that have not been received?

☐	Locked stores
☐	Matching of purchase invoices with goods received notes
☐	Authorisation of invoice payment
☐	Safeguarding of blank order documents

See **Answer** at the end of this chapter.

Interactive question 3: Purchase recording

Rhonda posts the invoices to the payables ledger.

Which **two** of the following would help prevent suppliers from being overpaid?

☐	Posting invoices to the receivables ledger
☐	Reconciliation of the payables ledger to the control account
☐	Authorisation of payments
☐	Bank reconciliations

See **Answer** at the end of this chapter.

3 Payment

Section overview

- Payments might be made to the wrong person.
- Payments should be authorised.

3.1 Risks and control objectives

The following risks arise at this stage of proceedings:

- False invoices are paid in error.
- Invoices are paid too soon.
- Payment is not correctly recorded.
- Credits are not correctly recorded.
- Payments are not recorded in the right period.

The key risk is that money might be paid out by the business inappropriately. The following objectives arise out of the risks:

- All **expenditure** is for goods that are **received.**
- All **expenditure** is **authorised.**
- All **expenditure** that is made is **recorded** correctly in the nominal and payables ledgers.
- **Payments** are **not made twice** for the same liability.

3.2 Controls

The arrangements for controlling payments will depend to a great extent on the nature of business transacted, the volume of payments involved and the size of the company.

Cheque and cash payments generally	The cashier should generally not be concerned with keeping or writing-up books of account other than those recording payments, nor should he have access to, or be responsible for the custody of, securities or title deeds belonging to the company.
	The person responsible for preparing cheques should not himself be a cheque signatory. Cheque signatories in turn should not be responsible for recording payments.

Cheque and bank transfer payments	• **Cheque and bank transfer requisitions**
	  – Appropriate supporting documentation (for example, invoices)
	  – Approval by appropriate staff
	  – Presentation to cheque signatories (in case of cheques)
	  – Instigation of bank transfer by appropriate staff
	
	• **Authority** to sign cheques
	  – Signatories should not also approve cheque requisitions
	  – Limitations on authority to specific amounts
	  – Number of signatories
	  – Prohibitions over signing of blank cheques
	
	• **Prompt dispatch** of signed **cheques**
	
	• **Obtaining** of paid **cheques** from **banks**
	
	• Payments **recorded promptly** in **cash book** and **nominal** and **payables ledgers**

Cash payments	• **Authorisation** of **expenditure** • **Cancellation** of **vouchers** to ensure they cannot be paid twice • **Limits** on **payments** • **Rules** on **cash advances** to employees, IOUs and cheque cashing

Worked example: Controls over cash payments

Build Co has a large number of suppliers and it takes deliveries most days. Deliveries are noted on goods received notes which are matched with invoices when they arrive. Invoices are entered to the payables ledger system, which is programmed with the credit terms given by each supplier and produces a payment listing each week when the computer prints all the necessary cheques.

Linda, the payments clerk, takes the cheques to the financial controller for authorisation and signature.

3.3 Tests of controls

The following controls may be used:

Payments cash book (authorisation)	• For a sample of payments: – Compare with paid cheques to ensure payee agrees. – Check that cheques are signed by the persons authorised to do so within their authority limits. – Check that bank transfer was authorised and initiated by appropriate person. – Check to suppliers' invoices for goods and services. Verify that supporting documents are signed as having been checked and passed for payment and have been stamped 'paid'. – Check to suppliers' statements. – Check to other documentary evidence, as appropriate (agreements, authorised expense vouchers, petty cash books etc).
Payments cash book (recording)	• For a sample of weeks: – Check the sequence of cheque numbers and enquire into missing numbers. – Trace transfers to other bank accounts, petty cash books or other records, as appropriate. – Check additions, including extensions, and balances forward at the beginning and end of the months covering the periods chosen. – Check postings to the payables ledger. – Check postings to the nominal ledger, including the control accounts.

When checking that bank and cash are **secure**, assurance providers should consider the security arrangements over blank cheques. Bank reconciliations are also a very important control and assurance providers should carry out the following tests on these.

Area	Tests of control
Bank reconciliations	• For a period which includes a reconciliation date reperform reconciliation (see Chapter 13). • Verify that reconciliations have been prepared at regular intervals throughout the year. • Scrutinise reconciliations for unusual items.
Petty cash payments	• For a sample of payments: – Check to supporting vouchers. – Check whether they are properly approved. – See that vouchers have been marked and initialled by the cashier to prevent their re-use.

Worked example: Tests of controls over cash payments

The auditors of Build Co have decided that it is important to check the computer control that ensures that suppliers' credit terms are used and payments are made on time. To do this they will use a computer assisted audit technique (CAAT). They will process a number of 'dummy' invoices from existing suppliers and check that the computer processes the payments at the correct time. CAATs will be covered in more detail in Chapter 11.

Interactive question 4: Cash payments

Which **two** of the following control activities are most likely to reduce the risk of payments being made twice for the same liability?

	Stamping '**Paid**' on invoices that have been paid
	Prompt dispatch of cheques
	Authorisation of payments
	Checking supplier statements before payments are made

See **Answer** at the end of this chapter.

4 Deficiencies

Section overview

- As outlined in Chapter 6, it is important to be able to identify the deficiencies of systems.

Try the following question.

Interactive question 5: Deficiencies of the purchases system

The auditor of Sunny plc has identified that there is no procedure to track purchase invoice due dates.

Which **one** of the following is the most likely consequence which might arise as a result of that deficiency?

	Prompt payment discounts may not be obtained.
	Goods not actually received may be paid for.
	Inferior goods may be purchased.
	Payments may be made to fictitious suppliers.

See **Answer** at the end of this chapter.

Summary and Self-test

Summary

Controls in the purchases system are focused on the following key points of the cycle

- **Ordering**

- **Goods inwards and recording of invoices**

- **Cash payments**

Risks:
- Goods for personal use
- Goods not on most advantageous terms

Risks:
- Goods may be misappropriated
- Invoices may be mislaid leading to non-payment
- Invoices are paid at wrong time/amount
- Payments/credits not recorded
- Record in wrong period

Risks:
- Payments made inappropriately
- Blank cheques (and therefore cash) stolen

Self-test

Answer the following questions.

1   For each of the following, state whether it is an objective relating to ordering, recording invoices or payment:

(a)   Orders are only made to authorised suppliers ☐ Ordering ☐ Recording invoices ☐ Payment

(b)   Liabilities are recognised for all goods and services received ☐ Ordering ☐ Recording invoices ☐ Payment

(c)   Orders are made at competitive prices ☐ Ordering ☐ Recording invoices ☐ Payment

(d)   All expenditure is authorised ☐ Ordering ☐ Recording invoices ☐ Payment

(e)   Cut-off is correctly applied ☐ Ordering ☐ Recording invoices ☐ Payment

(f)   Goods and services are only accepted if there is an authorised order ☐ Ordering ☐ Recording invoices ☐ Payment

2   List **four** examples of purchase documentation on which numerical sequence should be checked.

1   ....
2   ....
3   ....
4   ....

3   Why is numerical sequence on GRNs checked?

4   Give **five** examples of tests to be performed on the cash payments book.

1   ....
2   ....
3   ....
4   ....
5   ....

Now, go back to the Learning Objectives in the Introduction. If you are satisfied you have achieved these objectives, please tick them off.

Answers to Interactive questions

Answer to Interactive question 1

Approved list of suppliers

Check of goods inward by person other than orderer

Because the stores manager is entitled to make orders, pre-numbered order forms and safekeeping of order forms would have made no difference in this case.

Answer to Interactive question 2

Matching of purchase invoices with goods received notes

Answer to Interactive question 3

Reconciliation of the payables ledger to the control account

Authorisation of payments

Answer to Interactive question 4

Stamping '**Paid**' on invoices that have been paid

Authorisation of payments

Although checking supplier statements will help, the timing differences between the statement date and payments made may mean that this method is not foolproof

Answer to Interactive question 5

Prompt payment discounts may not be obtained

1

(a)	Orders are only made to authorised suppliers	✓	Ordering		Recording invoices		Payment	
(b)	Liabilities are recognised for all goods and services received		Ordering	✓	Recording invoices		Payment	
(c)	Orders are made at competitive prices	✓	Ordering		Recording invoices		Payment	
(d)	All expenditure is authorised		Ordering		Recording invoices	✓	Payment	
(e)	Cut-off is correctly applied		Ordering	✓	Recording invoices		Payment	
(f)	Goods and services are only accepted if there is an authorised order		Ordering	✓	Recording invoices		Payment	

2   Four from: (1) purchase requisitions, (2) purchase orders, (3) goods received notes, (4) goods returned notes, (5) suppliers' invoices

3   Sequence provides a control that purchases are completely recorded. Missing documents should be explained, or cancelled copies available otherwise the implication could be that goods have been received but not matched with an invoice and the liability in respect of that invoice is being omitted.

4   For a sample of payments:

1   **Compare** with paid cheques to ensure payee agrees

2   **Note** that **cheques** are **signed** by the **persons authorised** to do so within their authority limits

3   **Check** to **suppliers' invoices** for goods and services. Verify that supporting documents are signed as having been **checked** and **passed for payment** and have been stamped 'paid'

4   **Check** to **suppliers' statements**

5   **Check** to **other documentary evidence**, as appropriate (agreements, authorised expense vouchers, wages/salaries records, petty cash books etc)

CHAPTER 8

Employee costs

Introduction

Examination context

Topic List

1   Calculating wages and salaries

2   Recording of wages and salaries and deductions

3   Payment of wages and salaries

4   Deficiencies

Summary and Self-test

Answers to Interactive questions

Answers to Self-test

Learning objectives

Tick off

- Identify risks in a payroll system

- Identify relevant controls to mitigate risk

- Identify tests of those controls

- Recognise weaknesses in a payroll system

Specific syllabus references for this chapter are: 2f, g, h, 3f.

Syllabus links

You will have learnt about double entries relating to wages and salaries in Accounting.

Examination context

As payroll is an important practical area, your assessment might well include scenario internal controls questions in this area. The sample paper contained a number of questions focused on payroll controls.

In the assessment, candidates may be required to:

- show how specific internal controls in a payroll system mitigate risk and state their limitations
- identify internal controls for an organisation in a given scenario
- identify internal control strengths and weaknesses in a given scenario
- determine the extent to which tests of controls should be used in a set of circumstances

1 Calculating wages and salaries

Section overview

- A key risk is paying employees too much.
- A key control is authorisation (of time records or of changes to the payroll for example).

1.1 Risks and control objectives

When calculating wages and salaries, a company might recognise the following risks:

- The company may pay employees too much money.
- The company may pay employees who have left.

The controls put into place will be designed to mitigate these risks. Hence the objectives of the controls will be to prevent these risks from occurring. Here are the control objectives which might arise from the risks noted above:

- **Employees** are **only paid** for **work** that they have **done.**
- **Gross pay** has been **calculated correctly** and **authorised.**
- Net pay has been calculated correctly.

1.2 Controls

The following controls may be put into place to mitigate the risks noted above.

- **Staffing** and **segregation of duties**

- **Maintenance of personnel records** and regular checking of wages and salaries to details in personnel records

- **Authorisation**
    - Engagement and discharge of employees
    - Changes in pay rates
    - Overtime
    - Non-statutory deductions (for example pension contributions)
    - Advances of pay

- **Recording** of **changes** in **personnel** and **pay rates**

- **Recording** of hours worked by **timesheets, clocking** in and out arrangements

- **Review** of hours worked

- **Recording** of **advances** of **pay**

- **Holiday pay** arrangements

- **Answering queries**

- **Review** of **wages** against **budget**

Worked example: Calculating wages

The workforce at CleanCo Limited has negotiated a pay rise through discussions between the union and management. In relation to this pay rise, management will want to ensure that they have the following controls in place to ensure that employees are not paid too much or too little for their work:

- Increases should be authorised on an individual basis by Adrian Lewis, the Personnel Manager, who is in charge of payroll.

- Details of the pay rise should be entered into each employee's personnel file.

- As the computer system calculates pay automatically, the new details must be entered into the master file by Adrian Lewis using the private password which allows him to make such changes.

1.3 Tests of controls

- Check that the **wages** and **salary summary** is **approved** for payment.

- Confirm that procedures are operating for **authorising changes** in **rates of pay**, overtime, and holiday pay.

- Obtain evidence that staff **only start being paid when they join the company**, and are **removed** from the payroll **when they leave the company**.

- Check that the **engagement** of **new employees** and **discharges** have been **confirmed in writing**.

- Check **calculations** of wages and salaries are being **checked**.

- For wages, check **calculation** of **gross pay** with:

  – authorised rates of pay

  – production records. See that production bonuses have been authorised and properly calculated

  – clock cards, time sheets or other evidence of hours worked. Verify that overtime has been authorised

- For salaries, **verify that gross salaries and bonuses are in accordance with personnel records, contracts of employment** etc and that increases in pay have been properly authorised.

Worked example: Tests of controls over calculating pay

The auditors at CleanCo want to check that controls over the negotiated pay rise operated properly. They have a copy of the minutes of the meeting where the pay rise was agreed, the pay rise being a 3.25% increase across the board. This minute of agreement indicates that the pay rise was authorised by the directors.

The auditors select a sample of employees and request their personnel files. They recalculate the pay rise as compared to the previous pay rate (which they agree to the previous payroll).

They then review the standing data in the payroll system for each employee sampled to ensure that the computer system contains the correct pay rate. They check that each employee was paid the correct wage in the month following the pay rise.

Lastly, the auditors attempt (with permission) to change the standing data in the computer system to ensure that unauthorised amendments cannot be made.

Interactive question 1: Calculating pay

The following system of time records exists at Shepherd Limited. Staff members are required to fill in a manual timesheet as they arrive, stating the time of arrival and as they leave, stating the time of departure. Staff members are then paid an hourly rate on the basis of this record.

Requirement

Which **two** of the following outcomes could arise from this system?

☐ Employees may be paid at an inappropriate rate

☐ Employees may be paid for work they have not done

☐ Employees are paid for the hours they have worked

☐ Employee deductions may be inappropriate

See **Answer** at the end of this chapter.

2 Recording of wages and salaries and deductions

Section overview

- A risk is not recording wages and therefore making incorrect payments.
- The payroll should be prepared, checked and authorised.

2.1 Risks and control objectives

When considering recording wages and salaries, the company might recognise the following risks:

- The various elements of pay might not be recorded correctly in the payroll.
- Amounts paid to employees might not be reflected in the cash books.
- Pay might not be recorded correctly in the general ledger.

In addition, the company has a duty to pay over to HMRC the correct amounts in respect of tax and national insurance. If these are calculated wrongly, the company might face a large tax bill in the future of arrears and penalties. The company also has a duty to pay other deductions on behalf of employees, for example, pension deductions. Again, errors might mean future liabilities.

These lead to the following control objectives:

- **Gross** and **net pay** and **deductions** are **accurately recorded** on the payroll.
- **Wages and salaries paid** are **recorded correctly** in the **bank** and **cash records.**
- **Wages and salaries** are **correctly recorded** in the **general ledger.**
- All **deductions** have been **calculated correctly** and are **authorised.**
- The **correct amounts** are paid to **HMRC.**

2.2 Controls

Responsibility for the preparation of payroll should be delegated to a suitable person, and adequate staff appointed to assist him. The extent to which the staff responsible for preparing wages and salaries may perform other duties should be clearly defined. In this connection full advantage should be taken where possible of the division of duties, and checks available where automatic wage accounting systems are in use.

In addition there should be:

- bases for compilation of payroll (for example, clockcards, overtime records, agreed hours)

- arrangements for the preparation, checking (reconciling to payroll information) and approval of payroll

- procedures for dealing with non-routine matters

- maintenance of separate employees' personnel records

- one for one checking of payroll details back to independently maintained personnel records

- reconciliation of total pay and deductions between one pay day and the next

- comparison of actual pay totals with budget estimates or standard costs and the investigation of differences between them

- agreement of gross earnings and total tax deducted with taxation returns

Worked example: Preparation of payroll

The system of control over payroll production at Maybury plc operates as follows.

Anne, the payroll clerk, uses a well-known computerised payroll system. She enters the number of hours worked by each employee in the week per their clock cards. The computer then produces the payroll based on the standing data concerning pay rates and deductions. Anne prints off the payroll for the week, checks that the brought forward figures for tax and national insurance agree to the previous payroll and sends it to Sandra, who checks the payroll and authorises it.

Sandra also checks that the brought forward figures agree to the previous payroll and indicates that she has checked by initialling the appropriate column in the payroll. She compares a sample of net pays to the previous payroll and investigates any significant differences. She authorises it by signing it. She prepares the journals that will be posted to the cash books and general ledgers and passes these and the payroll to the finance department, so that the journals may be posted and the bank transfer list prepared.

2.3 Tests of controls

A key control assurance providers will be concerned with will be the reconciliation of wages and salaries. For wages, there should have been reconciliations with:

- the **previous week's payroll**
- **clock cards/time sheets/job cards**
- **costing analyses, production budgets**

The total of **salaries** should be **reconciled** with the **previous week/month** or the **standard payroll**.

In addition, assurance providers should confirm that important calculations have been checked by the clients and re-perform those calculations.

These include checking for wages for a number of weeks:

- **Additions** of **payroll**
- **Totals** of **payroll detail** selected to summary of payroll
- **Additions** and **cross-casts** of summary
- **Postings** of **summary** to **general ledger** (including control accounts)
- **Net cash column** to cash book

For salaries they include checking for a number of weeks/months:

- **Additions** of **payroll**
- **Totals** of **salaries details** to **summary**
- **Additions** and **cross-casts** of **summary**
- **Postings** of **summary** to **general ledger** (including control accounts)
- **Total** of **net pay column** to cash book

Assurance providers should **check** the **calculations** of **taxation** and **non-statutory deductions**. For PAYE and NI they should carry out the following tests:

- **Scrutinise** the **control accounts** maintained to see **appropriate deductions** have been **made**.
- **Check** that the **payments** to **HMRC** are **correct**.

They should check other deductions to appropriate records. For voluntary deductions, they should see the authority completed by the relevant employees.

Worked example: Test of controls over recording pay

An audit assistant on the audit of Maybury plc has been asked to test controls over the payroll. She has been given the following audit plan.

- Sample four separate weeks of payroll.
- Ensure that Sandra's signature appears, authorising payroll.
- Check for Sandra's initials showing the brought forward figures have been checked.
- Recheck the brought forward figures from the previous payroll.
- Cast a sample of lines in the payroll to ensure it is arithmetically accurate.
- Check the calculations of statutory deductions.
- Obtain journal sheet for posting to ledger and cash book and confirm the postings are correct.
- Trace postings to ledgers to ensure processed correctly.
- Check a sample of hours worked to original clock cards.

Interactive question 2: Recording pay

Personnel and wages records at Simonston Brothers Limited are maintained by Sam, the wages clerk, on a personal computer. Sam calculates the hours worked by each employee on a weekly basis, based on that employee's clock cards and enters them on the computer. The payroll program, using data from personnel records in respect of wage rates and deductions, produces the weekly payroll and a payslip for each employee.

Sam uses the payroll to prepare the bank transfer list, which he then sends to the company accountant. The accountant signs the transfer list and has it countersigned by a director. The wages clerk then processes the bank transfer on the computer.

Requirement

Which **two** of the following are deficiencies which exist in the wages system at Simonston Brothers Limited?

<!-- checkbox --> Sam records the salaries and organises the payment of wages.
<!-- checkbox --> There is no review of the payroll.
<!-- checkbox --> The bank transfer list is countersigned by a director.
<!-- checkbox --> The payroll and the time recording system are separate.

See **Answer** at the end of this chapter.

3 Payment of wages and salaries

Section overview
- There is a risk that payments are made incorrectly.
- Authorisation should prevent this.

3.1 Risks and control objectives

The key risks here are that people who are not employees are paid and those that are employees are not paid. Therefore the overriding control objective is that the correct employees are paid.

3.2 Controls

Payment of cash wages (this is increasingly rare)	• Segregation of duties
	
	  – Preparing the payroll net pay summary
	  – Filling of pay packets
	  – Distribution of wages
	
	• Authorisation of wage cheque cashed
	
	• Custody of cash
	
	  – When the wages cheque is cashed
	  – Security of pay packets
	  – Security of transit
	  – Security and prompt banking of unclaimed wages
	
	• Verification of identity
	
	• Recording of distributions

Payment of salaries	• Preparation and authorisation of cheques and bank transfer lists • Comparison of cheques and bank transfer list with payroll • Maintenance and reconciliation of wages and salaries control account

Worked example: Payment of wages

At Pynewood Limited, the bookkeeper calculates the wages and then prepares the bank transfer list. She then puts through the transfer herself. This system displays the following deficiency:

- There is no segregation of duties between preparing the payroll and preparing the bank transfer lists, and then again between preparing the lists and making the actual payment. This means that the bookkeeper could easily perpetrate a fraud of paying staff extra or paying non existent staff and keeping the proceeds.

3.3 Tests of controls

If wages are paid in cash:

- **Arrange to attend** the **pay-out** of wages to confirm that the official procedures are being followed.

- Before the wages are paid **compare payroll** with **wage packets** to ensure all employees have a wage packet.

- **Examine receipts** given by employees; **check unclaimed wages** are recorded in unclaimed wages book.

- **Check** that **no employee receives more than one wage packet**.

- **Check entries** in the **unclaimed wages book** with the entries on the payroll.

- **Check that unclaimed wages** are **banked regularly**.

- **Check** that unclaimed wages books show **reasons** why wages are unclaimed.

- **Check pattern** of **unclaimed wages** in unclaimed wages book; variations may indicate failure to record.

- For salaries, check that comparisons are being made between each month's payroll net pay summary and **examine paid cheques** or a **certified copy** of the **bank list** for employees paid by cheque or bank transfer.

Worked example: Tests of control over payment of wages

At HyperCo plc, all employees are salaried and are paid by direct transfer to their bank each month. The auditors will test that controls operate properly over this direct transfer by requesting a certified copy of the bank list for the payroll to see how the sum leaving the company's bank account is broken down and checking the individual amounts paid back to the payroll.

Interactive question 3: Payment of wages

Which **two** of the following control activities will reduce the risk of employees who have left being made up a pay packet which is collected by the leaver or an accomplice?

	Check that each employee only collects one pay packet
	Supervision of payout by member of staff who knows all the employees personally
	Authorisation of payroll
	Comparison of payroll with wage packets to ensure that they match

See **Answer** at the end of this chapter.

4 Deficiencies

Section overview

- Being able to identify the deficiencies of a system an important exam technique.

Interactive question 4: Deficiencies of a payroll system

The following describes the payroll system in operation at Whistling Co. For each process indicate whether the process indicates a strength or a deficiency of the system.

1	Employees each have an electronic card to swipe in order to enter and leave the factory premises. This 'swipe' system automatically updates time records in the payroll system.	☐ Strength	☐ Deficiency
2	There is no personnel department. Employees are engaged by department heads with the verbal consent of a director.	☐ Strength	☐ Deficiency
3	On leaving, employees are required to return their swipe cards.	☐ Strength	☐ Deficiency
4	The payroll has a variance function which reports items within the payroll falling outside the expected conventions which must be resolved by an authorised member of staff before the payroll can be finalised. The ability to resolve this report is controlled by a secret password.	☐ Strength	☐ Deficiency

See **Answer** at the end of this chapter.

Summary and Self-test

Summary

Controls in the employee costs system are focused on the following key points of the cycle

Setting wages

Risk:
- Employees are paid for work not done

Recording wages and deductions

Risks:
- Incorrect recording of wages and cash paid
- Incorrect deductions leading to future liabilities

Payment

Risks:
- Employees are not paid
- Non-employees are paid

Self-test

Answer the following questions.

1   List **six** procedures assurance providers should carry out if wages are paid in cash.

    1   ....

    2   ....

    3   ....

    4   ....

    5   ....

    6   ....

2   What are the most important authorisation controls over amounts to be paid to employees?

3   How should assurance providers confirm that wages have been paid at the correct rate to individual employees?

Now, go back to the Learning Objectives in the Introduction. If you are satisfied you have achieved these objectives, please tick them off.

Answers to Interactive questions

Answer to Interactive question 1

Shepherd has a simple control over how much work is being done by its employees. Therefore, employees should be being paid for the hours they have worked.

However, it is a very simple control, which relies on the integrity of the employees in recording the correct times they arrived and left the premises. There does not appear to be a supervisory control ensuring that employees are writing the correct times. Nor is there any provision for times when the employees are not working, for example, lunch hour or slack periods. Therefore it is possible that despite the presence of this control, employees may be paid for work they have not done.

Answer to Interactive question 2

Sam records the salaries and organises the pay packets. There is no review of the payroll.

Answer to Interactive question 3

Check that each employee only collects one pay packet. Authorisation of payroll.

Comparison of the payroll with the pay packets will only be effective if the payroll has been properly updated for the leaver. Supervision by a member of staff who knows all the staff will be necessary if the employees are not required to show identification to pick up wages, but will not necessarily stop a leaver picking up a wage packet if the supervisor does not know the staff member has left.

Answer to Interactive question 4

1   Strength. The fact that employees cannot access the factory to work without updating the time records automatically is a strength in the system.

2   Deficiency. It appears that the recruitment process is casual and there is not necessarily any written documentation resulting from the appointment of an employee. This could lead to errors in pay rates and payroll production that could be eliminated if written notice of an employee's start was given to the payroll department.

3   Strength. The fact that employees are required to return their cards when they leave means that they are effectively excluded from the time recording system and in practice cannot continue to be paid after they have left.

4   Strength. The fact that the payroll has parameters beyond which it seeks authorisation means that mistakes should be corrected before the payroll is finalised. In addition, there are application controls over correction of the payroll, strengthening this control.

1   Any from:

- **Arrange to attend** the **pay-out** of wages to confirm that the official procedures are being followed.

- Before the wages are paid **compare payroll** with **wage packets** to ensure all employees have a wage packet.

- **Examine receipts** given by employees; **check unclaimed wages** are recorded in unclaimed wages book.

- **Check** that **no employee receives more than one wage packet.**

- **Check entries** in the **unclaimed wages book** with the entries on the payroll.

- **Check that unclaimed wages** are **banked regularly.**

- **Check** that unclaimed wages book shows **reasons** why wages are unclaimed.

- **Check pattern** of **unclaimed wages** in unclaimed wages book; variations may indicate failure to record.

- **Verify** a sample of holiday pay **payments** with the **underlying records** and **check** the **calculation** of the amounts paid.

2   The most important authorisation controls over wages and salaries are controls over:

- engagement and discharge of employees
- changes in pay rates
- overtime
- non-statutory deductions
- advances of pay

3   Assurance providers should confirm that wages have been paid at the correct rate by checking calculation of gross pay to:

- authorised rates of pay
- production records
- clock cards, time sheets or other evidence of time worked

CHAPTER 9

Internal audit

Introduction

Examination context

Topic List

    1   What is internal audit?

    2   What does the internal audit function do?

Summary and Self-test

Answer to Interactive question

Answers to Self-test

Learning objectives

- Understand the role that internal audit plays in internal control

- Distinguish between the role of the internal auditor and the external auditor

The specific syllabus reference for this chapter is: 2d.

Syllabus links

Internal audit will be looked at again in the *Business and Finance* syllabus, and also in the *Audit and Assurance* syllabus.

Examination context

A question on this topic is likely to be included in your assessment as one of the questions on internal controls.

In the assessment, candidates may be required to identify the components of internal control in both manual and IT environments, including internal audit.

In addition, candidates may be required to:

- identify the role of the internal auditor in internal control
- identifying activities carried out by the internal auditor
- identify features which distinguish the internal auditor from the external auditor

1 What is internal audit?

Section overview

- The internal audit function assists management in achieving corporate objectives, particularly in achieving good corporate governance.

- Although many of the techniques internal and external auditors use are similar, the basis and reasoning of their work is different.

Definition

Internal audit function: An appraisal activity established or provided as a service to the entity. Its functions include, amongst other things, examining, evaluating and monitoring the adequacy and effectiveness of internal control.

Internal audit is generally a feature of large companies. It is a function, provided either by employees of the entity or sourced from an external organisation to assist management in **achieving corporate objectives**.

If the internal audit function exists to assist management in achieving corporate objectives, it is important to ask '**what are corporate objectives**?' Obviously, these will vary from company to company, and will be found, for example, in companies' mission statements and strategic plans.

In principle, all companies will want good management, and the internal audit function is a recognised way of ensuring good corporate governance.

The codes of corporate governance that indicate good practice for companies, such as the UK Corporate Governance Code (mandatory for UK listed companies) highlight the need for businesses to maintain **good systems of internal control** to manage the risks the company faces. **Internal audit** can play a **key role in assessing and monitoring** internal control policies and procedures.

The internal audit function can assist the board in other ways as well:

- By, in effect, acting as auditors for board reports not audited by the external auditors.

- By being the experts in fields such as auditing and accounting standards and assisting in implementation of new standards.

- By liaising with external auditors, particularly where external auditors can use internal audit work and reduce the time and therefore cost of the external audit. In addition, internal auditors can check that external auditors are reporting back to the board everything they are required to under auditing standards.

The UK Corporate Governance Code highlights the importance of internal audit by stipulating that directors of companies that do not have an internal audit department should reconsider the need for one annually.

1.1 Distinction between internal and external audit

An external audit is an audit carried out by an external, as opposed to an internal, auditor. Remember that the objective of an external audit of financial statements is to enable auditors to express an opinion on whether the financial statements are prepared (in all material respects) in accordance with the applicable financial reporting framework.

Contrast this with the definition of the internal audit function given at the beginning of this chapter. The external audit is focused on the financial statements, whereas the internal audit function is focused on the operations of the entire business.

C H A P T E R

9

The following table highlights the differences between internal and external audit.

	Internal audit	External audit
Reason	The internal audit function is an activity designed to add value and improve an organisation's operations.	An exercise to enable auditors to express an opinion on the financial statements.
Reporting to	Internal auditors report to the board of directors, or the audit committee, which is a sub committee of the board of directors concerned with financial and audit matters.	The external auditors report to the shareholders of a company on the truth and fairness of the financial statements.
Relating to	As demonstrated in the reason for their existence, an internal auditor's work relates to the operations of the organisation.	External audit's work relates to the financial statements. They are concerned with the financial records that underlie these.
Relationship with the company	Internal auditors are very often employees of the organisation, although sometimes the internal audit function is outsourced.	External auditors are independent of the company and its management. They are appointed by the shareholders.

The table shows that although some of the procedures that the internal audit function undertake are very similar to those undertaken by the external auditors, the **whole basis and reasoning of their work is fundamentally different**.

2 What does the internal audit function do?

Section overview

- The internal audit function has two key roles to play in relation to organisational risk management:
  - (a) ensuring the company's risk management system operates effectively
  - (b) ensuring that strategies implemented in respect of business risks operate effectively

- Internal auditors undertake operational audits.

- Internal auditors may also undertake special investigations on behalf of the directors.

- However, to preserve objectivity, internal auditors must not get involved in operational decision making matters.

The activities of the internal audit function usually involve:

- Monitoring internal controls (we shall consider this more in sections 2.1 and 2.2)

- Examining financial and operating information (for example, reviewing the accounting system and carrying out tests of detail on transactions and balances in the same way as the external auditor does)

- Review of the economy, efficiency and effectiveness of operations (this would include looking at non-financial controls of the organisation)

- Review of compliance with laws, regulations and other external requirements

- Special investigations, for instance, into suspected fraud

- Identifying and evaluating significant exposures to risk and contributing to the improvement of risk management and control systems

- Assessing the governance process in its accomplishment of objectives on ethics and values, performance management and accountability, communicating risk and control information to appropriate areas of the organisation and effectiveness of communication among those charged with governance, external and internal auditors, and management

2.1 Risk

We introduced the concept of the company facing risks in Chapter 5. All companies face risks arising from their activities, which cannot be eliminated, but such risks must be **managed** by the company.

Designing and operating internal control systems is a key part of a company's risk management. This will often be done by employees in their various departments, although sometimes (particularly in the case of specialised computer systems) the company will hire external expertise to design systems.

The internal audit function has a two-fold role in relation to risk management:

- Monitoring the company's overall risk management policy to ensure it operates effectively
- Monitoring the strategies implemented to ensure that they continue to operate effectively

2.2 Internal controls

The internal audit function is unlikely to assist in the development of systems because its key role will be in **monitoring the overall process** and in **providing assurance** that the **systems** which the departments have designed **meet objectives** and **operate effectively**.

It is important that the internal audit function retains **objectivity** towards these aspects of their role, which is why internal auditors would generally not be involved in the assessment of risks and the design of the system.

The fact that the control system should be monitored was discussed in Chapter 5. If there is an internal audit function, testing (and therefore monitoring) controls is likely to be an important part of their role. The tests that they carry out will be on the same lines as the tests outlined in the previous three chapters that external auditors will carry out. However, as internal auditors are focused on all the operations of the company, they are focusing on all controls, not just ones linked ultimately to the financial statements, so the scope of their testing will be far greater than that of the external auditors.

The work that internal auditors carry out on controls can be termed **operational audits**. These are audits of the operational processes of the organisation. They are also known as management or efficiency audits. Their prime objective is the monitoring of management's performance, ensuring company policy is adhered to.

There are two aspects of an operational assignment:

- Ensure policies are adequate
- Ensure policies work effectively

In terms of adequacy, the internal auditor will have to review the policies of a particular department by:

- reading them
- discussing them with members of the department

Then the auditor will have to assess whether the policies are adequate, and possibly advise the board of improvement.

The auditor will then have to examine the effectiveness of the controls by testing them, as discussed in the previous few chapters.

2.3 Other functions

The internal audit function may also carry out other work for the directors in a company. For instance, they might undertake special investigations in respect of a suspected fraud, or they might carry out traditional financial audits, similar to the exercise carried out by the external auditors.

However, the key issue to remember with regard to the internal audit function is the necessity for the department to retain objectivity in order to carry out its important monitoring role in respect of risk and controls. Therefore internal auditors will not become involved in the operational activities of the company.

Worked example: Internal audit

Ritzy Hotels plc (RH) is a listed company which owns a number of hotels in the UK. Each hotel is a subsidiary company of RH, for example, Ritzy Southampton Limited is the hotel in Southampton. RH charges each hotel a management charge, which is determined on a fixed calculation dependent on the number of rooms at the hotel. One of the things this management charge covers is the internal audit function, which is managed centrally by RH.

The internal audit function at RH is required to carry out cyclical operational audits at all the hotels. The London Hotel, which comprises 20% of group income, is audited annually. Other hotels are audited on a rotational basis, with each hotel being audited at least once every three years.

An 'audit' comprises a number of elements, all of which have to have been carried out (although not all at the same time) for the full cyclical audit to have been completed. These elements are:

- surprise cash counts in key cash transactions areas (reception, bar, restaurant)

- asset inspections, particularly linens and leisure facilities

- inventory count for certain assets, particularly the larder and bar

- tests of controls in key systems: sales, purchases, payroll (RH has a systems manual that all hotels are required to follow)

- health and safety control systems testing

- review of actual results against budget for the year

In addition, the internal audit function is sometimes required to carry out a special investigation. In 2010 there was a special investigation into VAT errors at one hotel. Currently, the directors of RH, concerned at the results of analytical review on bar income at one of the hotels, are considering implementing a discrepancy investigation at that hotel.

Interactive question: Internal audit activities

Lightening plc has an organisational structure which includes accounting, human resources, internal audit and audit committee. Which department should not be involved in determining pay rises?

A   Accounting
B   Human resources
C   Internal audit
D   Audit committee

See **Answer** at the end of this chapter.

Summary

The internal audit function is an appraisal activity established or provided as a service to the entity. Its functions include, amongst other things, examining, evaluating and monitoring the adequacy and effectiveness of internal control

Monitoring for **adequacy** and **effectiveness**

Therefore, must stay **objective**. Not involved in operational activities.

Self-test

Answer the following questions.

1   What is an internal audit function?

2   Name three key differences between external and internal audit.

    1   ....

    2   ....

    3   ....

3   It is possible to buy in an internal audit service from an external organisation.

☐ True

☐ False

4   As objectivity is a key issue for internal auditors, they are likely to routinely be involved in operational activities.

☐ True

☐ False

Now, go back to the Learning Objectives in the Introduction. If you are satisfied you have achieved these objectives, please tick them off.

Answer to Interactive question

C   The internal audit function must not become involved in operational activities.

1   The internal audit function is an appraisal activity established or provided as a service to the entity.

2   1   External report to members, internal to directors
     2   External report on financial statements, internal on systems, controls and risks
     3   External are independent of the company, internal often employed by it

3   True

4   False. The reverse is true.

CHAPTER 10

Documentation

Introduction
Examination context
Topic List
Summary and Self-test
Technical references
Answer to Interactive question
Answers to Self-test

Introduction

Learning objectives

- Understand the nature of working papers

- Understand the form and content of working papers

- Understand why assurance providers record their work

- Understand why and how assurance providers keep these records

The specific syllabus references for this chapter are: 3a, 1f.

Syllabus links

One reason for keeping working papers is to protect the assurance provider in the event of a negligence claim. This will be looked at in more detail in *Audit and Assurance*.

Examination context

This topic is likely to be examined on a regular basis and questions should be reasonably straightforward if you are well prepared.

There was one question in the sample paper on documentation, looking at the reasons behind preparing particular pieces of documentation and whether these reasons were valid.

In the assessment, candidates may be required to:

- define audit documentation
- state the reasons for preparing and keeping documentation relating to an assurance engagement
- state the form and content of working papers
- identify the advantages of automated working papers
- state the content of a permanent audit file and a current audit file

1 Purpose of documentation

Section overview

- Assurance providers should document the work they have done.

- This should be a record of the procedures performed, the evidence obtained and the conclusions reached.

- This provides evidence that the engagement was performed in accordance with any relevant standards, law or regulatory requirements.

- A record of work done also assists the team to plan and direct work, facilitates review by senior staff, provides accountability for work, provides a record of matters that are relevant to future engagements and enables experienced auditors to carry out any additional reviews necessary.

All assurance work must be documented: the working papers are the tangible evidence of the work done in support of the conclusion. Although the term 'working papers' continues to be used, modern audit practices are likely to retain little paper documentation on file, with most documents being retained electronically.

Audit documentation provides:

(a) evidence for the auditor's basis for a conclusion about the achievement of the overall objectives of the auditor

(b) evidence that the audit was planned and performed in accordance with ISAs and applicable legal and regulatory requirements

They must be prepared on a timely basis. Documentation prepared after the audit work has been performed is likely to be less accurate than timely documentation.

Definition

Audit documentation (working papers): The record of procedures performed, relevant evidence obtained and conclusions the auditor reached.

In addition, particularly in relation to audit, assurance providers record their work to:

- assist the audit team to plan and perform the audit

- assist relevant members of the team to direct and supervise work

- enable the audit team to be accountable for its work (and to prove adherence to ISAs in a litigious situation)

- retain a record of matters of continuing significance to future audits

- enable an experienced auditor to carry out quality control reviews

- enable an experienced auditor to conduct external inspections in accordance with applicable legal, regulatory or other requirements

Auditors may find it helpful to include in the audit documentation a summary of all significant matters arising during the audit and how these were addressed. This summary will facilitate effective and efficient reviews of the audit documentation. Additionally, it may assist the auditor's consideration of significant matters and help the auditor to consider if any individual ISA objectives have not been met.

CHAPTER

10

2 Form and content of documentation

Section overview

- Working papers should be headed in a certain way and contain certain information.
- They may be automated.

Working papers should be sufficiently complete and detailed to provide an overall understanding of the engagement.

However, assurance providers cannot record everything they consider. Therefore judgement must be used as to the extent of working papers, based on the following general rule (given in an audit context):

> Documentation that is sufficient to enable an experienced auditor, having no previous connection with the audit, to understand the nature, timing and extent of audit procedures performed to comply with the ISAs and applicable legal and regulatory requirements, the results of audit procedures performed and the audit evidence obtained, and significant matters arising during the audit, the conclusions reached thereon and significant professional judgements made in reaching those conclusions.

The form and content of working papers are affected by matters such as:

- the **size** and **complexity** of the entity

- the **nature** of the audit procedures to be performed

- the **identified risks** of material misstatement

- the **significance** of the audit evidence obtained

- the **nature and extent** of **exceptions** identified

- the **need to document** a conclusion or the **basis for a conclusion not readily determinable** from the documentation of the work performed or audit evidence obtained

- the **audit methodology** and tools used

Worked example: Audit file

An audit file will normally contain the following working papers:

- Information obtained in understanding the entity and its environment, including its internal control, such as the following:

  - Information concerning legal documents, agreements and minutes

  - Extracts from, or copies of, important legal documents, agreements and minutes

  - Information concerning the industry, economic and legislative environment within which the entity operates

  - Extracts from the entity's internal control manual

- Evidence of the planning process including audit plans and any changes thereto

- Evidence of the auditor's consideration of the work of the internal audit function and conclusions reached

- Analyses of transactions and balances

- Analyses of significant ratios and trends

- The identified and assessed risks of material misstatements

- A record of the nature, timing, extent and results of audit procedures

- Evidence that the work performed by assistants was supervised and reviewed

- An indication as to who performed the audit procedures and when they were performed

- Details of audit procedures applied regarding components whose financial statements are audited by another auditor

- Copies of communications with other auditors, experts and other third parties

- Copies of letters or notes concerning audit matters communicated to or discussed with management, including the terms of the engagement and material weaknesses in internal control

- Written representations received from the entity (these are covered in Chapter 12)

- Conclusions reached by the auditor concerning significant aspects of the audit, including how exceptions and unusual matters, if any, disclosed by the auditor's procedures were resolved or treated

- Copies of the financial statements and auditor's reports

- Notes of discussions about significant matters with management and others

- In exceptional circumstances, the reasons for departing from a basic principle or essential procedure of an ISA and how the alternative procedure performed achieved the audit objective

Working papers should show:

- the name of the client
- the reporting date
- the file reference of the working paper
- the name of the preparer
- the date of preparation
- the subject of the working paper
- the name of the reviewer
- the date of the review
- the objective of the work done
- the source of information

- how any sample was selected
- the sample size determined
- the work done
- a key to any audit ticks or symbols
- appropriate cross-referencing
- the results obtained
- analysis of errors
- other significant observations
- the conclusions drawn
- the key points highlighted

Worked example: Working paper

	A	B	C	D	E	F	G	H	I	J	K	L	M	N	O	P	Q	R
1	Client	①	Example Ltd							Prepared by	Farhana Haque ④		Date	16/2/X4 ⑦		E.3.1	E.3.1	
2	Subject	⑥	Payables							Reviewed by	Wendy Smith ⑤		Date	3/3/X4 ⑧				
3	Year end	②	31 December 20X3														③	
4																		
5	Objective	⑨	To ensure payables ledger balances fairly stated.															
6										⑩				⑩				
7	Procedures	⑪	Selected a sample of trade payables as at 31 December and reconciled the supplier's statement to the year end payables ledger balance. Vouched any reconciling items to source documentation.															
8																		
9	Results	⑬	See E.3.2 E.3.2															
10																		
11			One credit note, relating to Woodcutter Ltd, has not been accounted for.															
12			An adjustment is required. ⑭															
13																		
14			Dr	Trade payables			4,975											
15			Cr	Purchases				4,975 H.1.2	H.1.2									
16																		
17			One other error was found, which was immaterial, and which was the fault of the supplier.															
18			⑭															
19			In view of the error found, however, we should recommend that the client management checks supplier statement reconciliations at least on the larger accounts. Management letter point.															
20																		
21	Conclusion	⑮	After making the adjustment noted above, payables ledger balances are fairly stated as at 31 December 20X3.															
22																		

CHAPTER

10

	Client	Balance per payables ledger	Balance per supplier statement	Difference	Agreed	Reconciling item	Prepared by				
1	Client	Example Ltd					Prepared by	Farhana Haque	Date	16/2/X4	E.3.2
2	Subject	Payables					Reviewed by	Wendy Smith	Date	3/3/X4	
3	Year end	31 December 20X3									
4											
5	Client	Balance per payables ledger	Balance per supplier statement	Difference	Agreed	Reconciling item					
6		£	£	£		£					
7	A Ltd	300.00	300.00		✓						
8	B Ltd	747.00	732.00	15.00	✗	15.00					
9											
10		1,047.00									
11		^									

KEY

1. The **name** of the **client**
2. The reporting **date**
3. The **file reference** of the working paper
4. The **name** of the **person** preparing the working paper
5. The **date** the working paper was **prepared**
6. The **subject** of the working paper
7. The **name** of the person **reviewing** the working paper
8. The **date** of the **review**
9. The **objective** of the work done
10. The **sources of information**
11. The **work done**
12. A **key** to any audit ticks or symbols [none used here]
13. The **results obtained**
14. **Analysis** of **errors** or other significant observations
15. The **conclusions drawn**

The auditor shall record the identifying characteristics of specific items or matters being tested.

2.1 Automated and electronic working papers

Automated working paper packages have been developed which can make the documenting of audit work much easier. Such programs aid preparation of working papers, lead schedules, trial balance and the financial statements themselves. These are automatically cross referenced, adjusted and balanced by the computer.

The **advantages** of automated working papers are as follows:

- The risk of errors is reduced.

- The working papers are neater and easier to review.

- The time saved is substantial as adjustments can be made easily to all working papers, including working papers summarising the key analytical information.

In contrast to automated working papers, **electronic** working papers do not involve any automatic calculations (although these can be made use of if desired). Most audit firms nowadays – certainly all of the big firms – use electronic working papers.

Usually these take the form of a database containing all of the working papers (which may be Microsoft Office documents), which make up an electronic audit file. Electronic working papers can be cross-referenced within the program, and then signed off electronically by the preparer and by reviewers with various levels of authority. Written notes can be left for team members, and review points can be left electronically.

These days most documents are scanned and stored electronically rather than in paper form.

2.2 Filing working papers

Firms should have standard referencing and filing procedures for working papers, to facilitate their review.

For recurring audits, working papers may be split between permanent and current audit files, although this distinction is fading as audit files become automated, and 'permanent' documents can be scanned and carried in computer files year on year.

Permanent audit files (contain any information of continuing importance to the audit). These may contain:

- engagement letters
- new client questionnaire
- the memorandum and articles of association
- other legal documents such as prospectuses, leases, sales agreements
- details of the history of the client's business
- board minutes of continuing relevance
- previous years' signed accounts and analytical procedures
- accounting systems notes, previous years' control questionnaires

Current audit files (contain any information of relevance to the current year's audit). These should be compiled on a timely basis after the completion of the audit and should contain (amongst other things):

- financial statements
- accounts checklists
- management accounts details
- reconciliations of management accounts and financial statements
- a summary of unadjusted errors
- report to partner including details of significant events and errors
- review notes
- audit planning memorandum
- time budgets and summaries
- written representations from management
- notes of board minutes
- communications with third parties such as experts or other auditors

They also contain working papers covering each audit area. These should include the following:

- A lead schedule including details of the figures to be included in the accounts
- Problems encountered and conclusions drawn
- Audit plans
- Risk assessments
- Sampling plans
- Analytical procedures
- Details of tests of detail and tests of control

3 Safe custody and retention of documentation

Section overview

- Assurance providers should retain documents for a certain period of time.
- Documents must be kept secure during this period due to confidentiality requirements.

Judgement may have to be used in deciding the duration of holding working papers, and further consideration should be given to the matter before their destruction. ICAEW requires all firms should have a document retention policy and Registered Auditors to keep all audit working papers required by auditing standards for at least six years from the end of the accounting period to which they relate.

Given that assurance work must be kept confidential (as we shall see in Chapter 16), it is important that firms have good security procedures over their retained working papers. Paper documents must be kept securely, in locked premises. Electronic documents should be protected by electronic controls.

4 Ownership of and right of access to documentation

Section overview

- Working papers belong to the assurance providers.
- The report, once issued, belongs to the client.
- Assurance providers must keep working papers confidential.
- They may show working papers to the client at their discretion.
- They should obtain client permission before showing working papers to third parties.

ICAEW regulations, standards and guidance (available at icaew.com/en/members/regulations-standards-and-guidance) provides members with assistance in relation to documents and records: ownership, lien and rights of access.

Working papers are the property of the assurance providers. They are not a substitute for, nor part of, the entity's accounting records. However, the report becomes the property of the client once it has been issued.

Assurance providers must follow ethical guidance on the confidentiality of working papers. As working papers belong to the firm, the assurance providers are not required to show them to the client. However, the firm may show working papers to the client at their discretion, so long as the assurance process is not prejudiced.

Information should not be made available to third parties without the permission of the client. An example of when working papers might be shared with a third party is when a new firm is taking over an audit from the existing auditors.

Interactive question: Documentation

The auditor will prepare documentation in relation to the fieldwork carried out on an assurance engagement.

Indicate whether the following are, or are not, valid reasons for preparing such documentation.

(a)	To comply with the law.	☐ Valid	☐ Not valid	
(b)	To provide a record of matters of continuing significance to future audits.	☐ Valid	☐ Not valid	
(c)	To facilitate review by senior staff.	☐ Valid	☐ Not valid	
(d)	To prove adherence to ISAs in a litigious situation.	☐ Valid	☐ Not valid	

See **Answer** at the end of this chapter.

The table shows how the ownership of documents depends on the nature of the work being carried out.

Nature of work	Type of document	Who has ownership?
Auditing		
Preparation of auditor's report whether carried out under statutory provisions or not	Any documents prepared by member solely for purpose of carrying out his duties as auditor	Member
	Auditor's Report	Client
Accountancy		
Preparation of accounting records	Accounting Records	Client
Preparation of financial statements from client's records	Financial statements	Client
	Draft/office copy of financial statements	Member
	Correspondence with third parties	Member

Summary and Self-test

Summary

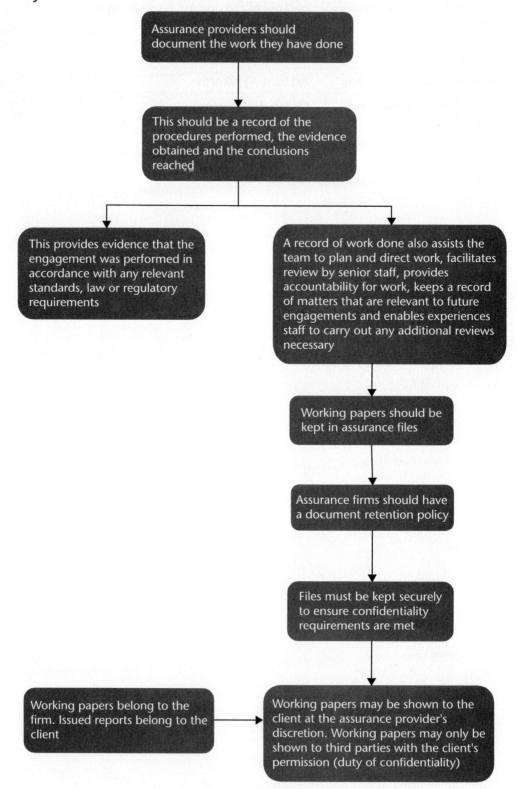

Assurance providers should document the work they have done

This should be a record of the procedures performed, the evidence obtained and the conclusions reached

This provides evidence that the engagement was performed in accordance with any relevant standards, law or regulatory requirements

A record of work done also assists the team to plan and direct work, facilitates review by senior staff, provides accountability for work, keeps a record of matters that are relevant to future engagements and enables experiences staff to carry out any additional reviews necessary

Working papers should be kept in assurance files

Assurance firms should have a document retention policy

Files must be kept securely to ensure confidentiality requirements are met

Working papers belong to the firm. Issued reports belong to the client

Working papers may be shown to the client at the assurance provider's discretion. Working papers may only be shown to third parties with the client's permission (duty of confidentiality)

Self-test

Answer the following questions.

1   State whether the following are advantages or disadvantages of standardised audit working papers:

(a)   Facilitate the delegation of work   ☐ Advantage   ☐ Disadvantage

(b)   Detract from proper exercise of professional judgement   ☐ Advantage   ☐ Disadvantage

(c)   Means to control quality   ☐ Advantage   ☐ Disadvantage

2   Complete the table, indicating in which file the working papers given below should be included.

Current audit file	Permanent audit file

- Engagement letters
- New client questionnaire
- Financial statements relating to year under review
- Accounts checklists
- Audit planning memo
- Board minutes of continuing relevance
- Accounting systems notes

3   Which **three** of the following are true?

A   Working papers belong to the auditor
B   The issued auditor's report belongs to the auditor
C   Auditors should retain working papers securely because of the duty of confidentiality
D   Auditors need client permission to share working papers with third parties

Now, go back to the Learning Objectives in the Introduction. If you are satisfied you have achieved these objectives, please tick them off.

Technical references

1 Nature and purposes of audit documentation

2 Form and content of documentation

3 Ownership of and right of access to documentation

ISA (UK) 230.2 – 3

ISA (UK) 230.8 – 11

ICAEW regulations, standards
and guidance at
www.icaew.com/regulations

Answer to Interactive question

(a) Not valid. It is not a legal requirement for the auditor to prepare working papers
(b) Valid
(c) Valid
(d) Valid

1   (a)   Advantage
    (b)   Disadvantage
    (c)   Advantage

2

Current audit file	Permanent audit file
Financial statements relating to year under review	Engagement letters
Accounts checklists	New client questionnaire
Audit planning memo	Board minutes of continuing relevance
	Accounting systems notes

3   A, C, D

CHAPTER 11

Evidence and sampling

Introduction

Examination context

Topic List

Summary and Self-test

Technical references

Answers to Interactive questions

Answers to Self-test

Learning objectives

- Understand the procedures for obtaining evidence

- Identify when tests of controls and substantive procedures will be used

- Recognise the strengths and weaknesses of particular forms of evidence

- Understand how much evidence to obtain

- Recognise when sufficient appropriate evidence has been obtained such that a conclusion can be drawn

Specific syllabus references for this chapter are: 3b, c, d, e, g.

Syllabus links

In Audit and Assurance you will focus on the drawing conclusions part of evidence, based on the collection of evidence that we focus on in this Assurance manual.

Examination context

This is a very important part of your syllabus and the issues discussed here and previously in Chapter 4 underpin the following two chapters as well. You can expect a number of practical and theoretical questions in the assessment covering audit evidence.

In the assessment, candidates may be required to:

- distinguish between tests of controls and substantive procedures

- identify and evaluate procedures used to obtain evidence

- select the appropriate means of obtaining evidence in a given scenario

- determine whether an audit test would be a test for overstatement or understatement in a given scenario

- identify factors affecting sample sizes

- identify weaknesses in methods of obtaining evidence

1 Evidence

Section overview

* Evidence must be sufficient and appropriate.

* Evidence is obtained in the form of substantive procedures and/or tests of controls.

* Evidence can be obtained by inspection, observation, inquiry and confirmation, recalculation, reperformance and analytical procedures.

* Substantive procedures will test for evidence of understatement or overstatement of account balances.

1.1 Overview of evidence from Chapter 4

You studied the basic principles of evidence in Chapter 4. These are the key points:

Evidence includes all the information contained within the accounting records underlying the financial statements, and other information gathered by the assurance providers, such as confirmations from third parties. Evidence is obtained in relation to the financial statement assertions which were set out in Chapter 4. There are two types of test; tests of controls (which we have looked at in detail in Chapters 5 to 9) and substantive procedures (which we will look at in more detail in Chapters 12 and 13).

ISA 500 states that evidence must be sufficient and appropriate.

* **Sufficiency** is the measure of the **quantity** of audit evidence.
* **Appropriateness** is the measure of the **quality** or relevance and **reliability** of the audit evidence.

We will look at the quantity of evidence obtained in section 2 below.

There are some general principles relating to the quality of evidence which were set out in Chapter 4.

Quality of evidence	
External	Evidence from **external sources** is more reliable than that obtained from the entity's records
Auditor	Evidence obtained **directly by assurance providers** is more reliable than that obtained indirectly or by inference
Entity	Evidence obtained from the entity's records is more reliable when related **control systems operate effectively**
Written	Evidence in the form of **documents (paper or electronic)** or **written representations** are more reliable than oral representations
Originals	Original documents are more reliable than photocopies, or facsimiles

1.2 Procedures to obtain evidence

Assurance providers obtain evidence by one or more of the following procedures outlined in ISA 500.

Procedures	Explanation	Strengths and weaknesses
Inspection of tangible assets	Inspection (physical examination) of tangible assets that are recorded in the accounting records confirms existence, but does not confirm rights and obligations or valuation. For example, machinery recorded in asset register can be inspected by assurance providers. Confirmation that assets seen are recorded in accounting records gives evidence of completeness. However, this is limited to assets assurance providers can see – if assets have been taken off site (hidden) they might not be picked up.	Inspection of assets is a good procedure, particularly in the case of assets that the entity could not function without (for example its production plant), but the weakness associated with inspection is that assets not used in daily production could be hidden from the assurance providers and not included in financial statements.
Inspection of documentation	Inspection of documents involves examining records or documents, for example, looking at a sales contract or a share certificate. What inspection of documents achieves depends on the nature of the document. For example, looking at a share certificate gives evidence of the existence of the investment. Looking at source documents (eg, sales invoices) and tracing to financial statements gives evidence of completeness (eg, of revenue). Inspection also provides evidence of valuation (for example, a purchase invoice gives evidence of the cost of inventory), rights and obligations (for example, a hire purchase agreement gives evidence in relation to ownership of non-current assets) and the nature of items (presentation and disclosure). It can also be used to compare documents (and hence test consistency of audit evidence) and confirm authorisation.	The strength of this procedure depends on what is being inspected to give evidence. For instance, inspection of a purchase invoice gives better quality evidence than inspection of sales invoice, because a purchase invoice is created by a third party.
Observation	This involves watching a procedure being performed (for example, post opening).	This procedure is relatively weak, as it only confirms that the procedure is being performed correctly when the assurance provider is watching.
Inquiry	This involves seeking information from client management or staff or external sources and evaluating responses.	The strength or weakness of this procedure will depend on of whom the inquiry is being made – a member of client staff could misrepresent matters to the assurance provider if they misunderstand the nature of the question, or they are seeking to conceal a misstatement or fraud.

Procedures	Explanation	Strengths and weaknesses
External confirmation (a particular form of inquiry)	This involves seeking confirmation from a third party eg, confirmation from bank of bank balances.	This can be a very strong procedure but there may be instances where the third party is motivated to misrepresent, for example an understated receivables balance might be confirmed because it favoured the customer.
Recalculation	Checking mathematical accuracy of client's records, for example, adding up ledger accounts.	Recalculation is evidence created by the assurance provider so is strong evidence.
Reperformance	Independently executing procedures or controls, either manually or through the use of computer assisted audit techniques (covered below).	Again, the fact that the assurance provider carries out the performance of a control himself makes it strong evidence.
Analytical procedures	Evaluating and comparing financial and/or non-financial data for plausible relationships and investigating unexpected fluctuations.	Evidence here is limited by the strength or weakness of the underlying accounting system. However, this can be a strong procedure if comparison is made to items that do not rely on the same accounting system or that the assurance provider can corroborate outside the accounting system.

Often these procedures will be used in conjunction with one another to provide a greater quality of evidence. For example, an assurance provider might observe controls in operation and then reperform the control himself to confirm that it operates as he has observed. Auditors will gather detailed evidence but other assurance providers may need less evidence.

1.3 Computer assisted audit techniques

With so many accounting systems now held on computer, the assurance provider may wish to make use of computer assisted audit techniques (CAATs). These have been mentioned before in your Study Manual, particularly in Chapter 5. There are three main types of CAAT that can be used:

- Test data
- Audit software
- Data analytics

1.3.1 Test data

Under this test of control, the assurance provider supervises the process of running data through the client's system. The stages in the use of test data are as follows:

- Note controls in client's system

- Decide upon test data, the options include:

    - Dummy data (the assurance provider must be very careful to reverse all effects)
    - Real data (the data may not contain all the errors necessary to test the controls rigorously)
    - Dummy data against a verified copy of the client's system (much safer)

- Run the test data

- Compare results with those expected

- Conclude on whether controls are operating properly

Worked example: Test data

Test data makes use of the client's own system. To carry out such a test the assurance provider identifies a control (or series of controls) in the client's system. The assurance provider then predicts the system's reaction to the test data. For example:

- An invoice which does not cast should be rejected when entered in the system
- An invoice with an invalid supplier code should be rejected
- Dates outside the current year should be rejected
- Valid data should be posted to the correct account

The assurance provider then runs the test data through the client's system (or a copy thereof) and compares the results with those expected. The results tell the assurance provider whether the controls within the system are operating correctly; the test is therefore a test of control.

1.3.2 Audit software

Audit software makes use of the assurance providers' own specialised software. There are a number of off-the-shelf packages available, or the assurance provider could have a tailor-made system. Audit software works on the basis of interrogating the client's system and extracting and analysing information. It can therefore carry out a whole range of substantive procedures, across all sorts of different data.

Examples of what audit software can do include:

- Extract a sample according to specified criteria:

    - Random
    - Over a certain amount
    - Below a certain amount
    - At certain dates

- Calculate ratios and select those outside set criteria (eg, more than 5% different from last year)

- Check calculations and casts performed by the system

- Prepare reports (eg, comparison of actual against budgeted figures)

- Follow items through a system and flag where they are posted

The procedures listed above are mostly substantive procedures, because they are substantiating the figures in the accounts. To generate more procedures that can be done using audit software, just think of the substantive procedures that you may wish to carry out, and consider whether the information is held on the client's computer (you can normally assume that it is). If the test does not require judgement, then it can almost certainly be carried out by audit software.

1.3.3 Data analytics

Definition

Data analytics: When used to obtain audit evidence in a financial statement audit, data analytics is the science and art of discovering and analysing patterns, deviations and inconsistencies, and extracting other useful information in the data underlying or related to the subject matter of an audit through analysis, modelling and visualisation for the purpose of planning and performing the audit.

(*Source: FRC (2017)* Audit Quality Thematic Review: The Use of Data Analytics in the Audit of Financial Statements)

Within an audit context this is sometimes known as Audit Data Analytics, or ADA.

Data analytics is a very hot topic in the auditing profession, and can be seen as part of the broader revolution wrought by 'big data'. Data analytics are fundamentally a modern, developed form of CAATs, and whereas CAATs never really changed the audit profession as a whole, it is possible that data analytics will do.

Auditors have for many years used computers to help them, developing the CAATs and audit software discussed above, but technology has not really been powerful enough to make these tools worth the time that needed to be invested in them. A key problem was the need to tailor the CAATs to each audit client, which could be costly. Many auditors did not use them.

In recent years, however, computing power has developed to the point where much more complex testing can be performed on data, but crucially **without the need to create tailor-made software**. Data analytics software came from the older audit software, but is standardised and more powerful. Now, standard data analytics techniques can simply be applied to a client's data, and since this is a much more efficient process than before, it is beginning to be adopted widely within the profession.

Auditors can generate intuitive visualisations of very complex data (eg, bubble, bar or pie charts), which they can then use in their analysis to spot trends that might otherwise have been missed.

Here are some examples of specific areas where ADA may be useful:

- Analyse all transactions in a population, stratify that population and identify outliers for further examination

- Reperform calculations relevant to the financial statements

- Match transactions as they pass through a processing cycle

- Assist in segregation of duties testing

- Compare entity data to externally obtained data

- Manipulate data to assess the impact of different assumptions.

- Analyses of revenue trends split by product or region

- Matches of orders to cash and purchases to payments

- Three-way matches between purchase/sales orders, goods received/despatched documentation and invoices

- 'Can do, did do testing' of user codes to test whether segregation of duties is appropriate, and whether any inappropriate combinations of users have been involved in processing transactions.

(FRC (2017): p7)

1.4 Analytical procedures

ISA (UK) 520, *Analytical Procedures* gives more detail on the use of analytical procedures as substantive procedures (optional) and at the overall review stage (compulsory) of an audit. The use of analytical procedures in planning (compulsory) is included in ISA 315 and was covered in Chapter 3. These ISAs apply to audits only, but all assurance providers may be able to use analytical procedures (indeed, they will be an important tool where less detailed evidence is required) and will need to consider the same general principles.

ISA 520 describes how the **auditor** must decide whether using substantive analytical procedures will be effective and efficient in **reducing audit risk** to an acceptably low level. Auditors may find it effective to use analytical data prepared by the entity's management, provided they are satisfied that it has been properly prepared.

There are a number of factors that the auditors should consider when using analytical procedures as substantive procedures:

- Objective of the analytical procedures (for example analytical procedures may be good at indicating whether a population is complete)

- Suitability of analytical procedures

- Reliability of the data

Factor	Issues to consider
Suitability	• Generally analytical procedures are more applicable to large volumes of transactions that tend to be predictable (for example, payroll). • It depends on the purpose of the test – for example, some analytical procedures will provide persuasive evidence and others will provide corroboration of other tests. • Other audit tests directed to the same assertions. • The auditor must decide if analytical procedures are suitable given the nature of the assertion and the assessment of risk associated with it.
Reliability of the data	• The source of the information used (third party or internal, for example) • The comparability of the information (for example, an industry standard may not be useful if the company is unusual within the industry) • Nature and relevance of the information used (for example, if comparing something to budget, is the budget realistic or more of a target?) • Whether there are controls over the production of the information used to ensure completeness, accuracy, validity
Precision	• The accuracy with which results in test area can be predicted (for example, compare gross margin with a less predictable item, for example, advertising) • The extent to which information can be disaggregated (for example, by division) • Availability of required information
Acceptable difference	This is influenced by materiality and the desired level of assurance. As assessed risk rises, the amount of difference from expected results considered acceptable without investigation will reduce.

When analytical procedures identify significant fluctuations or relationships that are inconsistent with other relevant information, or that are not the results that were expected, this must be investigated further.

The auditor shall make inquiries of management about the inconsistency or unexpected result and then corroborate those replies with other evidence.

If management responses cannot be corroborated or are unavailable, the auditor shall perform other audit procedures as necessary.

The auditor may consider testing the operating effectiveness of controls, if any, over the **preparation** of **information** used in applying analytical procedures. When such controls are effective, the auditor generally has greater confidence in the reliability of the information, and therefore in the results of analytical procedures.

The operating effectiveness of **controls** over **non-financial information** may often be tested in conjunction with other tests of controls. For example, in establishing controls over the processing of sales invoices, a business may include controls over the recording of sales units. In these circumstances the auditor may test the operating effectiveness of controls over the recording of unit sales in conjunction with tests of the operating effectiveness of controls over the processing of sales invoices.

The suitability of a particular analytical procedure will depend upon the auditor's assessment of how effective it will be in detecting a misstatement that may cause the financial statements to be materially misstated.

The ISA states that 'the auditor shall design and perform analytical procedures near the end of the audit that assist the auditor when forming an overall conclusion as to whether the financial statements are consistent with the auditor's understanding of the entity'.

The conclusions from these analytical procedures should corroborate the conclusions formed from other audit procedures on parts of the financial statements. This assists the auditor to draw reasonable conclusions on which to base the audit opinion. However, these analytical procedures may identify a previously unrecognised risk of material misstatement. In such circumstances the auditor is required to revise the auditor's assessment of the risks of material misstatement and modify the further planned audit procedures accordingly.

As we have discussed, analytical procedures should be used at the risk assessment stage. Possible sources of information about the client include:

- Interim financial information
- Budgets
- Management accounts
- Non-financial information
- Bank and cash records
- Sales tax returns
- Board minutes
- Discussions or correspondence with the client at the year end

Auditors may also use specific industry information or general knowledge of current industry conditions to assess the client's performance.

As well as helping to determine the nature, timing and extent of other audit procedures, such analytical procedures may also indicate aspects of the business of which the auditors were previously unaware. Auditors are looking to see if developments in the client's business have had the expected effects. They will be particularly interested in changes in audit areas where problems have occurred in the past.

1.5 Directional testing

For any item in the final statements which is being tested there are two possibilities. It could be fairly stated or misstated.

If it is misstated there are again two possibilities. It could be:

- overstated; or
- understated.

When testing for overstatement (or existence/occurrence) a different approach is used from testing for understatement (or completeness).

Worked example: Two invoices

Imagine two invoices, each for £1,000.

Invoice 1 is a fraudulent invoice for the purchase of a non-current asset, and should not have been posted. As a result, non-current assets are overstated by £1,000 (before depreciation). To find this misstatement the auditor can either:

- look at all the purchase invoices and try to identify the fraudulent one; or

- look at the figure for non-current assets in the financial statements and gradually follow the audit trail until arriving at persuasive supporting evidence.

One might think that either of these approaches would work. If the fraudulent invoice had been suppressed in some way, however, it would be impossible to find it by looking through the invoices. It follows therefore that, when testing for overstatement, the auditor should start with the figures given, and follow the audit trail until coming to the supporting documentation.

To summarise, the pattern for overstatement testing is as follows:

Now consider invoice 2, a sales invoice which has been omitted resulting in an understatement of revenue by £1,000. In this case, selecting a sample from the final revenue figure in the financial statements will be no use. As the item has been omitted, it will be impossible to select it and test it.

So in order to test for understatement the auditor will have to select from a population which will give the chance of selecting omitted items. Such a population has been described as 'a reciprocal population'. For invoice 2, that population would be the entity's dispatch notes, provided that the auditor is satisfied that all despatches are 'captured' on dispatch notes at the point of dispatch.

A reciprocal population for **accounts payable** is more difficult to arrive at. Paragraph A27 of ISA 500 suggests that when testing accounts payable for understatement, such a population could be:

- subsequent disbursements
- unpaid invoices
- suppliers' statements
- unmatched receiving reports

The pattern for understatement (or completeness) testing can be summarised as follows.

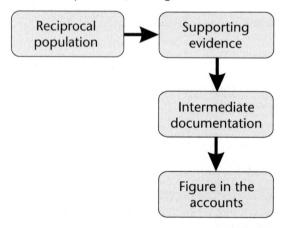

Traditionally directional testing has been used as a mechanism for reducing the amount of testing done. If in a double entry bookkeeping system there is a debit for every credit, the trial balance balances and all debit entries (expenses and assets) are tested for overstatement, and all credit entries (revenue, liabilities, equity and reserves) are tested for understatement, it is possible to draw the conclusion that, if no misstatements are found, all items are fairly stated.

The 'normal' approach adopted, therefore, is to test debits for overstatement and credits for understatement.

However, note that the majority of high profile corporate scandals (including Enron) have involved the overstatement of income rather than its understatement. Money laundering schemes would also tend to show similar characteristics. It is important therefore to assess the true risks, rather than automatically apply a formula.

Interactive question 1: Evidence

In respect of an assurance engagement, which one of the following is the least persuasive method of gathering evidence?

A   Inspection of a purchase invoice
B   Inspection of a sales invoice
C   Inspection of inventory by the auditor
D   Reperformance of a supplier statement reconciliation undertaken by the client

See **Answer** at the end of this chapter.

1.6   Audit of accounting estimates

The auditor often has to audit estimated figures, such as those for product warranties, depreciation, inventory or receivables allowances, where the values included in the financial statements are not the result of transactions with third parties (which are fairly reliable) but result from judgements made by management. Yet these figures can have a very significant effect on reported profits.

There is a risk that management may be biased in the judgements it makes when calculating estimated figures. The auditor must therefore approach these values with professional scepticism regarding the judgements made.

The audit approach required is set out in ISA (UK) 540, *Auditing Accounting Estimates, Including Fair Value Accounting Estimates, and Related Disclosures*. Essentially, if risk assessment procedures have identified a risk of material misstatement due to accounting estimates, the auditor can respond by undertaking one or more of the following methods.

Method	Example
Test the process that management used to estimate the figure and the data on which it is based	Management may use a formula to calculate the allowance for receivables. The auditor can test this by: • checking the calculation • considering if anything this year is likely to have changed the estimate
Use a point estimate	The auditors may use an available or proprietary model, or introduce different assumptions, or engage a specialist to develop a model.
Review events occurring up to the date of the auditor's report	If a settlement is reached after the year end regarding a claim against the company which requires a provision, the auditor can use the evidence of the agreement to establish the correct figure for the financial statements. In this case there is usually no need to use the other two methods.
Test the operating effectiveness of controls over how management made the accounting estimate, with associated substantive procedures	If there are strong controls over the estimation, and the estimate is derived from the routine processing of data by the entity's accounting system.

Having done the detailed work on the accounting estimate, the auditor checks the reasonableness of the figure and then reaches a conclusion about whether it is fairly stated.

This sort of work is clearly needed in an audit assignment, where estimates such as provisions required for damages in a lawsuit might be required, but the work is also very relevant to a number of other types of assurance engagement. Reports on a business plan often require an accounting estimate to be checked. The techniques used in these assignments will be the same as for audit assignments.

2 Selecting items to test

Section overview

- Assurance providers usually seek evidence from less than 100% of items of the balance or transaction being tested.

- Every item in the population of items being sampled must have an equal chance of being selected in the sample.

- The greater the risk of the area being sampled, the higher the sample size will be.

- When drawing conclusions from sampling, the auditor must identify which discovered misstatements affect the overall balance.

2.1 The concept of sampling

Assurance providers do not normally examine all the information available to them; it would be impractical to do so and using sampling will produce valid conclusions provided it is carried out properly.

ISA (UK) 530, *Audit Sampling* states that 'the objective of the auditor, when using audit sampling, is to provide a reasonable basis for the auditor to draw conclusions about the population from which the sample is selected'. Remember that the ISA relates specifically to audits, but all assurance providers may use sampling.

Definitions

Audit sampling: The application of audit procedures to less than 100% of items within a population of audit relevance such that all sampling units have a chance of selection in order to provide the auditor with a reasonable basis on which to draw conclusions about the entire population.

Population: The entire set of data from which a sample is selected and about which an auditor wishes to draw conclusions.

Some testing procedures do **not** involve sampling, such as:

- **testing all** items in a population (100% examination)
- testing all items with a **certain characteristic**, as selection is not representative

Assurance providers are unlikely to test 100% of items when carrying out tests of control, but 100% examination may be appropriate for certain substantive procedures. For example, if the population is made up of a small number of high value items and there is a high risk of material misstatement then 100% examination may be appropriate.

The ISA requires distinguishes between **statistical sampling** and **non-statistical methods**.

Definitions

Statistical sampling: An approach to sampling that has the following characteristics:

(a) random selection of the sample items; and
(b) the use of probability theory to evaluate sample results, including measurement of sampling risk.

Non-statistical sampling: A sampling approach that does not have characteristics (a) and (b) is considered non-statistical sampling.

The auditor may alternatively select certain items from a population because of specific characteristics they possess. The results of items selected in this way cannot be projected onto the whole population but may be used in conjunction with other audit evidence concerning the rest of the population.

- **High value or key items.** The auditor may select high value items or items that are suspicious, unusual or prone to error.

- **All items over a certain amount**. Selecting items this way may mean a large proportion of the population can be verified by testing a few items.

- **Items to obtain information** about the client's business, the nature of transactions, or the client's accounting and control systems.

2.2 Design of the sample

When designing the sample, ISA 530 requires the auditor to 'consider the **purpose** of the audit procedure and the **characteristics of the population** from which the sample will be drawn', and to consider the sampling and selection methods.

When designing an audit sample, the auditor's consideration includes the specific purpose to be achieved and the combination of audit procedures that is likely to best achieve that purpose. The auditor also needs to consider the nature and characteristics of the audit evidence sought and possible deviation or misstatement conditions. This will help them to define **what constitutes a deviation or misstatement** and **what population to use** for sampling.

Definitions

Misstatement: A difference between the amount, classification, presentation, or disclosure of a reported financial statement item and the amount, classification, presentation, or disclosure that is required for the item to be in accordance with the applicable financial reporting framework. Misstatements can arise from error or fraud.

Error: An unintentional misstatement in financial statements, including the omission of an amount or a disclosure.

The population from which the sample is drawn must be **appropriate and complete** for the specific audit objectives. Auditors must **define** the **sampling unit** in order to obtain an efficient and effective sample to achieve the particular audit objectives.

Definition

Sampling units: The individual items constituting a population.

Worked example: Sampling units

- Cheques listed on deposit slips
- Credit entries on bank statements
- Sales invoices
- Receivables balances
- A monetary unit (an example of monetary unit sampling is given in section 2.3)

ISA 530 requires that the auditor 'shall select items for the sample in such a way that each sampling unit in the population has a chance of selection'. This requires that **all items** in the population have an opportunity to be selected.

As we saw above, in obtaining evidence, the auditor should use professional judgement to assess audit risk and design audit procedures to ensure this risk is reduced to an acceptably low level. In determining the sample size, the auditor shall determine a sample size sufficient to reduce sampling risk is reduced to an acceptably low level.

Definitions

Sampling risk: The risk that the auditor's conclusion based on a sample may be different from the conclusion if the entire population were subjected to the same audit procedure.

Non-sampling risk: The risk that the auditor reaches an erroneous conclusion for any reason not related to sampling risk. For example, the use of inappropriate procedures, or misinterpretation of audit evidence and failure to recognise a misstatement or deviation.

2.2.1 Factors influencing sample sizes

ISA 530 gives examples of factors which influence sample sizes for tests of controls and tests of details:

Tests of controls	
Factor	**Effect on sample size**
An increase in the extent to which the auditor's risk assessment takes into account relevant controls	Increase
An increase in the tolerable rate of deviation	Decrease
An increase in the expected rate of deviation of the population to be tested	Increase
An increase in the auditor's desired level of assurance that the tolerable rate of deviation is not exceeded by the actual rate of deviation in the population	Increase
An increase in the number of sampling units in the population	Negligible effect

Tests of details	
Factor	**Effect on sample size**
An increase in the auditor's assessment of the risk of material misstatement	Increase
An increase in the use of other substantive procedures directed at the same assertion	Decrease
An increase in the auditor's desired level of assurance that tolerable misstatement is not exceeded by actual misstatement in the population	Increase
An increase in tolerable misstatement	Decrease
An increase in the amount of misstatement the auditor expects to find in the population	Increase
Stratification of the population when appropriate	Decrease
The number of sampling units in the population	Negligible effect

The greater the auditor's desired level of assurance that the results of the sample are in fact indicative of the actual misstatement in the population, the larger sample sizes have to be. In other words, if the auditor is placing a great deal of relevance on this (it is not corroborating other evidence, for example) the higher the sample size will have to be.

Definitions

Tolerable misstatement is a monetary amount set by the auditor in respect of which the auditor seeks to obtain an appropriate level of assurance that the monetary amount set by the auditor is not exceeded by the actual misstatement in the population.

Tolerable rate of deviation is a rate of deviation from prescribed internal control procedures set by the auditor in respect of which the auditor seeks to obtain an appropriate level of assurance that the rate of deviation set by the auditor is not exceeded by the actual rate of deviation in the population.

Tolerable misstatement is considered during the planning stage and, for substantive procedures, is related to the auditor's judgement about materiality. The smaller the tolerable misstatement, the greater the sample size will need to be.

(a) For tests of controls, the auditor makes an assessment of the **expected rate of deviation** based on the auditor's understanding of the relevant controls or on the examination of a small number of items from the population. If the expected rate of deviation is unacceptably high, the auditor will normally decide not to perform tests of controls.

(b) For tests of details, the auditor makes an assessment of the **expected misstatement** in the population, If the expected misstatement is high, 100% examination or use of a large sample size may be appropriate when performing tests of details.

The level of sampling risk that the auditor is willing to accept affects the sample size required. The lower the risk the auditor is willing to accept, the greater the sample size will need to be.

Worked example: Designing the sample

Sarah is planning the audit of receivables at Manufacturing Company Limited (MCL). MCL makes all its sales on credit, and the receivables ledger is extensive. However, Sarah has adjudged the area to be low risk as most customers pay their debts promptly and controls over the receivables ledger and credit control are good. In previous years, testing has revealed that few misstatements are discovered. She therefore applies a low sample number.

During the course of testing, Sarah discovers a much higher number of misstatements than she was expecting. She therefore increases her sample and extends her test.

In practice, most auditing firms use computer programs to set sample sizes, based on risk assessments and materiality.

2.3 Selecting the sample

There are a number of selection methods available.

(a) **Random selection** ensures that all items in the population have an equal chance of selection eg, by use of random number tables or computerised generator.

(b) **Systematic selection** involves selecting items using a constant interval between selections, the first interval having a random start. When using systematic selection assurance providers must ensure that the population is not structured in such a manner that the sampling interval corresponds with a particular pattern in the population.

(c) **Haphazard selection** may be an alternative to random selection provided assurance providers are satisfied that the sample is representative of the entire population. This method requires care to guard against making a selection that is biased, for example towards items that are easily located, as they may not be representative. It should not be used if assurance providers are carrying out statistical sampling.

(d) **Sequence or block selection**. Sequence sampling may be used to check whether certain items have particular characteristics. For example, an auditor may use a sample of 50 consecutive cheques to check whether cheques are signed by authorised signatories rather than picking 50 single cheques throughout the year. Sequence sampling may, however, produce samples that are not representative of the population as a whole, particularly if misstatements only occurred during a certain part of the period, and hence the misstatements found cannot be projected onto the rest of the population.

(e) **Monetary Unit Sampling (MUS).** This is a selection method that ensures that every £1 in a population has an equal chance of being selected for testing. The advantages of this selection method are that it is easy when computers are used, and that every material item will automatically be sampled. Disadvantages include the fact that if computers are not used, it can be time consuming to pick the sample, and that MUS does not cope well with errors of understatement (as the computer cannot select a £ which is not there) or negative balances.

Worked example: MUS

You are auditing trade accounts receivable and are testing for overstatement. Total trade account receivables is £500,000 and performance materiality is £50,000. You will select the balances containing each 50,000th £1 from the following ledger.

Customer	Balance	Cumulative total	Selected
A	30,000	30,000	
B	35,000	65,000	Yes
C	45,000	110,000	Yes
D	**52,000**	**162,000**	**Yes**
E	13,000	175,000	
F	**50,000**	**225,000**	**Yes**
G	23,000	248,000	
H	500	248,500	
I	41,500	290,000	Yes
J	47,000	337,000	Yes
K	**54,000**	**391,000**	**Yes**
L	17,000	408,000	Yes
M	**80,000**	**488,000**	**Yes**
N	12,000	500,000	Yes
	500,000		

Material items are shown **in bold** and have all automatically been selected. The cumulative column shows you when the next 50,000th £1 has been reached.

Interactive question 2: Factors affecting sample size

When determining a sample size for tests of detail there are a number of factors that an auditor should take into account.

For each of the following factors, select whether it would cause the sample size to increase or decrease.

(a) Decrease in the assessed level of tolerable misstatement. ☐ Increase ☐ Decrease

(b) Increase in the assessed risk level. ☐ Increase ☐ Decrease

(c) Discovery of more misstatements than were anticipated during testing. ☐ Increase ☐ Decrease

See **Answer** at the end of this chapter.

3 Drawing conclusions from sampling

Section overview

- The purpose of sampling a set of items was to enable the auditors to project the conclusion to the whole population.

- Auditors must consider the nature of the misstatement and whether it is fair to project that misstatement.

- If the projected misstatement exceeds tolerable misstatement then sampling risk must be reassessed and further audit procedures must be considered.

When the auditors have tested a sample of items, they must then draw conclusions from that sample. The purpose of audit sampling is to enable conclusions to be drawn from an entire population on the basis of testing a sample drawn from it.

To begin with, the auditors must consider whether the items in question are **true misstatements**, as they defined them before the test. For example, when testing receivables, a sampled misposting between customer accounts will not affect whether the auditors conclude the valuation of total receivables is true and fair.

When the expected audit evidence regarding a specific sample item cannot be found, the auditor shall perform the procedure on a replacement item. In such cases, the item is not treated as a misstatement.

The **qualitative** aspects of misstatements are also considered, including the **nature and cause** of the misstatement. Auditors must also consider any possible effects the misstatement might have on **other parts of the audit** including the general effect on the financial statements and on the auditors' assessment of the accounting and internal control systems.

Where common features are discovered in misstatements, the auditors may decide to identify all items in the population that possess the common feature (eg, location), thereby producing a sub-population. Audit procedures could then be extended in this area.

On some occasions the auditor may decide that the misstatement is an anomaly.

Definition

Anomaly: A misstatement or deviation that is demonstrably not representative of misstatements or deviations in a population.

To be considered anomalous, the auditors have to be certain that the misstatements are not representative of the population. Extra work will be required to prove that a misstatement is an anomaly.

The auditors must project the misstatement results from the sample onto the relevant population. The auditors will **estimate the probable misstatement** in the population by extrapolating the misstatements found in the sample.

For substantive procedures, auditors will then **estimate any further misstatement** that might not have been detected because of the imprecision of the technique (in addition to consideration of the qualitative aspects of the errors).

Auditors must also consider the effect of the projected misstatement on other areas of the audit. The auditors should compare the projected population misstatement (net of adjustments made by the entity in the case of substantive procedures) to the tolerable misstatement taking account of other relevant audit procedures.

If the projected population misstatement **exceeds** or is close to tolerable misstatement, then the auditors must re-assess sampling risk. If it is unacceptable, they shall consider extending auditing procedures or performing alternative procedures. However, if after alternative procedures the auditors still believe the actual misstatement rate is higher than the tolerable misstatement rate, they should re-assess control risk if the test is a test of controls; if the test is a substantive procedures, they should consider whether the financial statements need to be adjusted.

Worked example: Drawing conclusions from sampling

Adrian carried out a supplier statement reconciliation on Peabody Ltd, testing the completeness and valuation assertions. This means that he compared the statements sent by suppliers to Peabody Ltd with the details on Peabody's own payables ledger. Tolerable misstatement has been set at £10,000. The sample was 10 payables ledger balances totalling £35,024 out of a total of £375,297. Adrian found that of these, 8 reconciliations proved that the balance on the ledger was correct, one showed that an invoice had been misposted to a different supplier's account and one showed that an invoice had not been posted at all.

When considering the results of his sample, Adrian decided that he can disregard the misposting, as, although it means that two accounts were individually misstated, the overall balance was not affected by this mistake. In the case of the invoice that had simply been omitted in error however, Adrian had to conclude that this misstatement of £250, which does affect the overall total balance, could be repeated in the overall population with the potential for causing material misstatement. Adrian projected the total population misstatement based on the sample and compared the outcome with tolerable misstatement. In this case he found that the projected misstatement of £2,679 was considerably below the tolerable misstatement of £10,000 and concluded that no further action was required. He concluded from his testing that the trade payables balance in the financial statements was fairly stated.

Interactive question 3: Drawing conclusions from sampling

Danielle has carried out a receivables circularisation on Donothing plc to gain evidence about the existence and valuation of the receivables balance stated in the draft statement of financial position. Identify whether the following conclusions drawn by her are correct or not.

(a) An amount disagreed by Lazy Limited because an invoice had been paid two days before the year end and cleared shortly after the year end, did not constitute a misstatement for the purposes of drawing a conclusion for the whole population. ☐ True ☐ False

(b) An amount disagreed by Sloth Limited because a credit note had been issued by Donothing plc a month before the year end did not constitute a misstatement for the purposes of drawing a conclusion for the whole population. ☐ True ☐ False

(c) An amount disagreed by Busy Limited because they had paid the balance some time earlier, which further enquiry revealed had been posted to a different customer account, did constitute a misstatement for the purposes of drawing a conclusion for the whole population. ☐ True ☐ False

See **Answer** at the end of this chapter.

4 Evaluation of misstatements

> **Section overview**
>
> - ISA (UK) 450, *Evaluation of Misstatements Identified During the Audit* requires the auditor to evaluate the effect of identified misstatements on the audit and evaluate the effect of any uncorrected misstatements on the financial statements.
> - All non-trivial misstatements must be communicated to management and if uncorrected, to those charged with governance.

The auditor is required to **evaluate the effect of identified misstatements on the audit** in ISA (UK) 450, *Evaluation of Misstatements Identified during the Audit*. Under this ISA, the auditor must also **evaluate the effect of any uncorrected misstatements on the financial statements**.

During the audit, auditors must accumulate any non-trivial misstatements identified and determine whether the audit plan or overall audit strategy need to be revised based on these. Additional audit procedures shall be performed where management has examined and corrected balances at the auditor's request.

The auditor is required to communicate all misstatements on a timely basis to the appropriate level of management and request that management corrects the misstatements. The auditor is required to request a written representation from management whether they believe the effects of uncorrected misstatements to be immaterial to the financial statements as a whole. If management have corrected material misstatements, then doing this may help them to fulfil their governance responsibilities, including reviewing the effectiveness of internal control.

If management refuses to correct some or all of the misstatements then the auditor shall:

- obtain an understanding of management's **reasons** for not making the corrections
- determine whether uncorrected misstatements are **material** individually or in aggregate
- **communicate** individual uncorrected misstatements to those charged with governance and request that these be corrected, mentioning any effect on the opinion in the auditor's report
- request a **written representation** from management (and if appropriate those charged with governance) that they believe the effects of the uncorrected misstatements are immaterial, individually and in aggregate, to the financial statements as a whole

In determining whether uncorrected misstatements are material, the auditor must consider the **size** and **nature** of the misstatements, along with the particular **circumstances** of their occurrence. Certain circumstances may cause the auditor to evaluate misstatements as material, even if they are lower than materiality for the financial statements as a whole. Examples of circumstances include, but are not limited to, the extent to which the misstatement:

- affects compliance with regulatory requirements
- affects compliance with debt covenants or other regulatory requirements
- masks a change in earnings or other trends
- affects ratios used to evaluate the entity's financial position, results of operations or cash flows
- increases management's compensation, for example by ensuring the requirements for the award of bonuses are met

Interactive question 4: Material misstatements

Which **two** of the following should be determined as material uncorrected misstatements?

A   An isolated misposting between two supplier accounts which is below materiality
B   A misstatement which is below materiality and results in director's bonus targets being met
C   An immaterial misstatement of assets which results in a debt covenant not being breached
D   The monthly bank reconciliation was not prepared in August as the cashier was on holiday

See **Answer** at the end of this chapter.

Summary and Self-test

Summary

Evidence can be obtained by:
- Inspection
- Observation
- Inquiry
- Confrontation
- Recalculation
- Reperformance
- Analytical procedures

The strengths and weaknesses of these methods depend on associated issues relating to the quality of evidence – for example, of whom the inquiry was made, client staff or third parties

Evidence will often be obtained from a sample of a population, rather than testing every item within it

Factors affecting sample size include:
- The degree of assessed risk
- The level of tolerable misstatement

To draw a conclusion from a sample, auditors must distinguish between true misstatements and other misstatements

Auditors must communicate misstatements to management and request that these be corrected

Self-test

Answer the following questions.

1   Which **one** of the following procedures would give the most persuasive evidence that a control operated as the assurance providers had been advised?

   A   Inspection of the controls handbook
   B   Inquiry of the staff operating the control
   C   Observation of the staff operating the control
   D   Reperformance of the control by audit staff

2   Indicate the purpose of the primary test for each type of account in directional testing.

   (a) Assets   ☐ Overstatement   ☐ Understatement

   (b) Liabilities   ☐ Overstatement   ☐ Understatement

   (c) Income   ☐ Overstatement   ☐ Understatement

   (d) Expense   ☐ Overstatement   ☐ Understatement

3   Identify the significant relationships in the list of items below.

   (a) Payables   (b) Interest   (c) Purchases   (d) Revenue

   (e) Amortisation   (f) Loans   (g) Receivables   (h) Intangibles

4   Identify whether the following statements are true or false.

		True	False
(a)	The risk that the auditor's conclusion, based on a sample, may be different from the conclusion if the entire population were subjected to the same audit procedure is sampling risk.	☐	☐
(b)	The risk that the auditor might use inappropriate procedures or might misinterpret audit evidence and thus fail to recognise a misstatement or deviation is non-sampling risk.	☐	☐

5   Identify whether the following examples of sample selection are random, haphazard or systematic.

		Random	Haphazard	Systematic
(a)	Barry is selecting a sample from the list of receivables balances. He selects the second, and thereafter every 7th balance.	☐	☐	☐
(b)	Carol is selecting a number of purchase invoices to carry out a directional test. She selects them by flicking through the files and selecting an invoice occasionally.	☐	☐	☐

Now, go back to the Learning Objectives in the Introduction. If you are satisfied you have achieved these objectives, please tick them off.

Technical references

1 Evidence

- Procedures to obtain evidence   ISA (UK) 500.A14 – A25
- Analytical procedures   ISA (UK) 520 + ISA (UK) 315.6
- Accounting estimates   ISA (UK) 540.13

2 Selecting items to test

- The concept of sampling   ISA (UK) 500.A54 + ISA (UK) 530.4 – 5
- Design of the sample   ISA (UK) 530.5 – 8, Appx 2, Appx 3
- Selecting the sample   ISA (UK) 530 Appx 1

3 Drawing conclusions from sampling   ISA (UK) 530.14, A18 – A23

4 Evaluation of misstatements   ISA (UK) 450.5 – 15 + ISA (UK) 450.A16

Answers to Interactive questions

Answer to Interactive question 1

B   A sales invoice is an internally generated document and therefore provides a poor source of evidence. It would be better to obtain information about sales from the customers.

Answer to Interactive question 2

They would all cause the sample size to increase.

Answer to Interactive question 3

(a)   True – this is just a timing difference.

(b)   False – this indicates that the credit note may not have been processed to the receivables ledger, which would be an error that could also be true of other potential credits due on the ledger.

(c)   False – this error does not affect the overall balance on the ledger.

Answer to Interactive question 4

B, C Although these two items are below materiality, the particular circumstances surrounding their occurrence make them material misstatements. D relates to a test of controls.

1 D Reperformance by the auditor would give the strongest evidence of this being the case.

2 (a) Overstatement
   (b) Understatement
   (c) Understatement
   (d) Overstatement

3 (a) and (c)
   (b) and (f)
   (d) and (g)
   (e) and (h)

4 (a) True
   (b) True

5 (a) Systematic
   (b) Haphazard

CHAPTER 12

Written representations

Introduction

Examination context

Topic List

Summary and Self-test

Technical references

Answer to Interactive question

Answers to Self-test

Introduction

Learning objectives

- Understand the purpose and nature of written representations from management
- Understand when oral representations should be confirmed in writing
- Understand how reliable these written representations are as a form of assurance evidence

The specific syllabus reference for this chapter is: 3h.

Syllabus links

You will need to understand the purpose, content and reliability of written representations as assurance evidence when you go on to draw assurance conclusions and look at assurance reports in Audit and Assurance.

Examination context

There was one question on the sample paper, relating to written representations, dealing with their purpose. You should not expect more than one or two questions on this area in your assessment.

In the assessment, candidates may be required to:

- identify the purposes of a written representation letter
- identify the circumstances in which written representations may be sought

1 Written representations as assurance evidence

Section overview

- The auditor shall request management to provide certain general written representations: that it has prepared the financial statements in accordance with the applicable financial reporting framework, that it has provided the auditor with all relevant information and access, and that all transactions have been recorded and reflected in the financial statements.

- Some ISAs require the auditor to request written representations. In addition to this, the auditor may decide that it needs more. These written **representations from management** should be restricted to one or more specific assertions in the financial statements.

- Any written representations should be **compared** with other evidence and their **sufficiency** assessed.

Assurance providers receive many representations during the engagement, both unsolicited and in response to specific questions. Some of these representations may be critical to obtaining sufficient appropriate evidence.

ISA (UK) 580, *Written Representations* deals with the auditor's responsibility to obtain written representations from management and, where appropriate, those charged with governance in an audit of financial statements. The principles of the ISA (outlined in this section) are also valid for other assurance work.

Definition

Management is the person(s) with executive responsibility for the conduct of the entity's operations. For some entities in some jurisdictions, management includes some or all of those charged with governance, for example, executive members of a governance board, or an owner-manager.

In ISA 580 references to management also include those charged with governance where this is appropriate.

Written confirmation of oral representations avoids confusion and disagreement. Such matters should be discussed with those responsible for giving the written confirmation, to ensure that they understand what they are confirming. Written confirmations are normally required of senior management.

1.1 General matters

Written representations are required for general matters; for example, that the accounting records have been made fully available to the auditors.

There are a number of elements that ISA 580 requires auditors to confirm in writing, namely that management (usually the directors in the UK, who have statutory duties in respect of financial statements) has:

- fulfilled its responsibility for the preparation of the financial statements in accordance with the applicable financial reporting framework, including where relevant their fair presentation, as set out in the terms of the audit engagement

- provided the auditor with all relevant information and access as agreed in the terms of the audit engagement

- recorded and reflected all transactions in the financial statements

The confirmation with regard to responsibility and approval of the financial statements is normally done when the auditors receive a signed copy of the financial statements, which incorporate a relevant statement of responsibilities.

The written representations are dated as near as possible, but not after, the date of the auditor's report on the financial statements.

1.2 Other written representations

In addition to general written representations about management's responsibilities, the auditors are required to request specific written representations by other ISAs and also where the auditor determines they are necessary to support other audit evidence.

Written representations cannot be used instead of other (better) evidence which the auditors expect to exist.

2 When other written representations are required

Section overview

- Specific written representations may be required in a variety of situations.

- If written representations do not agree with other audit evidence, other audit procedures should be performed and the implications considered.

Other written representations may include the following matters.

- Whether the selection and application of accounting policies are appropriate

- Whether matters such as the following, where relevant under the applicable financial reporting framework, have been recognised, measured, presented or disclosed in accordance with that framework:

    – Plans or intentions that may affect the carrying value or classification of assets and liabilities

    – Liabilities, both actual and contingent

    – Title to assets, the liens on assets, and assets pledged as collateral

    – Aspects of laws, regulations and contractual agreements that may affect the financial statements, including non-compliance

- Whether all deficiencies in internal control of which management is aware have been communicated to auditors

- Specific written representations required by other ISAs

- Support for management's judgement or intent in relation to a specific assertion

Worked example: Other written representations required

Keira is working on the audit of Prejudiced plc. In the prior year, there had been a large amount of obsolete inventory at the year end due to a decision by management to amend the design of their major product to improve the safety of the product. Keira has been asked to ensure that management provide written representation that they have no intention of making any similar amendments to their products this year that would impact on existing inventory in this way. This representation would be corroborated by reviewing minutes of management meetings.

There may be occasions when there are doubts over the **reliability** of written representations. If the auditor has concerns over the competence, integrity, ethical values or diligence of management, the auditor shall determine the effect that such concerns may have over the reliability of representations (oral and written) and audit evidence in general.

If written representations are **inconsistent with other audit evidence**, the auditor shall perform audit procedures in an attempt to resolve the matter. If the matter remains unresolved, the auditor shall reconsider its assessment of management and determine the effect that this may have on the reliability of representations (oral or written) in general.

3 Example of a written representation letter

Section overview

- Here is an example of a written representation letter from management.

(Entity Letterhead)

(To Auditor) (Date)

This representation letter is provided in connection with your audit of the financial statements of ABC Company for the year ended 31 December 20X1 for the purpose of expressing an opinion as to whether the financial statements are presented fairly, in all material respects, (or give a true and fair view) in accordance with International Financial Reporting Standards.

We confirm that (to the best of our knowledge and belief, having made such inquiries as we considered necessary for the purpose of appropriately informing ourselves):

Financial Statements

- We have fulfilled our responsibilities, as set out in the terms of the audit engagement dated [insert date], for the preparation of the financial statements in accordance with International Financial Reporting Standards; in particular the financial statements are fairly presented (or give a true and fair view) in accordance therewith.

- Significant assumptions used by us in making accounting estimates, including those measured at fair value, are reasonable. (ISA 540)

- Related party relationships and transactions have been appropriately accounted for and disclosed in accordance with the requirements of International Financial Reporting Standards. (ISA 550)

- All events subsequent to the date of the financial statements and for which International Financial Reporting Standards require adjustment or disclosure have been adjusted or disclosed. (ISA 560)

- The effects of uncorrected misstatements are immaterial, both individually and in the aggregate, to the financial statements as a whole. A list of the uncorrected misstatements is attached to the representation letter. (ISA 450)

- Any other matters that the auditor may consider appropriate.

Information provided

- We have provided you with:
  - Access to all information of which we are aware that is relevant to the preparation of the financial statements such as records, documentation and other matters;
  - Additional information that you have requested from us for the purpose of the audit; and
  - Unrestricted access to persons within the entity from whom you determined it necessary to obtain audit evidence.

- All transactions have been recorded in the accounting records and are reflected in the financial statements.

- We have disclosed to you the results of our assessment of the risk that the financial statements may be materially misstated as a result of fraud. (ISA 240)

- We have disclosed to you all information in relation to fraud or suspected fraud that we are aware of and that affects the entity and involves:
  - Management;
  - Employees who have significant roles in internal control; or
  - Others where the fraud could have a material effect on the financial statements. (ISA 240)

- We have disclosed to you all information in relation to allegations of fraud, or suspected fraud, affecting the entity's financial statements communicated by employees, former employees, analysts, regulators or others. (ISA 240)

- We have disclosed to you all known instances of non-compliance or suspected non-compliance with laws and regulations whose effects should be considered when preparing financial statements. (ISA 250A)

- We have disclosed to you the identity of the entity's related parties and all the related party relationships and transactions of which we are aware. (ISA 550)

- Any other matters that the auditor may consider necessary.

....
Management   Management

Interactive question: Written representations

Which **two** of the following are purposes of a written representation letter from management?

☐ Confirmation that management has received the signed audit report

☐ Confirmation that management has fulfilled its responsibility for the preparation of the financial statements

☐ Confirmation of all representations made by management in the course of the audit

☐ Confirmation that management has recorded and reflected all transactions in the financial statements

☐ Confirmation that management understands the terms of the engagement

See **Answer** at the end of this chapter.

Summary

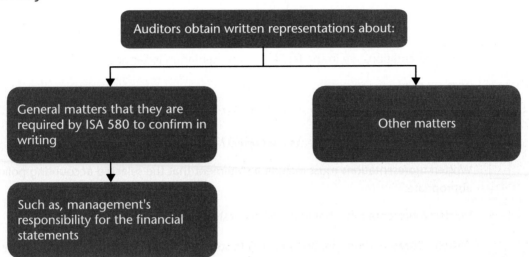

Auditors obtain written representations about:

General matters that they are required by ISA 580 to confirm in writing

Such as, management's responsibility for the financial statements

Other matters

Self-test

Answer the following questions.

1   Written representations include a statement that management has provided the auditor with all relevant information.

☐   True

☐   False

2   All written representations are in the form of a representation letter addressed to the shareholders.

☐   True

☐   False

3   Which **two** of the following statements are correct?

☐   Written representations must include a statement that the selected accounting policies are appropriate.

☐   Written representations should be corroborated with other sources of evidence.

☐   Written representations are an appropriate source of evidence when other evidence does not exist because it has been accidentally destroyed.

☐   The written representation should be dated on or before the date of the auditor's report.

Now, go back to the Learning Objectives in the Introduction. If you are satisfied you have achieved these objectives, please tick them off.

Technical references

CHAPTER

12

Answer to Interactive question

Confirmation that management has fulfilled its responsibility for the preparation of the financial statements.

Confirmation that management has recorded and reflected all transactions in the financial statements.

Answers to Self-test

1 True

2 False – the representation letter is addressed to the auditor.

3 Written representations should be corroborated with other sources of evidence.

The written representation should be dated on or before the date of the auditor's report.

CHAPTER 13

Substantive procedures – key financial statement figures

Learning objectives

- Understand the nature of tests on balances carried out by assurance providers and the objectives of those tests ☐

- Identify suitable tests in a given business scenario ☐

- Understand when a matter should be referred to a senior member of staff ☐

Specific syllabus references for this chapter are: 3f, i.

Syllabus links

The results of the tests outlined here will be the basis for the drawing conclusions part of your Audit and Assurance paper.

Examination context

Questions about assurance evidence could be set in the context of any balances outlined in this chapter.

In the assessment, candidates may be required to:

- select appropriate audit procedures for a given financial statement assertion
- identify the features of external confirmation requests
- identify why the results of a physical inventory count may differ from inventory records
- identify the procedures which should be undertaken to confirm the existence of cash at bank
- evaluate the results of audit work and identify issues that should be referred to a senior colleague

1 Non-current assets

1.1 Tangible non-current assets

You should be aware of the major classes of tangible non-current assets from your *Accounting* studies. Examples of tangible non-current assets include land, buildings, plant, vehicles, fittings and equipment.

The major risks of the tangible non-current asset balances in the financial statements being misstated are due to:

- the company not actually owning the assets (rights and obligations assertion)

- the assets not actually existing or having been sold by the company (existence assertion)

- omission of assets owned by the company (completeness assertion)

- the assets being overvalued, either by inflating cost or valuation, or by undercharging depreciation (valuation assertion)

- the assets being undervalued, by not including an appropriate revaluation in a policy of revaluation or by overcharging depreciation (valuation assertion)

- the assets being incorrectly presented in the financial statements (presentation and disclosure assertion)

The objective of assurance tests in respect of non-current assets is therefore to prove that these assertions about the assets are correct. There are several sources of information about non-current assets that can be used (you should consider the strengths and weaknesses of all the sources of evidence listed in this chapter according to the criteria we set out in Chapter 11):

- The non-current asset register (which many companies maintain as a control over the assets they own)

- Purchase invoices for assets purchased within the year

- Sales invoices for assets sold within the year

- Registration documents or other documents of title such as title deeds for property

- Valuations carried out by employees or third party valuers

- Leases or hire purchase documentation in respect of assets

- Physical inspection of the assets themselves by the auditor

- Depreciation records or calculations (these are often kept with the asset register)

Worked example: Non-current asset assurance engagement

Peter is carrying out a non-current asset assurance engagement at Manufacturing Company Limited (MCL). MCL owns the property from which it operates. It has a lot of fixed plant, which it replaced three years ago, and owns several industrial vehicles for moving inventory between locations at its premises. It also owns a number of cars, which its staff have as company cars, and a great deal of office furniture, fittings and computers in the office complex attached to the factory.

Peter is concerned with concluding that the non-current assets declared in the financial statements are complete, exist, are owned by the company and are valued appropriately.

Completeness

Peter will:

- obtain a schedule of non-current assets from the client

- agree the figures per the schedule to the financial statements and accounting records (nominal ledger)

- compare the schedule to the asset register to ensure that the schedule reflects all the assets owned by the company

- select a number of assets physically present on site and ensure that they are contained in the asset register

- confirm the additions on the schedule are correct

Existence

Peter will:

- select a sample of assets contained in the asset register and verify that they are physically present on site

Rights and obligations

Peter will:

- select a sample of assets in the asset register and vouch them to the registration documents available for those assets (vehicles – registration documents (although these indicate who is the 'registered keeper', who is not necessarily the owner), building – title deeds, plant and fixtures – purchase invoice, ensuring that it is not a lease)

- review sales invoices for sold assets to ensure that ownership has been transferred

Valuation

Peter will:

- confirm the cost or valuation of a sample of assets to purchase invoices or valuation certificates

- confirm the brought forward depreciation levels of those assets (if relevant) to prior year audit files or by reviewing the brought forward asset register files

- confirm the annual depreciation in respect of those assets is appropriate (by reference to the accounting policy on depreciation published in the financial statements), and correctly calculated (by recalculation or by using analytical procedures)

- review to ensure that depreciation has been correctly calculated on disposed assets, and recalculate profit or loss on sale of those assets

Presentation and disclosure

- Peter will review the financial statements to ensure that the disclosure requirements relating to non-current assets have been met.

Other matters

- Peter is likely to focus asset testing on asset additions, as these will comprise a large proportion of the cost of non-current assets as they will have been depreciated the least.

- Peter will use sampling on some classes of assets and not others. For example, in this instance, property is likely to be a material balance and therefore will be vouched 100%. Other classes of assets are likely to be sampled as the overall total contains a large number of assets.

Worked example: Self-constructed assets

Katie is working on the audit of Quickshop plc, a large supermarket chain. She has been allocated the audit of non-current assets. One aspect of this audit is the fact that the company has built four new superstores during the year, which have been capitalised into non-current assets. The key objectives she is working on are that all the relevant costs have been capitalised (completeness) and that the self-built stores are valued correctly at cost (valuation).

Completeness

Katie will:

- obtain architect's certificates for the stores, certifying that the work is complete

- obtain a schedule of all the costs capitalised into the stores; this is also likely to have been verified by the contractor, giving comfort that the costs are complete

Valuation

Katie will:

- vouch a sample of costs to appropriate sources of evidence, for example, labour costs to payroll records or contractor bills, materials costs to purchase invoices or contractor bills, finance costs to statements from lenders (for example, bank statements)

- in respect of finance costs, Katie will review bank statements to ensure that all relevant finance costs have been included

Interactive question 1: Non-current assets

Which **three** of the following might an auditor vouch when testing the rights and obligations of a company in respect of a vehicle?

	A purchase invoice
	A registration document
	A hire-purchase agreement
	An asset register

See **Answer** at the end of this chapter.

1.2 Intangible non-current assets

Examples of intangible assets include licences, development costs and purchased brands.

The major risks of misstatement of the intangible non-current asset balances in the financial statements are due to:

- expenses being capitalised as non-current assets inappropriately (existence assertion)

- intangible assets being carried at the wrong cost or valuation due to inflating the cost or valuation (valuation assertion)

- intangible assets being carried at the wrong cost or valuation due to charging inappropriate amortisation, wrongly amortising or not amortising (valuation assertion)

- intangible assets being carried at the wrong cost or valuation due to impairment reviews not being carried out appropriately (valuation assertion)

The objective of tests in respect of intangible non-current assets is therefore to prove that these assertions about the assets are correct. The following sources of information can be used:

- Accounting standards/auditor's knowledge of accounting standards for what constitutes an intangible asset

- Purchase invoices or documentation (particularly for, say, purchased intangibles)

- Client calculations and schedules

- Specialist valuations

- Auditor understanding of the entity for signs of impairment factors

2 Inventory

Section overview

- Key areas when testing inventory are:
  - attending an inventory count (existence)
  - valuation at the lower of cost and net realisable value (valuation)
  - in some cases, confirmation of ownership (rights and obligations)

The major risks of misstatement of the inventory balance in the financial statements are due to:

- inventory that does not exist being included in the financial statements (existence)

- not all inventory that exists being included in the financial statements (completeness)

- inventory being included in the financial statements at full value when it is obsolete or damaged (valuation)

- inventory being included in the financial statements at the wrong value, whether due to miscalculation of cost or the fact that cost has been used although net realisable value is lower than cost (valuation)

- inventory that actually belongs to third parties being included in the financial statements (rights and obligations)

- inventory which has actually been sold is included in the financial statements (cut-off)

The objective of assurance tests in respect of inventory is therefore to prove that these assertions about the assets are correct. The following sources of information can be used:

- The company's controls over inventory counting
- The auditors' attendance at the annual inventory count
- Confirmations with third parties holding inventory or having inventory stored for them by the company
- Purchase invoices for inventory
- Work-in-progress records for inventory
- Post-year-end sales invoices for inventory
- Post-year-end price lists for inventory
- Post-year-end sales orders

Inventory may lend itself to analytical review as there is a relationship between inventory, revenue and purchases.

2.1 Inventory count

Attendance at an inventory count can be very important. In order to confirm the amount of inventory in existence, rather than undertake a count itself, assurance providers usually rely on the controls that a company has in operation over its inventory or its annual inventory count.

It is important that the assurance provider is satisfied that controls are such that it can be concluded that the count, or the overall inventory controls, are capable of ensuring the correct amount of inventory is reflected in the financial statements.

In terms of inventory counts, the assurance provider will be looking for the following sorts of controls.

Review of inventory count instructions	
Organisation of count	**Supervision** by senior staff, including senior staff not normally involved with inventory
	Tidying and **marking** inventory to help counting
	Restriction and **control** of the production process and inventory movements during the count
	Identification of damaged, obsolete, slow-moving, third party and **returnable** inventory
Counting	**Systematic counting** to ensure all inventory is counted
	Teams of **two counters,** with one counting and the other checking, or two **independent counts**
Recording	**Serial numbering, control** and **return** of all inventory sheets
	Inventory sheets being **completed** in **ink** and **signed**
	Information to be recorded on the **count records** (location and identity, count units, quantity counted, conditions of items, stage reached in production process)
	Recording of **quantity, conditions** and **stage of production** of **work-in-progress**
	Recording of last numbers of **goods inwards** and **outwards** records and of internal transfer records
	Reconciliation with **inventory records** and **investigation** and correction of any **differences**

Some companies have better day-to-day controls over inventories than others and many have complex systems of perpetual counting rendering an annual year-end count unnecessary. In order to rely on such a system of perpetual counting, the assurance provider needs to confirm that the controls over this system are strong.

If perpetual inventory counting is used, assurance providers will check that management does the following.

(a) Ensures that all inventory lines are counted at least once a year.

(b) Maintains **adequate inventory records** that are kept up-to-date. Assurance providers may compare sales and purchase transactions with inventory movements, and carry out other tests on the inventory records, for example checking casts and classification of inventory.

(c) Has **satisfactory procedures** for **inventory counts** and **test-counting**. Assurance providers should confirm the inventory count arrangements and instructions are as rigorous as those for a year-end inventory count by reviewing instructions and observing counts. Assurance providers will be particularly concerned with **cut-off**; that there are no inventory movements whilst the count is taking place, and inventory records are updated up until the time of the inventory counts.

(d) **Investigates** and **corrects** all **material differences**. Reasons for differences should be recorded and any necessary corrective action taken. All corrections to inventory movements should be authorised by a manager who has not been involved in the detailed work; these procedures are necessary to guard against the possibility that inventory records may be adjusted to conceal shortages.

Audit plan: Perpetual inventory count

Attend one of the inventory counts (to observe and confirm that instructions are being adhered to)

Follow up the **inventory counts attended** to compare quantities counted by the assurance providers with the inventory records, obtaining and verifying explanations for any differences, and checking that the client has reconciled count records with book records

Review the **year's counts** to confirm the extent of counting, the treatment of discrepancies and the overall accuracy of records (if matters are not satisfactory, assurance providers will only be able to gain sufficient assurance by a full count at the year-end)

Assuming a full count is not necessary at the year-end, **compare** the **listing of inventory with the detailed inventory records**, and carry out other procedures (**cut-off, analytical review**) to gain further comfort

2.2 Cost vs NRV

Management should **compare cost and net realisable value** for each item of inventory. Where this is impracticable, the comparison may be done by group or category.

Net realisable value is likely to be less than cost when there has been:

- an **increase in costs** or a fall in selling price
- **physical deterioration**
- **obsolescence** of products
- a **marketing decision** to manufacture and sell products at a loss
- **errors in production or purchasing**

For work in progress, the **ultimate selling price** should be **compared** with the **carrying value** at the year-end plus **costs** to be **incurred** after the year-end to bring work in progress to a finished state. The example below shows the test carried out to identify whether NRV is lower than cost.

Worked example: Audit of inventory

Rajeev is carrying out the audit of inventory at Icket Ltd. Icket produces various lines of tableware on behalf of high street stores. It also sells tableware to wholesalers and has a small retail outlet. Icket is not entitled to sell branded products to wholesalers and it makes approximately 10% more inventory of branded products than ordered to ensure it meets quality control standards of the stores. This 10% is therefore obsolete once sales of a line to a store are finished. Each high street store has an allocated sales manager at Icket who keeps records of what sales have been made of each line and when the line is coming to an end. One high street store customer, Argus, maintains a store of approved inventory at Icket's premises, which it calls off as required. Icket carried out an annual inventory count at the year-end.

The key issues for Rajeev when auditing inventory are:

- to ensure that obsolete inventory is not included at full cost in the financial statements

- to ascertain that inventory included in the financial statements exists and that all existing and valuable inventory is included, including the inventory held at the retail outlet

- to ensure that inventory belonging to Argus is not included in the financial statements

- to ensure that inventory is held at the appropriate value in the financial statements

Existence

Rajeev will:

- obtain a copy of the count instructions issued to employees of Icket and review them to assess whether controls over the count appear strong enough to ensure that the correct amount of inventory will be reflected in the financial statements

- assess the key issues arising at the count; for instance, what the high value inventory is, what the risks are (outlined above), or whether there are any specific issues that will make counting complex (not in this case)

- plan his count attendance, including sample sizes and target inventory lines

- attend the inventory count, at which he will carry out sample counts to ensure that the counters are counting properly, the instructions are being adhered to, procedures for obsolete and damaged inventory are being followed, Argus inventory is properly separated and noted, and to gain an overall impression of the level and state of the inventories and conclude whether the count has been carried out properly

- trace a sample of items on the final inventory sheets back to original count documents and ensure all count documents are reflected in the final sheets

Completeness

Rajeev will:

- follow up items sampled at the inventory count to ensure that they are included in the final inventory sheets, and therefore the financial statements

- follow up Argus items sampled at the inventory count to ensure that they are not included in the final inventory sheets, and therefore the financial statements

- carry out a 'cut-off' test, ensuring that year-end deliveries and sales have not been double counted or not counted (for example, by including an item in inventory and in sales, or by excluding a consignment of goods received from inventory and purchases). This will be done by selecting the goods inwards and outwards notes on either side of the year-end and tracing them to invoices, ledgers and inventory sheets to ensure they are recorded correctly

Rights and obligations

Rajeev will:

- send a confirmation letter to Argus, asking them to confirm the level of inventory held at Icket on the year-end date

- compare the answer to this letter to Icket's records, and, if necessary, reconcile any differences, liaising with Icket's Argus sales manager. If there are any substantial differences, this could indicate a problem with controls over this area of which Rajeev should inform a senior audit team member

Valuation

Rajeev will:

- check that the calculations of valuation on the final inventory sheets have been made correctly

- select samples of raw materials, work in progress and finished goods from Icket's final inventory sheets

- ascertain the accounting policy for inventory cost from the financial statements (for example, FIFO) and confirm it is reasonable and appropriate

- trace the cost of the raw materials sample to purchase invoices to ensure cost has been recorded correctly and on the right basis

- in addition, for work in progress and finished goods samples, ensure that an appropriate level of raw material has been costed, by reviewing production records

- confirm labour costs allocated to work in progress and finished goods by reference to production records and payroll

- review Icket's overhead allocation to ensure only appropriate costs are included (for example, not idle time) and perform analytical procedures comparing overhead allocation to previous years

- compare valuation of cost for finished goods sample to post-year end selling prices, by reference to sales orders or invoices, to ensure inventory is held at the lower of cost and NRV

- follow up items noted as obsolete or damaged at the inventory count to ensure that valuation has been appropriately adjusted to reflect NRV

- for branded goods in excess of customer requirements, ensure that valuation has been entered as zero (these goods should be identifiable from sales manager's records)

Interactive question 2: Inventory

Which **one** of the following procedures should be undertaken to confirm the existence of inventory?

- ☐ Attendance at inventory count
- ☐ Follow up of inventory count sheets to final inventory sheets
- ☐ Trace items of inventory to purchase invoices
- ☐ Cast the final inventory sheets

See **Answer** at the end of this chapter.

---

3 Receivables

Section overview

- Key areas when testing receivables are:
    - confirming debt owed by customers with customers (existence, rights and obligations)
    - confirming debt is still likely to be collected (valuation)

The major risks of misstatement of the receivables balance in the financial statements are due to:

- debts being uncollectable (valuation)
- debts being contested by customers (existence, rights and obligations)

The objective of assurance tests in respect of receivables is therefore to prove that these assertions about the assets are correct. The following sources of information can be used:

- Receivables ledger information
- Confirmations from customers
- Cash payments received after the year end

If the company makes a similar number of sales annually to a fairly established customer base then analytical procedures may give good results.

3.1 Confirmations from customers

When it is reasonable to expect customers to respond, the assurance providers should ordinarily plan to obtain direct confirmation of receivables to individual entries in an account balance. Direct confirmation of receivables in an audit is covered by ISA (UK) 505, *External Confirmations*. External confirmations are not compulsory in an audit of financial statements.

The verification of trade receivables by external confirmation is a means of providing relevant and reliable audit evidence to satisfy the objective of checking whether customers exist and owe *bona fide* amounts to the company (**existence** and **rights and obligations**).

Confirmation should take place immediately after the year end and hence cover the year end balances to be included in the statement of financial position. If this is not possible it may be acceptable to carry out the confirmation **prior to the year end** provided that the auditor obtains further evidence relating to the remainder of the period.

Confirmation is essentially an act of the **client**, who alone can authorise third parties to divulge information to the auditor. If the client refuses to allow the auditor to send a confirmation request, the auditor shall inquire as to management's reasons for the refusal and evaluate the implications on the auditor's risk assessment. Alternative audit procedures must be performed. If these do not generate relevant and reliable audit evidence or the auditor concludes that management's refusal is unreasonable, the auditor must communicate with those charged with governance and determine the implications for the auditor's opinion.

When confirmation is undertaken the method of requesting information from the customer may be either 'positive' or 'negative'.

- Under the **positive** method the customer is requested to give the balance or to confirm the accuracy of the balance shown or state in what respect he is in disagreement.

- Under the **negative** method the customer is requested to reply only if the amount stated is disputed. This method generally provides less reliable audit evidence than the positive method as a lack of response could mean that the customer does not dispute the balance, or it could mean that the customer did not receive the confirmation request, or ignored it.

The positive method is generally preferable as it is designed to encourage definite replies from those contacted. The risk that customers might reply without actually confirming the balance can be mitigated by not providing the balance for confirmation and requesting that the customer fills the balance in. However, this approach can lead to a lower response rate as it involves more work on the part of the customer. The negative method should only be used when:

- assessed risk of material misstatement is low.
- the relevant controls are operating effectively.
- a large number of small balances is involved.
- a substantial number of errors is not expected.
- the auditor has no reason to believe that customers will disregard the request.

The statements will normally be prepared by the client's staff, from which point the assurance providers, as a safeguard against the possibility of fraudulent manipulation, must maintain strict control over the checking and despatch of the statements.

Precautions must also be taken to ensure that undelivered items are returned, not to the client, but to the assurance providers' own office for follow up by them.

Worked example: Positive request for confirmation with balance provided

MANUFACTURING CO LIMITED

15 South Street

London

Date

Messrs (customer)

In accordance with the request of our auditors, Arthur Daley LLP, we ask that you kindly confirm to them directly your indebtedness to us at (insert date) which, according to our records, amounted to £.......... as shown by the enclosed statement.

If the above amount is in agreement with your records, please sign in the space provided below and return this letter direct to our auditors in the enclosed stamped addressed envelope.

If the amount is not in agreement with your records, please notify our auditors directly of the amount shown by your records, and if possible detail on the reverse of this letter full particulars of the difference.

Yours faithfully,

For Manufacturing Co Limited

Reference No: ....

....

(Tear off slip)

The amount shown above is/is not * in agreement with our records as at (insert date)

Account No .... Signature ....

Date .... Title or position ....

* The position according to our records is shown overleaf.

Notes

1   The letter is on the client's paper, signed by the client.
2   A copy of the statement is attached (although that will not always be the case).
3   The reply is sent directly to the auditor in a pre-paid envelope.

Assurance providers will normally only contact a sample of customers although it must be based upon a complete list of all customers. In addition, when constructing the sample, the following classes of account should receive special attention:

- **Old unpaid accounts**
- **Accounts written off** during the period under review
- **Accounts with credit balances**
- **Accounts settled by round sum payments**

Similarly, the following should not be overlooked:

- **Accounts with nil balances**
- **Accounts** that have been **paid** by the date of the examination

Assurance providers will have to carry out further work in relation to those receivables who:

- **disagree** with the **balance stated** (positive and negative confirmation)
- **do not respond** (positive confirmation only)

In the case of disagreements, where the customer balance was stated, the customer response should have identified specific amounts that are disputed.

There is a **dispute** between the client and the customer. The reasons for the dispute would have to be identified, and specific allowances for receivables made if appropriate against the debt.

Cut-off problems exist, because the client records the following year's sales in the current year or because goods returned by the customer in the current year are not recorded in the current year. Cut-off testing may have to be extended.

The customer may have sent the **monies before** the year-end, but the monies were **not recorded** by the client as receipts until **after** the year-end. Detailed cut-off work may be required on receipts.

Monies received may have been posted to the **wrong account** or a cash-in-transit account. Assurance providers should check if there is evidence of other misposting. If the monies have been posted to a cash-in-transit account, assurance providers should ensure this account has been cleared promptly.

Customers who are also suppliers may **net off balances** owed and owing. Assurance providers should check that this is allowed.

Teeming and lading (stealing monies and **incorrectly posting** other receipts so that no particular customer is seriously in debt), is a fraud that can arise in this area. If assurance providers suspect teeming and lading has occurred, detailed testing will be required on cash receipts, particularly on prompt posting of cash receipts.

When the positive request method is used the assurance providers must follow up by all practicable means those customers who **fail to respond**. Second requests should be sent out in the event of no reply being received within two or three weeks and if necessary this may be followed by telephoning the customer, with the client's permission.

After two, or even three, attempts to obtain confirmation, a list of the outstanding items will normally be passed to a responsible company official, preferably independent of the sales accounting department, who will arrange for them to be investigated.

Where their confirmation is carried out before the year end, assurance providers will have to reconcile the balance agreed to the year-end balance by reviewing ledger records, invoices and receipts.

All confirmations, regardless of timing, must be properly recorded and evaluated. All **balance disagreements** and **non replies** must be **followed up** and their effect on total receivables evaluated.

Differences arising that merely represent **invoices** or **cash in transit** (normal timing differences) generally do not require adjustment, but disputed amounts, and errors by the client, may indicate that further substantive work is necessary to determine whether material adjustments are required.

3.2 Alternative procedures to verify existence/rights and obligations

If it proves impossible to get confirmations from individual customers, alternative procedures must be performed which may include the following.

Check receipt of cash after date

Verify valid purchase orders, although these will not necessarily have led to an invoice

Examine the account to see if the balance outstanding represents specific invoices and **confirm** their **validity** to despatch notes

Obtain explanations for **invoices remaining unpaid** after subsequent ones have been paid

Check if the **balance** on the account is **growing**, and if so, why

Test company's control over the issue of **credit notes** and the **write-off of irrecoverable receivables**

C
H
A
P
T
E
R

13

3.3 Irrecoverable receivables

A significant test of irrecoverable receivables will be reviewing the **cash received after** date. This will provide evidence of collectability of debts (and hence **valuation**). It also provides some evidence of correctness of title (**rights and obligations**), although ideally it should be carried out as well as a receivables confirmation (the main test on rights and obligations as outlined above).

3.4 Other receivables

A company may also have other receivables, such as royalties. It should be possible to verify such items to third party evidence, such as correspondence from the relevant partner, or by cash received after date.

Worked example: Audit of receivables

Sajeeda is working on the audit of General Stationery plc (GSP), a company that sells a large range of standard stationery items to businesses by mail order. GSP has a large receivables ledger. Although GSP has many established clients, it also receives a number of one-off or short-term customers, as some companies tend to shop around for the best deals on stationery at the time. GSP's controls over new customers and sales orders are good in principle, but controls testing has revealed weaknesses in their operation. In addition, some problems with goods despatch and invoicing were also discovered during controls testing. It has been concluded that substantial tests of detail are required in this area with quite a large sample of customer accounts being taken.

The major risks of misstatement of GSP's receivables balance arise from:

- customers disputing the balances due to requested credits and general problems with recording sales on customer accounts

- there being a high instance of irrecoverable receivables

Completeness

Sajeeda will:

- obtain a listing of receivables, and ensure that it casts correctly and agrees with the receivables balance in the financial statements and the sales ledger control account total in the nominal ledger

- check a sample of customers on the list against the individual sales ledger accounts

Rights and obligations/existence

Sajeeda will:

- select a sample of receivables balances and carry out confirmation procedures at the year end, using the positive approach, providing a statement of the customer's account

- follow up replies appropriately depending on their content

Valuation

Sajeeda will:

- obtain an analysis of aged debt at the year end from receivables ledger records and review it for debt in excess of GSP's published credit terms

- carry out an analysis of after-date receipts to observe whether any old debt remains outstanding at audit date

- if so, collate a list of old debt as yet unpaid and compare the results of any confirmation replies that are covered by the list

- cross-refer her list to any list of debt written off in the financial statements

- discuss old debts not written off with the credit controller to see what steps GSP has taken to recover the debt

- consider whether any of the debt requires writing off in the financial statements. This amount should be entered on a list of potential adjustments. If material, it should be referred to senior audit team members

It is the middle of the final audit visit to GSP. Sajeeda has received 54 out of 56 replies to her confirmation requests. Of these replies, 30 agree the balance stated and 24 dispute the balance. Customers who have not yet replied have been sent three reminders each.

Sajeeda will:

- pass the two outstanding requests to a senior official unconnected with sales for further follow up

- perform reconciliations on the 24 disputed balances, using the information given on the reply and the information available in the sales and receipts records of GSP

Of the 24 disputes, Sajeeda finds that 10 relate to timing differences with regard to receipts. She confirms that all of these receipts clear GSP's bank within reasonable time after the year end by checking the paying in records and bank statements. She can conclude that these 10 accounts are fairly stated.

The remaining 14 have differences resulting from requested credits, for damaged goods (some going back over six months), for invoices in relation to which there were no goods delivered and for invoices relating to different customers.

Sajeeda will:

- discuss the requested credits with the appropriate sales manager to determine why credits have not been issued and form an opinion as to whether these debts and related sales may need writing off

- trace invoices disputed due to lack of goods delivered, try and trace back to despatch notes to ascertain whether GSP states the goods were delivered and form an opinion as to whether these debts and related sales may need writing off

- consider the implications in terms of inventory movements if goods are being invoiced but not delivered – is inventory overstated; is a fraud being carried out where goods are being stolen?

- refer to copy invoices to confirm whether invoices were in fact sent to the wrong customers. These errors, while indicating a lack of control over invoicing, do not affect the overall total of receivables, as they are genuine sales to other customers

Sajeeda should:

- highlight to senior audit team members that performing substantive procedures has confirmed conclusions that controls in the area have been ineffective and proved that there is a problem with the receivables balance, and that the sample may have to be extended and further substantive procedures carried out in this area

Interactive question 3: Audit of receivables

Which **one** of the following procedures should be undertaken to confirm the rights and obligations of trade receivables?

- Review of cash received after date
- Tests of controls over ordering
- Receivables external confirmation
- Recalculation of specific allowance for doubtful debts

See **Answer** at the end of this chapter.

4 Bank

> **Section overview**
>
> - Key areas when testing the statement of financial position bank figure are:
>   - Confirming bank balances directly with the bank (existence, valuation, rights and obligations)
>   - Confirming reconciling differences calculated by the client are reasonable (completeness, valuation)
>   - Confirming any material cash balances held at the client are correctly stated (valuation)

The major risks of misstatement of the bank and cash balance in the financial statements are due to:

- not all bank balances owned by the client being disclosed (rights and obligations/existence)
- reconciliation differences between bank balance and cash book balance being misstated (valuation)
- material cash floats being omitted or misstated (completeness/existence)

The objective of tests in respect of bank is therefore to prove that these assertions about the assets are correct. The following sources of information can be used:

- Cash book
- Confirmation from the bank
- Bank statements
- Bank reconciliation carried out by the client

4.1 Direct confirmation with bank

Testing of bank balances will need to cover **completeness, existence, rights and obligations and valuation**. All of these elements can be tested directly through the device of obtaining third party confirmations from the client's banks and reconciling these with the accounting records, having regard to cut off. The assurance providers should update details of bank accounts held.

The form and content of a confirmation request letter (bank letter) will depend on the purpose for which it is required and on local practices.

The most commonly requested information is in respect of balances due to or from the client entity on **current, deposit, loan and other accounts**. The request letter should provide the account description number and the type of currency for the account.

It may also be advisable to request information about **nil balances** on accounts, and accounts which were closed in the twelve months prior to the chosen confirmation date. The client entity may ask for confirmation not only of the balances on accounts but also, where it may be helpful, other information, such as the maturity and interest terms, unused facilities, lines of credit/standby facilities, any offset or other rights or encumbrances, and details of any collateral given or received.

The client entity and its assurance providers are likely to request confirmation of **contingent liabilities**, such as those arising on guarantees, comfort letters, bills and so on.

Banks often hold **securities** and other items in safe custody on behalf of customers. A request letter may thus ask for confirmation of such items held by the confirming bank.

The procedure is simple but important.

(a) The banks will require **explicit written authority** from their client to disclose the information requested.

(b) The **assurance providers' request** must **refer** to the **client's letter** of authority and the date thereof. Alternatively it may be countersigned by the client or it may be accompanied by a specific letter of authority.

(c) In the case of joint accounts, **letters of authority** signed by all **parties** will be necessary.

(d)   Such **letters** of **authority** may either **give permission** to the bank to disclose information for a specific request or grant permission for an indeterminate length of time.

(e)   The request should **reach** the **branch manager** at least **two weeks in advance** of the client's **year-end** and should state both that year-end date and the previous year-end date.

(f)   The **assurance providers** should themselves **check** that the bank response covers all the information in the standard and other responses.

4.2   Bank reconciliation

Care must be taken to ensure that there is no **window dressing**, by checking **cut off** carefully. Window dressing in this context is usually manifested as an attempt to overstate the liquidity of the company by:

(a)   keeping the cash book open to take credit for **remittances actually received** after the year-end, thus enhancing the balance at bank and reducing receivables, as cash is more liquid than debt; and

(b)   **recording cheques paid** in the period under review which are not actually despatched until after the year-end, thus decreasing the balance at bank and reducing payables. This can contrive to present an artificially healthy looking current ratio.

With the possibility of (a) above in mind, where lodgements have not been cleared by the bank until the new period, the **assurance providers** should **examine the paying in slip** to ensure that the amounts were actually paid into the bank on or before the end of the reporting period.

As regards (b) above, where there appears to be a particularly **large number of outstanding cheques** at the year-end, the **assurance providers** should check whether these were **cleared within** a **reasonable time** in the new period. If not, this may indicate that despatch occurred after the year-end.

4.3   Cash count

Planning is an essential element of cash counts, for it is an important principle that all cash balances are counted at the same time as far as possible. Cash in this context may include unbanked cheques received, IOUs and credit card slips, in addition to notes and coins. Often such cash balances are unlikely to be material, but in certain businesses they may be.

As part of their planning procedures the **assurance providers** will hence need to determine the **locations** where cash is held and which of these locations (if any) warrant a count.

Planning decisions will need to be recorded on the current audit file including:

* The **precise time** of the count(s) and location(s)
* The **names** of the **audit staff** conducting the counts
* The **names** of the **client staff** intending to be present at each location

Where a location is not visited it may be expedient to obtain a letter from the client confirming the balance.

The following matters apply to the count itself.

* All cash/petty **cash books** should be **written up** to date in ink (or other permanent form) at the time of the count.

* All **balances** must be **counted** at the **same time**.

* At **no time** should the **assurance providers** be left **alone** with the cash and negotiable securities.

* **All cash counted** must be **recorded** on working papers subsequently filed on the current audit file. Reconciliations should be prepared where applicable (for example imprest petty cash float).

Worked example: Audit of bank

Tracey is working on the audit of the bank reconciliation at IT Limited (ITL), a computer systems company. She has obtained the following bank reconciliation.

Bank reconciliation at 31 December 20X6

	£	£
Balance per bank statement		79,938
Less unpresented cheques		
Cheque number		
13539	(24,933)	
13540	(54,388)	
13542	(64,420)	
13543	(3,492)	
13544	(1,849)	
13545	(53,944)	
13546	(940)	
		(203,966)
		(124,028)
Bal c/f		(124,028)
Add outstanding lodgements		
Date in cash book		
27.12	355	
28.12	103,344	
31.12	39,455	
31.12	5,301	
		148,455
Balance per financial statements		24,427

The bank letter confirmed the balance per bank given in the bank reconciliation.

Tracey will:

- trace unpresented cheques to bank statements after the year end to confirm what date they cleared the bank

- review paying in books and bank statements in respect of the lodgements, to see what date they were paid into the bank

- enquire why a substantial lodgement remained unbanked for three days prior to the year end

---

Interactive question 4: Bank balance

Which **one** of the following will be confirmed by obtaining a bank letter from a specific bank?

- [ ] That the bank balance stated on the bank reconciliation is correct.
- [ ] That the unpresented cheques listed on the bank reconciliation were sent out pre year-end.
- [ ] That the company possesses only the bank accounts it declares.
- [ ] That the cash floats of the company are fairly stated.

See **Answer** at the end of this chapter.

5 Payables

Section overview

- Key areas when testing payables are:
    - ensuring that all liabilities are included (completeness)
    - confirming that all liabilities are *bona fide* owed by the company (rights and obligations)

The major risks of misstatements of payables in the financial statements are due to:

- the entity understating its liabilities in the financial statements (completeness)
- cut-off between goods inward and liability recording being incorrect (cut-off)
- (more rarely) non-existent liabilities being declared (existence, rights and obligations)

The objective of tests in respect of payables is therefore to prove that these assertions about the liabilities are correct. The following sources of information can be used:

- Payables ledger records
- Confirmations from suppliers

Analytical procedures could point to understatement if the account balance is inexplicably reduced from previous years.

5.1 Supplier statements

The most important test when considering **trade payables** is comparison of suppliers' statements with payables ledger balances.

When selecting a sample of payables to test, assurance providers must be careful not just to select suppliers with large year-end balances. Remember, it is errors of **understatement** that assurance providers are primarily interested in when reviewing payables, and errors of understatement could occur equally in payables with low or nil balances as with high.

When comparing **supplier statements** with **year-end payables ledger balances**, assurance providers should include within their sample payables with nil or negative **payables ledger** balances. Assurance providers should be particularly wary of low balances with major suppliers. Remember the client has no incentive to record liabilities before being invoiced. The sample should be selected from the client's list of suppliers, not the payables ledger.

You may be wondering, as we normally carry out a circularisation confirmation of receivables, whether we would also circularise suppliers. The answer is generally no.

The principal reason for this lies in the nature of the purchases cycle: third party evidence in the form of suppliers' invoices and, even more significantly, **suppliers' statements**, are part of the standard documentation of the cycle. The assurance providers will hence concentrate on these documents when designing and conducting their tests.

In the following circumstances the assurance providers may, however, determine that a confirmation is necessary. In these cases confirmation requests should be sent out and processed in a similar way to accounts receivable confirmation requests. 'Positive' replies will be required where:

- **suppliers' statements** are, for whatever reason, **unavailable** or **incomplete**

- **weaknesses in internal control** or the nature of the client's business make possible a material misstatement of liabilities that would not otherwise be picked up

- it is thought that the **client** is **deliberately** trying to **understate payables**

- the **accounts** appear to be **irregular** or if the nature or size of balances or transactions is abnormal

5.2 Other payables/accrued expenses

Companies may have other **payables** and the tests carried out on them will vary according to what the nature of that account is. Remember that you are primarily testing for understatement. Consider whether you can obtain third party evidence about the balance. You may have to think laterally about the specific balance.

An **accrual** is a type of payable, and is made when an expense has been incurred in the current period, but will not be paid for until the next period. Typically, an accrual is made when a company not only has not paid for the item, but has not even received an invoice at the period end. In order to include these expenses the company draws up a list of accruals. Examples of accruals include recurring items, such as utility expenses and bank interest, as well as one-offs such as the audit fee.

The amount of some accruals may be known precisely, but in some cases the amount to accrue has to be **estimated**. In cases where the invoice covers a period straddling the year end, it may be necessary to **prorate** an expense ie, to accrue for only the proportion of the expense which falls before the period end (eg, the two months of a three-month phone bill which relates to the reporting period).

The audit of accruals focuses primarily on **cut-off** and **completeness**. Here, cut-off means that the amount accrued relates to the reporting period eg, that two months of the three-month phone bill have been accrued (up to the period end) rather than two and half months, which would be inaccurate. Cut-off can therefore be **tested** by the auditor making her own estimate of the accrual and comparing this with the amount accrued by the entity.

Completeness means that no accruals have been missed. This can be **tested** by reviewing the entity's purchase invoices received after the period end. Any invoices which relate to the reporting period should be accrued for.

Worked example: Audit of payables

Ugo is working on the audit of payables at Seriously Dodgy Limited (SDL). He has carried out analytical procedures on the payables balance, comparing it with prior years, month by month balance owing levels, levels of purchases during the year and the change in inventory levels from beginning to end of the year.

Ugo has enquired about obtaining supplier statements at the year-end, and the **payables ledger** clerk has directed him to a file where they are kept. She tells him that not all the suppliers send statements, so they only reconcile the ones they get. Ugo confirms this with the audit file from the previous year. On examination of the file, however, Ugo notes that at least three suppliers which sent statements last year have apparently not sent statements this year. In addition, SDL has started major accounts with three new suppliers in the year, none of which has sent a statement.

As a result of this, and the results of his analytical procedures, which indicate that there may be a discrepancy between the level of purchases and the published payables at the year end, he suspects that SDL may be trying to understate payables.

Ugo therefore alerts senior audit staff members to his suspicions and makes a recommendation that a supplier circularisation be carried out as a one-off exercise.

Interactive question 5: Audit of payables

Indicate whether the following statements are true or false.

	True	False
(a) Supplier statements are a strong source of evidence as they are third party evidence; however, as the assurance provider receives them through the medium of the client, the assurance provider must treat supplier statements with professional scepticism.	☐	☐
(b) Payables may be tested by cash payments after date as these give an indication that debts were owed and the value of those debts has not been understated.	☐	☐

See **Answer** at the end of this chapter.

6 Long-term liabilities

Section overview

- Risks include failure to make correct disclosures and miscalculation of interest.
- There should be third party evidence from lender.

We are concerned here with long-term liabilities comprising debentures, loan stock and other loans **repayable** at a date **more than one year after the year-end**. The major risks of misstatement of long-term liabilities are:

- that not all long-term liabilities have been disclosed (completeness)

- that interest payable has not been calculated correctly and included in the correct accounting period (accuracy and cut-off)

- that disclosure is incorrect (presentation and disclosure)

A complication for the assurance provider is that debenture and loan agreements frequently contain conditions with which the company must comply, including restrictions on the company's total borrowings and adherence to specific borrowing ratios.

The following sources of information exist:

- Schedule of loans/prior year audit file information
- Statutory books, such as register of debentures, articles of association
- Loan agreements
- Bank letter and direct confirmations from other lenders
- Cash book
- Board minutes
- Client schedules and calculations
- Accounting policies in the financial statements

Plan: Long-term liabilities

Obtain/prepare schedule of loans outstanding at the end of the reporting period showing, for each loan: name of lender, date of loan, maturity date, interest date, interest rate, balance at the end of the period and security

Compare opening balances to previous year's working papers

Test the clerical accuracy of the analysis

Compare balances to the **nominal ledger**

Check name of **lender** etc, to **register** of **debenture holders** or equivalent (if kept)

Trace additions and **repayments** to **entries** in the **cash book**

Confirm repayments are in accordance with **loan agreement**

Examine cancelled cheques and **memoranda of satisfaction** for **loans repaid**

Verify that **borrowing limits** imposed either by Articles or by other agreements are **not exceeded**

Examine signed Board minutes relating to **new borrowings/repayments**

Obtain direct confirmation from **lenders** of the amounts outstanding, accrued interest and what security they hold

Verify interest charged for the period and the adequacy of accrued interest

Confirm assets charged have been **entered** in the **register of charges** and **notified** to the **Registrar**

Review restrictive covenants and provisions relating to default·
- **Review** any **correspondence** relating to the loan
- **Review confirmation** replies for non-compliance
- If a **default appears** to exist, **determine** its **effect**, and schedule findings

Review minutes, cash book to **check** if all **loans have been recorded**

7 Statement or profit or loss items

Section overview
- A key area when testing statement of profit or loss items is completeness.

7.1 Revenue

It was stated in Chapter 6 that revenue will often be tested by testing controls. Subsequent testing on revenue will usually involve analytical procedures, as revenue is the area of the business the company is most likely to have information and analysis about. In addition, revenue has predictable relationships with other items in the financial statements, notably receivables, about which it is possible to obtain strong third party evidence as outlined above.

Revenue can also be tested by vouching individual transactions. If the major risk with revenue at a particular client is that it is overstated, this would involve selecting individual items of revenue recorded in the nominal ledger and tracing back to source documents, such as sales invoice, then despatch notes.

7.2 Purchases

As noted in Chapter 7, purchases are often tested by testing controls in that area. Additional or alternative substantive procedures will often include the use of analytical procedures due to the strong relationships that purchases has with other items in financial statements, notably inventory and payables.

In addition, individual transactions can be tested, commencing with goods received notes and tracing transactions through the system to ensure completeness.

7.3 Payroll costs

Analytical procedures are often carried out on payroll costs as there are strong relationships between numbers of staff, pay rates and overall costs and also tax/NI rates and pay.

Tests of details to verify if payroll costs might include checking for a sample of payroll records that time worked has been correctly included (to clockcards), employees exist (personnel records) and are being paid at the correct rate (contracts/personnel records) and that the payroll is calculated correctly (by reperforming calculations).

Payments from the payroll to staff and tax authorities can be verified to bank statements. Postings from the payroll to the nominal ledger should also be checked.

7.4 Interest paid/received

Interest paid/received can usually be tested by inspecting bank statements, or confirmations from other lenders.

7.5 Expenses

Other expenses in the statement of profit or loss can be tested by analytical procedures, and also by vouching specific transactions to purchase invoices.

7.6 Summary of matters which should be reported to more senior staff

The following table applies to any of the areas of the financial statements covered in this chapter, and gives examples of matters which should be reported to more senior staff.

Matters which should be referred to a senior member of staff
Conclusions of audit procedures performed. This is crucial if the conclusion is negative eg, that controls in the area being tested are ineffective.
Exceptional items discovered when performing procedures eg, transactions outside the normal course of business, and transactions above or below market rates.
Any **unusual** accounting entries noticed. These could be misstatements, or may be subject to different reporting requirements eg, related party transactions.
Any **indications of possible money laundering**. It may be necessary for the junior to report the matter to the firm's MLRO rather than to more senior staff.
Issues which need to be **discussed with the client**. Different firms have different norms here; in some it is usual for the junior member of staff to discuss issues with the client staff, but in others this would always be done by a senior member of staff. Junior staff should generally behave in accordance with their firm's expectations, referring matters up to senior staff as appropriate. Where the junior member of staff discusses issues directly with the client staff, the client's responses should be clearly recorded in the audit file. If these responses appear unclear or ambiguous, this should be raised and discussed with a senior member of staff.
Anything which the junior member of staff is **unsure about** or does not understand. It may not be always necessary to raise an exception on the audit file, so the matter should first be discussed with more senior staff. This is important both for the junior's professional development and also because it may be that they do not understand the matter because it contains a misstatement.

CHAPTER

13

Summary

Non-current assets

Key issues:
Existence, rights and obligations, completeness, valuation

Sources of information:
Third party valuations, invoices, auditor inspection (strong)
Client schedules and calculations (not so strong)

Inventory

Key issues:
Existence, valuation

Sources of information:
Auditor attendance at count, invoices, third party confirmations (strong)
Client controls over count, client production schedules (not so strong)

Receivables

Key issues:
Rights and obligations, valuation

Sources of information:
Third party confirmations, cash payments after date (strong)

Payables

Key issues:
Completeness

Sources of information:
Supplier statements (strong, but open to tampering by client)

Bank

Key issues:
Completeness, existence, rights and obligations, valuation

Sources of information:
Confirmation from bank, bank statements (strong)
Client schedules, reconciliations (not so strong)

Long-term liabilities

Key issues:
Completeness, accuracy, disclosure

Sources of information:
Loan documentation, statutory books, confirmations from lenders (strong)
Client schedules, board minutes, client calculations (not so strong)

Statement of profit or loss

Key issue:
Completeness

Self-test

Answer the following questions.

1   Complete the table, showing which tests on tangible non-current assets are designed to provide evidence about which financial statement assertion.

Completeness	Existence
Accuracy, valuation and allocation	**Rights and obligations**

(a)   Inspect assets

(b)   Verify to valuation certificate

(c)   Refer to title deeds

(d)   Compare assets in ledger to non-current asset register

(e)   Review depreciation rates

(f)   Verify material on self-constructed assets to invoices

(g)   Examine invoices after the year end

(h)   Review repairs in nominal ledger

2   Should the following inventory counting tests take place before, during or after the count?

	Before	During	After
(a) Check client staff are following instructions	☐	☐	☐
(b) Review previous year's inventory count arrangements	☐	☐	☐
(c) Assess method of accounting for inventories	☐	☐	☐
(d) Trace counted items to final inventory sheets	☐	☐	☐
(e) Check replies from 3rd parties re inventory held for them	☐	☐	☐
(f) Conclude whether count has been properly carried out	☐	☐	☐
(g) Gain an overall impression of levels/values of inventory	☐	☐	☐
(h) Consider the need for expert help	☐	☐	☐

3   Which of the following is not a reason why NRV of inventory should be lower than cost?

A   An increase in costs or a fall in selling price
B   Physical deterioration
C   A marketing decision to manufacture and sell products at a loss
D   Errors in recording or counting

4   The negative method of receivables' external confirmation should only be used if the client has a good internal control and a small number of large receivables accounts.

☐   True

☐   False

5   Complete these two sentences of the audit tests performed to verify the bank reconciliation.

   (a) Trace cheques shown as outstanding on the .... to the ....
        .... prior to the year end and ....
        ....

   (b) Obtain satisfactory explanations for all items in the .... for which
        there is no corresponding entry in the .... and ....
        ....

6   At which **two** of the following locations would auditors expect to see more substantial cash floats?

   ☐ Hotels

   ☐ Retail outlets

   ☐ Manufacturing company

   ☐ Solicitor's practice

7   Nil balances should not be included in a supplier statement test.

   ☐ True

   ☐ False

Now, go back to the Learning Objectives in the Introduction. If you are satisfied you have achieved these objectives, please tick them off.

1 Receivables

- Confirmations from customers   ISA (UK) 505

Answer to Interactive question 1

A purchase invoice, a registration document and a hire-purchase agreement.

Answer to Interactive question 2

Attendance at inventory count.

Answer to Interactive question 3

Receivables external confirmation.

Answer to Interactive question 4

That the bank balance stated on the bank reconciliation is correct. The others are incorrect for the following reasons:

- That the unpresented cheques listed on the bank reconciliation were sent out pre year-end. (These will not be accounted for in the bank's year-end balance; only bank statements after the reporting period will indicate whether these may have been held back.)

- That the company possesses only the bank accounts it declares. (As the company may have bank accounts with a different bank.)

- That the cash floats of the company are fairly stated. (As cash floats at the company are not within the scope of the bank letter.)

Answer to Interactive question 5

(a) True. Assurance providers must always behave with professional scepticism, not assuming that documents such as supplier statements have been tampered with, but bearing in mind that it is a possibility if indications arise supporting that suggestion.

(b) False. Cash payments after date do not prove that the balance is not understated, as the client may control the payments it makes and conceal correspondence from suppliers requesting full payment.

Answers to Self-test

1

Completeness	Existence
(d) Compare assets in ledger to non-current asset register	(a) Inspect assets
(h) Review repairs in nominal ledger	
Accuracy, valuation and allocation	**Rights and obligations**
(b) Verify to valuation certificate	(c) Refer to title deeds
(e) Review depreciation rates	(g) Examine invoices after the year end
(f) Verify material on self-constructed assets to invoices	

2   (a) During   (b) Before   (c) Before   (d) After
    (e) After   (f) During   (g) During   (h) Before

3   D   Errors in recording or counting

4   False

5   (a) Bank reconciliation, cash book, after date bank statements

    (b) Bank statements, cash book, bank reconciliation

6   Hotels and retail outlets

7   False

CHAPTER 14

Codes of professional ethics

Introduction

Examination context

Topic List

1 Professional ethics

2 IESBA Code

3 ICAEW Code

4 FRC *Ethical Standard*

Summary and Self-test

Answer to Interactive question

Answers to Self-test

Introduction

Learning objectives

- Be aware of the key ethical codes to which ICAEW members are subject and the sources that influence them
- Understand the difference between principles and rules based systems
- Understand why ethics are important to accountants
- Know the key features of IESBA and ICAEW Codes
- Know the fundamental principles of IESBA and ICAEW Codes

Specific syllabus references for this chapter are : 4a, b, c, d, e.

Syllabus links

You will build on the principles of professional ethics you learn here in your Audit and Assurance paper.

Examination context

Ethics is 20% of the syllabus, and therefore in the sample paper, there were ten questions on ethics. These were a combination of questions about general ethical concepts and principles, which we shall look at in this chapter, and more detailed ethical threats and safeguards, which we shall look at in the next two chapters.

In the assessment, candidates may be required to:

- state the role of ethical codes and their importance to the profession
- recognise the differences between a rules based ethical code and one based upon a set of principles
- identify the key features of the system of professional ethics adopted by IESBA and ICAEW
- identify the fundamental principles underlying the IESBA and the ICAEW *Code of Ethics*

1 Professional ethics

Section overview

- Accountants require an ethical code because they hold positions of trust, and people rely on them.

- Accountants work in the public interest, which extends beyond clients to people associated with those clients and the general community.

- ICAEW members are subject to ICAEW guidance (influenced by IESBA guidance) and FRC standards.

- Guidance tends to be issued in the form of principles rather than hard and fast rules.

1.1 Need for ethics

Professional accountants have a responsibility to consider the public interest and maintain the reputation of the accounting profession. Personal self-interest must not prevail over these duties. The IESBA and ICAEW Codes of Ethics help accountants to meet these obligations by setting out ethical guidance to be followed.

Acting in the public interest involves having regard to the legitimate interests of clients, government, financial institutions, employees, investors, the business and financial community and others who rely upon the objectivity and integrity of the accounting profession to support the propriety and orderly functioning of commerce.

In summary, then, the key reason accountants need to have an ethical code is that **people rely on them and their expertise**. It is important to note that this reliance extends beyond clients to the general community.

Accountants deal with a range of issues on behalf of clients. They often have access to confidential and sensitive information. Auditors (and other assurance providers) claim to give an independent view. It is therefore critical that accountants (particularly those giving assurance) are independent.

Compliance with a shared set of ethical guidelines gives protection to accountants as well, as they cannot be accused of behaving differently from (that is, less well than) other accountants.

1.2 Sources of ethical guidance

ICAEW members (and trainees) and employees of member firms are subject to the ICAEW *Code of Ethics*. This is influenced by the guidance of IFAC (the International Federation of Accountants, of which ICAEW is a member), which is actually issued by the IESBA (a body of IFAC) as the IESBA *Code of Ethics for Professional Accountants*. This is referred to here as the IESBA *Code of Ethics*. You should already be aware of this body as it is the same body that issues International Standards on Auditing, which we have been studying in this Study Manual.

UK auditors are also subject to the FRC's *Ethical Standard* (formerly the 'Ethical Standards for Auditors'). The FRC is the Financial Reporting Council in the UK, which also issues auditing standards (adopted from IFAC, which creates them).

1.3 Rules- or principles-based guidance?

The ethical guidance we shall look at tends to be in the form of a principles-based framework. It contains some rules (as we shall see in the next chapter), but in the main it is flexible guidance. It can be seen as being a framework of principles rather than a set of rules. There are a number of advantages of a framework of principles over a system of ethical rules, which are outlined in the following table.

Factor	Explanation
Active consideration and demonstration of conclusions	A framework of principles places the onus on the accountant to actively consider independence for every given situation, rather than just agreeing a checklist of forbidden items. It also requires him to demonstrate that a responsible conclusion has been reached about ethical issues.
Broad interpretation of ethical situations	A principles-based framework prevents auditors interpreting legalistic requirements narrowly to get around ethical requirements. There is an element to which rules engender deception whereas principles encourage compliance.
Individual situations covered	A principles-based framework allows for the variations that are found in individual situations. Each situation is likely to be different.
Flexible to changing situation	A principles-based framework can accommodate a rapidly changing environment, such as the one that assurance providers are involved in.
Can incorporate prohibitions	However, a principle-based framework can contain certain prohibitions where these are necessary.

2 IESBA Code

Section overview

- The IESBA Code contains a number of fundamental principles.

- It also gives guidance on the meaning of independence and the approach accountants should take to ethical questions.

- The IESBA Code sets out a number of general threats to independence and categories of safeguards.

The IESBA Code contains a number of fundamental principles. It then goes on to outline key issues of ethics, such as independence, and highlight general and specific threats to independence and the safeguards that can be implemented to reduce those threats. A key issue to remember is that if it is impossible to reduce a threat to an acceptable level, the threat must be avoided (for example, by not accepting an engagement).

2.1 Fundamental principles

The fundamental principles as follows.

- **Integrity.** To be straightforward and honest in all professional and business relationships.

- **Objectivity.** To not allow bias, conflict of interest or undue influence of others to override professional or business judgements.

- **Professional competence and due care.** To maintain professional knowledge and skill at the level required to ensure that a client or employer receives competent professional service based on current developments in practice, legislation and techniques, and act diligently and in accordance with applicable technical and professional standards.

- **Confidentiality.** To respect the confidentiality of information acquired as a result of professional and business relationships and, therefore, not disclose any such information to third parties without proper and specific authority, unless there is a legal or professional right or duty to disclose, nor use the information for the personal advantage of the professional accountant or third parties.

- **Professional behaviour.** To comply with relevant laws and regulations and avoid any action that discredits the profession.

Professional accountants shall conduct themselves with courtesy and consideration towards all with whom they come into contact when performing their work.

In marketing and promoting themselves and their work, professional accountants shall not make:

- exaggerated claims for the services they are able to offer, the qualifications they possess, or experience they have gained; or

- disparaging references or unsubstantiated comparisons to the work of others.

2.2 Independence

IESBA Code

'It is in the public interest and, therefore, required by this Code of Ethics, that members of assurance teams and firms be independent of assurance clients and that any threats that the firm has reason to believe are created by a network firm's interests and relationships be evaluated.'

The Code discusses independence in the light of the wider term 'assurance engagements' and separately in relation to audits.

The guidance states its purpose in a series of steps. It aims to help firms and members:

Step 1

Identify threats to independence

Step 2

Evaluate whether the threats are insignificant

Step 3

Apply safeguards, when necessary, to eliminate the threats or reduce them to an acceptable level.

It also recognises that there may be occasions **where no safeguard is available**. In such a situation, it is only appropriate to:

- **eliminate the interest** or activities causing the threat; or
- **decline the engagement**, or discontinue it.

Definitions

Independence of mind: The state of mind that permits the expression of a conclusion without being affected by influences that compromise professional judgement, allowing an individual to act with integrity, and exercise objectivity and professional scepticism.

Independence in appearance: The avoidance of facts and circumstances that are so significant that a reasonable and informed third party would be likely to conclude, weighing all the specific facts and circumstances, that a firm's, or a member of the assurance team's, integrity, objectivity or professional scepticism has been compromised.

The degree of independence required is highest for an audit engagement, with less stringent requirements for non-audit engagements at an audit client, and engagements at non-audit clients.

2.3 Threats and safeguards

The following general points are made in the Code. We shall look at more specific guidance in the following chapters.

There are five general sources of threat identified by the Code. The FRC's Ethical Standard (*section 1*) identifies a sixth threat (the management threat):

- **Self-interest** threat (for example, having a financial interest in a client)

- **Self-review** threat (for example, auditing financial statements prepared by the firm)

- **Advocacy** threat (for example, promoting the client's position by dealing in its shares)

- **Familiarity** threat (for example, an audit team member having family at the client)

- **Intimidation** threat (for example, threats of replacement due to disagreement)

- **Management** threat (for example, doing work that should be carried out by management, such as the design and implementation of IT systems)

There are two general categories of safeguard identified by the Code:

- Safeguards created by the profession, legislation or regulation
- Safeguards within the work environment

Examples of safeguards created by the profession, legislation or regulation:

- Educational training and experience requirements for entry into the profession

- Continuing professional development requirements

- Corporate governance regulations

- Professional standards

- Professional or regulatory monitoring and disciplinary procedures

- External review by a legally empowered third party of the reports, returns, communication or information produced by a professional accountant

Examples of safeguards in the work environment:

- Involving an additional professional accountant to review the work done or otherwise advise as necessary

- Consulting an independent third party, such as a committee of independent directors, a professional regulatory body or another professional accountant

- Rotating senior personnel

- Discussing ethical issues with those in charge of client governance

- Disclosing to those charged with governance the nature of services provided and extent of fees charged

- Involving another firm to perform or re-perform part of the engagement

The team and the firm should be independent **during the period of the engagement.**

The period of the engagement is from the commencement of work until the signing of the final report being produced. For a **recurring audit**, independence may only cease on **termination of the contract** between the parties.

3 ICAEW Code

Section overview

- The ICAEW Code is relevant to professional accountants in all of their professional and business activities.

- The ICAEW Code incorporates the IESBA *Code of Ethics*, but also contains additional rules deemed appropriate by ICAEW.

The ICAEW Code states that 'professional accountants are expected to follow the guidance contained in the fundamental principles in all of their professional and business activities whether carried out with or without reward and in other circumstances where to fail to do so would bring discredit to the profession.'

Therefore the Code may apply not only to the job of the professional accountant but also to the life of the professional accountant, particularly if he is involved in matters relevant to his profession, such as keeping the books for a private club of which he is a member.

The Code also states that professional accountants are required to follow the spirit as well as the letter of the guidance. In other words, a specific matter being excluded from the guidance does not mean that the accountant does not have to think about it; rather he must determine if the spirit of the guidance would also apply to that situation.

The ICAEW Code implements the IESBA Code above so that following it ensures compliance with the IESBA Code.

4 FRC *Ethical Standard*

Section overview

- The FRC has issued an ethical standard with which UK auditors must comply when carrying out audits.

- The ethical standard was drafted with the IESBA *Code of Ethics* in mind.

As noted above, the FRC has issued an ethical standard (ES) with which UK auditors must comply when carrying out UK audits. The current *Ethical Standard* brings together in one document the guidance which was previously contained within five separate 'Ethical Standards for Auditors'.

There is also an ES with provisions available for smaller entities, which is not examinable. This offers exemptions and special rules to the auditors of smaller entities.

These standards were developed with regard to the IESBA *Code of Ethics* and also the EC Recommendation on the independence of statutory audits.

Interactive question: Ethical codes

There are two main approaches to a code of professional ethics: a rules-based ethical code and a code based on a set of principles.

Indicate whether the following statements are true or false.

(a) A code based on a set of principles rather than rules is more flexible in a rapidly changing environment. ☐ True ☐ False

(b) ICAEW's *Code of Ethics* is principles based. ☐ True ☐ False

(c) A code based on a set of rules requires accountants to evaluate and address threats to independence. ☐ True ☐ False

See **Answer** at the end of this chapter.

Summary and Self-test

Summary

Accountants require an ethical code because they hold positions of trust and people rely on them

A principles based system:
- Allows flexibility
- Allows broad interpretation
- Encourages evaluation
- Allows for individual situations
- Can contain rules

The IESBA Code is principles based. It contains a number of fundamental principles and then goes on to focus on the importance of independence, and threats of self-interest, self-review, advocacy, familiarity and intimidation

The ICAEW Code is compulsory for members in their professional lives and where actions in their personal life would discredit the profession. It implements the IESBA Code

The FRC has issued its Ethical Standard, with which UK auditors must comply when carrying out UK audits. This standard applies the principles of the IESBA Code

Self-test

Answer the following questions.

1   Which **two** of the following statements are correct?

   (a)   Accountants must have ethical codes because people rely on accountants.

     ☐ Yes

     ☐ No

   (b)   A set of ethical principles gives protection to accountants as it means they are all working to the same guidelines.

     ☐ Yes

     ☐ No

   (c)   Rules-based codes provide better protection to users of accountancy services because every potential situation arising is covered by them.

     ☐ Yes

     ☐ No

2   Are the following statements true or false?

   (a)   The principle of integrity can be defined as the accountant not allowing bias, conflict of interest or undue influence of others to override his choice of actions.

     ☐ True

     ☐ False

   (b)   Accountants may use information obtained during the course of their professional work for personal use so long as they do not disclose it to others in breach of their duty of confidentiality.

     ☐ True

     ☐ False

   (c)   Professional accountants should be technically up to date so as to give appropriate advice to clients.

     ☐ True

     ☐ False

3   The following are examples of which types of general threats to independence?

   (a)   The financial statements of Dropdown Ltd have been prepared by Glazer Brothers LLP, their audit firm.

   (b)   Know how plc has intimated to the audit firm that if they do not receive an unqualified auditor's opinion for the year 20X6, they may put the audit out to tender.

4   The ICAEW Code implements the IESBA Code.

     ☐ True

     ☐ False

5   The FRC's Ethical Standard applies to UK audits and assurance work.

     ☐ True

     ☐ False

Now, go back to the Learning Objectives in the Introduction. If you are satisfied you have achieved these objectives, please tick them off.

Answer to Interactive question

(a) True – it is an advantage of the principles-based approach

(b) True – it implements the IESBA Code, which is principles-based

(c) False – a rules based system tends to remove the need to evaluate, as accountants can just check whether certain rules are being met or not, rather than applying the principles to given situations.

Answers to Self-test

1   (a) and (b) are correct; (c) is incorrect, as this would be true of a principles-based system, not a rules-based system

2   (a) is false; this is a description of objectivity. (b) is false; accountants are not entitled to use confidential information for their own personal good. (c) is true

3   (a)   Self-review
      (b)   Intimidation

4   True

5   False – they apply to UK audits only.

CHAPTER 15

Integrity, objectivity and independence

Introduction

Examination context

Topic List

Summary and Self-test

Answers to Interactive questions

Answers to Self-test

Introduction

Learning objectives

Tick off

- Understand the concepts of integrity, objectivity and independence

- Recognise the importance of integrity, objectivity and independence

- Identify threats to integrity, objectivity and independence

- Identify safeguards for integrity, objectivity and independence

- Be able to suggest sensible measures to resolve ethical conflicts

- Be able to suggest how conflicts of interest between employee duty and professional duty may be resolved

Specific syllabus references for this chapter are: 4f, g, h, l, m, n, o.

Syllabus links

All these ethical matters will be considered further in Audit and Assurance.

Examination context

As we saw in the previous chapter, ethics is an important area for your exam. The sample paper contained six practical, scenario-based questions about issues relating to independence. In addition, there was a question on a conflict for an employed accountant working in industry between the needs of his employer and his professional duty.

In the assessment, candidates may be required to:

- determine an appropriate course of action in situations that may impair or threaten integrity and objectivity

- respond appropriately to the request of an employer to undertake work outside the confines of an individual's expertise or experience

- identify the principal types of threat to independence which arise in a set of given circumstances

- identify safeguards to eliminate or reduce threats to independence

- suggest how a conflict of loyalty between the duty a professional accountant has to their employer and the duty to their profession could be resolved

1 Integrity, objectivity and independence

Section overview

- Independence and objectivity matter because of the trust clients and the public have in the assurance provider.

- Safeguards should be applied when independence and objectivity are put at risk.

- If the risks are too great for safeguards to be effective, then the assurance provider should not accept or should withdraw from the engagement.

We looked at the importance of independence in the IESBA Code in the previous chapter. The fundamental principles of integrity and objectivity were also introduced. In this chapter we shall look more closely at these three issues, the threats to them that exist and the safeguards that can be applied to reduce the risks to a level determined to be acceptable by partners in the audit firm. Remember, however, that the ethical principles state that some risks cannot be reduced by safeguards and should therefore be avoided.

Definitions

Integrity: This means that an accountant must be straightforward and honest. It implies fair dealing and truthfulness.

Objectivity: This is a state of mind that excludes bias, prejudice and compromise and that gives fair and impartial consideration to all matters that are relevant to the task in hand, disregarding those that are not.

Independence is related to and underpins objectivity – it is freedom from situations and relationships that make it probable that a reasonable and informed third party would conclude that objectivity either is impaired or could be impaired.

In other words, objectivity relates to the state of the accountant's mind, and independence relates to the circumstances surrounding the situation, such as financial, employment, business and personal relationships that affect the assurance provider in connection with the client or potential client.

1.1 Why do independence and objectivity matter so much?

Independence and objectivity matter because of the following.

- The **expectations** of those directly affected, particularly the members of the company. The audit should be able to provide **objective** assurance that the directors can never provide on the financial statements.

- The **public interest**. Companies are public entities, governed by rules requiring the disclosure of information.

Potential general threats to independence and objectivity were outlined in Chapter 14. We shall look at more specific threats in the next section.

What can the auditor do to preserve objectivity? The simple answer is to **withdraw from any engagement** where there is the **slightest threat** to objectivity. However, there are disadvantages in this strict approach.

- Clients may lose an auditor who knows their business.
- It denies clients the freedom to be advised by the accountant of their choice.

The better approach was set out in Chapter 14 too. It is to identify threats to independence, evaluate how significant they are and then apply safeguards if they are significant. We shall look in more detail at safeguards in the next section also.

2 Threats and safeguards

Section overview

- Examples of threats to independence and potential safeguards are given here, categorised by the main type of threat they represent. You should note that some matters can present several types of threat.

- Hard and fast rules are shown in bold.

This section is based on the ICAEW *Code of Ethics* and the FRC *Ethical Standard*. It examines a number of specific threats to independence on assurance engagements. They are outlined here, categorised by type of risk and appropriate safeguards. You should, however, note that certain issues fall into several types of threat, not simply one. Where this is the case, issues have been listed under the dominant threat but other threats are noted. Where relevant, rules relating to each threat are set out. We shall also look at how these risks might apply to particular situations, such as when considering whether to accept a new client.

2.1 Self-interest threat

The *Code of Ethics* highlights a great number of areas in which a self-interest threat might arise.

Figure 15.1: Self-interest threat

2.1.1 Financial interests

Definitions

Financial interest: An interest in equity or other security, debenture, loan or other debt instrument of an entity, including rights and obligations to acquire such an interest and derivatives directly related to such interest.

Direct financial interest: A financial interest:

- owned directly by and under the control of an individual or entity (including those managed on a discretionary basis by others); or

- beneficially owned through a collective investment vehicle, estate, trust or other intermediary over which the individual or entity has control, or the ability to influence investment decisions.

Indirect financial interest: A financial interest beneficially owned through a collective investment vehicle, estate, trust or other intermediary over which the individual or entity has no control or ability to influence investment decisions.

Immediate family: A spouse (or equivalent) or a dependent.

Assurance team:

(a) All members of the engagement team for the assurance engagement.
(b) All others within a firm who can directly influence the outcome of the assurance engagement.

A financial interest in a client constitutes a substantial self-interest threat. **The parties listed below are not allowed to own a direct financial interest or an indirect material financial interest in a client:**

- The **assurance firm**

- Any **partner** in the assurance firm

- Any **person in a position to influence** the conduct and outcome of the engagement (eg, a member of the assurance team)

- An **immediate family member of such a person**

The following safeguards will therefore be relevant:

- Disposing of the interest
- Removing the individual from the team if required
- Keeping the client's audit committee informed of the situation
- Using an engagement quality control reviewer to review work carried out if necessary

Assurance firms should have quality control procedures requiring staff to disclose relevant financial interests for themselves and immediate family members. They should also foster a culture of voluntary disclosure on an ongoing basis so that any potential problems are identified on a timely basis.

2.1.2 Close business relationships

A close business relationship will involve a common commercial interest, which in addition to a self-interest threat, could cause advocacy or intimidation threats and a perceived loss of independence.

Examples of when an assurance firm and an assurance client have an inappropriately close business relationship include:

- Operating a joint venture between the firm and the client, or between the firm and a director or other senior manager of the client

- Arrangements to combine one or more services or products of the firm with one or more services or products of the assurance client and to market the package with reference to both parties

- Distribution or marketing arrangements under which the firm acts as distributor or marketer of the assurance client's products or services or *vice versa*

- Other commercial transactions, such as the audit firm leasing its office space from the assurance client

Again, it will be necessary for the partners to judge the materiality of the interest and therefore its significance. However, **unless the financial interest is clearly immaterial and the relationship to the firm and its client clearly insignificant, an assurance provider should not participate in such a venture with an assurance client.** Appropriate safeguards are therefore to end the assurance provision or to terminate the (other) business relationship.

If an individual member of an assurance team had such an interest, he should be removed from the assurance team.

Generally speaking, **purchasing goods and services from an assurance client in the ordinary course of business on an arm's length basis does not constitute a threat to independence.** However, if there is a substantial number of such transactions, there may be a threat to independence and safeguards may be necessary.

The FRC *Ethical Standard* (section 2) states that for **audit clients and firms,** there should be no business relationships except for the purchase of goods and services in the ordinary course of business and on an arm's length basis, and which are not material or clearly inconsequential to either party.

2.1.3 Employment with assurance client

Dual employment (the same person being employed by both an assurance firm and a client) **is not permitted**.

It is also possible that staff might transfer between an assurance firm and a client, or that negotiations or interviews to facilitate such movement might take place. Both situations are a threat to independence:

- An assurance team member might be motivated by a desire to impress a future possible employer (objectivity is therefore affected)

- A former partner turned Finance Director has too much knowledge of the firm's systems and procedures

These sorts of situations can also present self-review, intimidation and familiarity threats. The extent of the threat to independence depends on various factors, such as the role the individual has taken up at the client, the extent of his influence on the assurance service previously, and the length of time that has passed between the individual's connection with the assurance service and the new role at the client.

Various safeguards may be considered:

- Modifying the assurance strategy

- Ensuring the assurance engagement is assigned to someone of sufficient experience as compared with the individual who has left

- Involving an additional professional accountant not involved with the engagement to review the work done

- Carrying out a quality control review of the engagement

There is a significant threat to objectivity if a partner of an audit firm accepts a key management position at a client of the firm.

The FRC *Ethical Standard* (section 2) states that when a **partner** leaves the firm and is appointed as a director or to a key management position with an audit client, having acted as audit engagement or independent/key partner in relation to that audit at any time in the previous two years, the firm should resign as auditors. The auditors should not reaccept appointment until two years have elapsed since that partner's involvement in the audit or the former partner leaves the audit client, if earlier.

When any other former member of an engagement team joins an audit client as director/key management within two years of being involved with the audit, the firm should consider whether the composition of the audit team is appropriate.

An individual who has moved from the firm to a client should not be entitled to any benefits or payments from the firm unless these are made in accordance with pre-determined arrangements. The individual should not continue to participate (or appear to) in the firm's business or professional activities. If money is owed to the individual, it should not be so much as to compromise the independence of the assurance engagement.

A firm should have quality control procedures setting out that an individual involved in serious employment negotiations with an audit client should notify the firm and that this person would then be removed from the engagement. In addition, the FRC *Ethical Standard* (section 2) states that a review of the employee's work on the current and, where appropriate, most recent audit should take place.

2.1.4 Partner on client board

A partner or employee of an assurance firm should not serve on the board of an assurance client. This can also cause a self-review and/or a management threat.

It may be acceptable for a partner or an employee of an assurance firm to perform the role of company secretary for an assurance client, if the role is essentially administrative.

2.1.5 Family and personal relationships

Definition

Close family: A parent, child or sibling who is not an immediate family member.

Family or close personal relationships between assurance firm and client staff could seriously threaten independence. Each situation has to be evaluated individually. Factors to consider are:

- The individual's responsibilities on the assurance engagement
- The closeness of the relationship
- The role of the other party at the assurance client

When an immediate family member of a member of the assurance team is a director, an officer or an employee of the assurance client in a position to exert significant influence over the subject matter information of the assurance engagement, the individual should be removed from the assurance team.

The firm should also consider whether there is any threat to independence if an employee who is not a member of the assurance team has a close family or personal relationship with a director, an officer or an employee of an assurance client.

A firm may wish to establish quality control policies and procedures under which staff should disclose if a close family member employed by the client is promoted within the client.

If a firm inadvertently violates the rules concerning family and personal relationships they should consider applying additional safeguards, such as undertaking a quality control review of the assurance engagement and discussing the matter with the audit committee of the client, if there is one.

2.1.6 Gifts and hospitality

Unless the value of gifts or hospitality are such that a reasonable and informed third party, weighing all the specific facts and circumstances, would consider them trivial and inconsequential, a firm or a member of an assurance team should not accept them.

Worked example: Receiving a benefit

Katie, a trainee at West LLP, chartered accountants, is attending the inventory count at Designs Limited, a company that manufactures fashion lines for a number of famous high street stores. During the course of the count, the stores manager tells Katie that after the inventory count, staff are entitled to purchase goods at cost to the value of £30 each. He invites her to take part in this company perk.

In this case, Katie has not been offered a gift, she has been invited to spend £30. However, the benefit that this would confer on her could be substantial. Given the customary mark ups in the fashion industry, cost price could be as low as 25% of ultimate selling price, so in effect, Katie would be receiving a benefit of £90. While this is likely to be immaterial and insignificant to the financial statements of Designs Limited, it could be significant to a trainee in an audit firm. Katie should certainly not accept any such offer without confirming with her engagement partner that it is appropriate to do so. She may be able to determine herself that the best course of action is not to accept the benefit.

In this case, a benefit of £90 is **not clearly insignificant**, and therefore Katie should decline the offer.

In addition, you should note that this practice could represent an audit risk, as it means that there will be inventory movements after the inventory count but before the end of the year, and unless there are strong controls over recording these sales, both inventory and sales could be misstated. Such a benefit to employees is unlikely to cause a material misstatement, but Katie should probably observe the controls over the sales and make a note of the practice for the audit file.

The FRC *Ethical Standard* (section 4) extends this prohibition to immediate family members or persons able to influence the audit and states that hospitality should not be accepted from an audit client unless it is reasonable in terms of its frequency, nature and cost.

2.1.7 Loans and guarantees

The advice on loans and guarantees falls into two categories:

- The client is a bank or other similar institution
- Other situations

If a **loan** or a guarantee of a loan is **made by an audit client which is a bank** (or other similar institution), then this is **not acceptable if the loan is not made under normal lending procedures** (ie, in the normal course of business).

If the **loan is made under normal lending procedures**, then this **is acceptable provided that appropriate safeguards are applied**. An example of a safeguard would be having the work reviewed by a professional accountant from a network firm that is neither involved with the audit nor received the loan.

If a **loan is made by a bank client to a member of the audit team under normal lending procedures**, then this **is acceptable and no safeguards are necessary**. An example of this would be if a member of the team had a home mortgage, bank overdraft, car loan or credit card with a bank client.

If a loan is made or guaranteed **by a client that is not a bank or other similar institution to either the firm or to a member of the audit team**, then **the self-interest threat created would be so significant that no safeguards could reduce the threat to an acceptable level**, unless the loan or guarantee is immaterial to both (a) the firm or the member of the audit team and the immediate family member, and (b) the client.

Finally, **if the firm, a member of the audit team or an immediate family member, makes or guarantees a loan to a client**, then **the self-interest threat created would be so significant that no safeguards could reduce the threat to an acceptable level**, unless the loan or guarantee is immaterial to both (a) the firm or the member of the audit team or the immediate family member, and (b) the client.

2.1.8 Overdue fees

In a situation where there are overdue fees, the assurance provider runs the risk of, in effect, making a loan to a client, whereupon the guidance above becomes relevant. The ICAEW Code states that, generally, the payment of overdue fees should be required before the assurance report for the following year can be issued.

Firms should guard against fees building up and being significant by discussing the issues with those charged with governance (more specifically, the audit committee), and, if necessary, the possibility of resigning if overdue fees are not paid.

2.1.9 Percentage or contingent fees

Definition

Contingent fee: A fee calculated on a predetermined basis relating to the outcome of a transaction or the result of the services performed by the firm. A fee that is established by a court or other public authority is not a contingent fee.

A firm shall not enter into any fee arrangement for an assurance engagement under which the amount of the fee is contingent on the result of the assurance work or on items that are the subject matter of the assurance engagement.

2.1.10 High percentage of fees

Definition

Public interest entity:

- a listed entity; and

- an entity (a) defined by regulation or legislation as a public interest entity or (b) for which the audit is required by regulation or legislation to be conducted in compliance with the same independence requirements that apply to the audit of listed entities. Such regulation may be promulgated by any relevant regulator, including an audit regulator.

A firm should be alert to the situation arising where the total fees generated by an assurance client represent a large proportion of a firm's total fees. Factors such as the structure of the firm and the length of time it has been trading will be relevant in determining whether there is a threat to independence. It is also necessary to beware of situations where the fees generated by an assurance client present a large proportion of the revenue of an individual partner.

Safeguards in these situations might include:

- Discussing the issues with the audit committee
- Taking steps to reduce the dependency on the client
- Obtaining external/internal quality control reviews
- Consulting a third party such as ICAEW

The Code states that where an audit client is a **public interest entity** and, for **two consecutive years**, the **total fees** from the client and its related entities represent **more than 15% of the total fees received by the firm** expressing the opinion on the financial statements of the client, the firm shall:

- Disclose this fact to those charged with governance of the audit client

- Carry out an engagement quality control review of the second year engagement, either before the audit opinion is issued (a 'pre-issuance review') or after it is issued (a 'post-issuance review')

If total fees significantly exceed 15%, then only a pre-issuance review may be sufficient.

The FRC *Ethical Standard* contains stricter requirements here. Section 4 of the *Ethical Standard* states that if total fees (audit and non-audit services) are expected to **regularly exceed 10%** of the annual fee income of the audit firm (**5% in the case of a listed company**) the audit engagement partners should **disclose that fact to the ethics partner and those charged with governance** of the audit client and consider whether appropriate safeguards should be applied to reduce the threat to independence. In the case of non-listed companies, an independent quality control review of the engagement should be undertaken before the report is signed. In the case of a listed client, the safeguards might be stricter, such as seeking to reduce non-audit work provided.

If total fees (audit and non-audit services) are expected to **regularly exceed 15% (10% for a listed entity)** of gross practice income, **the firm should not act as the auditors** of that entity, and should resign or refuse reappointment, as appropriate.

The FRC *Ethical Standard* also features a further requirement in relation to the total amount of fees received from non-audit services. For public-interest (listed) entities, **total fees from non-audit services must not exceed 70%** of the audit fee (or rather, of the average audit fee over the last three years).

It will be difficult for new firms establishing themselves to keep within these limits and firms in this situation should make use of the safeguards outlined above.

2.1.11 Lowballing

When a firm quotes a significantly lower fee level for an assurance service than would have been charged by the predecessor firm, there is a significant self-interest threat. If the firm's tender is successful, the firm must apply safeguards such as:

- Maintaining records such that the firm is able to demonstrate that appropriate staff and time are spent on the engagement

- Complying with all applicable assurance standards, guidelines and quality control procedures

The FRC *Ethical Standard* (section 4) observes that 'the audit engagement partner shall be satisfied and able to demonstrate that the audit engagement has assigned to it sufficient partners and staff with appropriate time and skill to perform the audit in accordance with all applicable Auditing and Ethical Standards, irrespective of the audit fee to be charged'.

The FRC *Ethical Standard* also states that the audit engagement partner should ensure audit fees are not influenced or determined by the provision of non-audit service to the audited entity.

As a result of the EU Audit Regulation (June 2016), a limit is also placed on the total fees received from non-audit services in comparison with the audit. The FRC *Ethical Standard* states that the total non-audit fees must be no more than 70% of the average audit fee from the last three years.

2.2 Self-review threat

Figure 15.2: Self-review threat

The key area in which there is likely to be a self-review threat is where an assurance firm provides services other than assurance services to an assurance client (providing multiple services). There is a great deal of guidance in the rules about various other services accountancy firms might provide to their clients, and these are dealt with below.

2.2.1 Service with an assurance client

Individuals who have been a director or officer of the client, or an employee in a position to exert direct and significant influence over the subject matter information of the assurance engagement in the period under review or the previous two years, should not be assigned to the assurance team. The FRC *Ethical Standard* (section 2) states that **the person should not be assigned to a position in which he or she is able to influence the conduct and outcome of the audit for two years following the date of leaving the audit client**.

Here the key threat is self-review where a member of the engagement team has to report on work they prepared originally, or elements of the financial statement they had responsibility for at the client, but there is also a risk of self-interest and familiarity threats.

The FRC *Ethical Standard* also covers the situation where audit staff are temporarily 'loaned' to a client which is forbidden unless it is not in a management position and the client acknowledges its responsibility for directing and supervising that work. The role should not include making management decisions or exercising discretionary authority to commit the client to a particular position or accounting treatment. The agreement should only be for a short period of time and should not result in the individual performing non-audit services that are disallowed under the FRC *Ethical Standard* (section 5). When an audit staff member returns to the firm after such a secondment, he should not be given a role in the audit involving any function or activity that he performed/supervised while at the client.

If an individual had been closely involved with the client prior to the time limits set out above, the assurance firm should consider the threat to independence arising and apply appropriate safeguards, such as:

- Obtaining a quality control review of the individual's work on the assignment
- Discussing the issue with the audit committee

2.2.2 Preparing accounting records and financial statements

There is clearly a significant risk of a self-review threat if a firm prepares accounting records and financial statements and then audits or reviews them.

On the other hand auditors routinely assist management with the preparation of financial statements and give advice about accounting treatments and journal entries.

Therefore, assurance firms must analyse the risks arising and put safeguards in place to ensure that the risk is at an acceptable level. Safeguards include:

- Using staff members other than assurance team members to carry out work

- Implementing policies and procedures to prohibit the individual providing such services from making any managerial decisions on behalf of the assurance client

- Requiring the source data for the accounting entries to be originated by the assurance client

- Requiring the underlying assumptions to be originated and approved by the assurance client

The rules are more stringent when the client is listed. The FRC *Ethical Standard* (section 5) states that **firms should not prepare accounts or financial statements for listed clients** (in the past there was an exception which allowed firms to prepare accounts in an 'emergency', but this has been removed).

The EU Audit Regulation (June 2016) reiterated this guidance by prohibiting auditors from bookkeeping, preparing accounting records or preparing financial statements for public interest entities.

2.2.3 Valuation services

Definition

Valuation comprises the making of assumptions with regard to future developments, the application of appropriate methodologies and techniques, and the combination of both to compute a certain value, or range of values, for an asset, a liability or for a business as a whole.

If an audit firm performs a valuation that will be included in financial statements audited by the firm, a self-review threat arises and also a management threat might arise.

The FRC *Ethical Standard* (section 5) states that **audit firms shall not carry out valuations which either:**

- **have a material effect on a listed company's financial statements, either separately or in aggregate with other valuations provided; or**

- **involve a significant degree of subjective judgement and have a material effect on the financial statements either separately or in aggregate with other valuations provided to any other audited entity.**

If the valuation is for an immaterial matter, the audit firm should apply safeguards to ensure that the risk is reduced to an acceptable level. Matters to consider when applying safeguards are the extent of the audit client's knowledge of the relevant matters in making the valuation and the degree of judgement involved, how much use is made of established methodologies and the degree of uncertainty in the valuation. Safeguards might include:

- Second partner review
- Confirming that the client understands the valuation and the assumptions used
- Ensuring the client acknowledges responsibility for the valuation
- Using separate personnel for the valuation and the audit

The EU Audit Regulation (June 2016) stated that **valuation services**, including those performed in relation to actuarial or litigation support services, are **prohibited for public interest entities**. This guidance is reflected in the FRC *Ethical Standard*.

2.2.4   Taxation services

The Code divides taxation services into four categories:

- Tax return preparation
- Tax calculations for the purpose of preparing the accounting entries
- Tax planning and other tax advisory services
- Assistance in the resolution of tax disputes

Tax return preparation does not generally threaten independence, as long as management takes responsibility for the returns.

Tax calculations for the purpose of preparing the accounting entities may not be prepared for public interest entities, except in emergency situations. For non-public interest entities, it is acceptable to do so provided that safeguards are applied.

Tax planning may be acceptable in certain circumstances eg, where the advice is clearly supported by a tax authority or other precedent. However, if the effectiveness of the tax advice depends on a particular accounting treatment or presentation in the financial statements, the audit team has reasonable doubt about the accounting treatment, and the consequences of the tax advice would be material, then the service should not be provided.

Assistance in the resolution of tax disputes may be provided, depending on whether the firm itself provided the service which is the subject of the dispute, and whether the effect is material on the financial statements. Safeguards include using professionals who are not members of the audit team to perform the service, and obtaining advice on the service from an external tax professional.

The audit firm:

- Provides advice to the audit client in one or more specific matters at the request of the client

- Undertakes a substantial proportion of the tax planning or compliance work for the audit client

- Promotes tax structures or products to the audit client, the effectiveness of which is likely to be influenced by the manner in which they are accounted for in the financial statements

The FRC *Ethical Standard* (section 5) observes that providing taxation services can cause self-review, self-interest, management and advocacy threats. **Safeguards** to mitigate these threats include:

- Tax services being provided by partners and staff with no involvement in the audit of financial statements

- Tax services being reviewed by an independent tax partner or senior tax employee

- Obtaining external independent advice on tax work

- Tax computations prepared by audit staff members being reviewed by a partner/staff member of appropriate experience who is not a member of the audit team

- An audit partner not involved in the audit engagement reviews whether the tax work has been properly and effectively addressed in the context of an audit of the financial statements

In addition, there are a number of rules set out in the FRC *Ethical Standard* (section 5).

The audit firm shall not:

- **Promote tax structures or products or undertake an engagement to provide tax advice to an audit client where the audit engagement partner has, or ought to have, reasonable doubt as to whether the relevant accounting treatment involved is based on established interpretations or is appropriate, having regard to the requirement for the financial statements to give a true and fair view in accordance with the relevant financial reporting framework**

- **Undertake an engagement to provide tax services to an audited entity wholly or partly on a contingent fee basis where the outcome of those tax services is dependent on the application of tax law which is uncertain or not yet established**

- **Undertake an engagement to provide tax services to an audited entity where the engagement would involve the audit firm undertaking a management role**

- **Undertake an engagement to prepare current or deferred tax calculations to an audited entity that is a listed entity or significant affiliate for the purpose of preparing accounting entries that are material to the relevant financial statements, with the exception of emergency situations**

- **Undertake an engagement to provide tax services to an audited entity where this would involve acting as an advocate, before an appeals tribunal or court in the resolution of an issue that is material to the financial statements or where the outcome of the tax issue is dependent on a future or contemporary audit judgement**

Finally, as a result of the EU Audit Regulation (June 2016) the following taxation services are prohibited in relation to auditors of public interest entities:

- Preparation of tax forms

- Payroll tax

- Customs duties

- Identification of public subsidies and tax incentives (unless support from the statutory auditor or the audit firm in respect of such services is required by law)

- Support regarding tax inspections by tax authorities (unless support from the statutory auditor or the audit firm in respect of such inspections is required by law)

- Calculation of direct and indirect tax and deferred tax

- Provision of tax advice

The FRC *Ethical Standard* (which implements this Regulation) does however state that if these services have no direct effect (or only an inconsequential effect) on the financial statements, then the services are not necessarily prohibited.

2.2.5 Internal audit services

Providing internal audit services to an audit client creates a **self-review threat** if the internal audit work is relied upon in the external audit. The **key issue is whether the audit firm's personnel assume a management responsibility**. If they do, then **the threat created would be so significant that no safeguards could reduce the threat to an acceptable level.**

Examples of internal audit services that involve assuming management responsibilities include:

- Setting internal audit policies
- Directing and taking responsibility for the actions of the entity's internal audit employees
- Deciding which recommendations resulting from internal audit activities shall be implemented
- Reporting the results of the internal audit activities to those charged with governance
- Performing procedures that form part of the internal control
- Taking responsibility for designing, implementing and maintaining internal control

Safeguards include ensuring that:

- The client designates an appropriate and competent resource to be responsible at all times for internal audit activities.

- The client's management reviews, assesses and approves the scope, risk and frequency of the internal audit services.

- The client's management determines which recommendations to implement and manages the implementation process.

The FRC *Ethical Standard* (section 5) states that the key threats in providing internal audit services are self-review and management. It states that **an audit firm shall not undertake to provide internal audit services to an audited entity where it is reasonably foreseeable that:**

- **for the purposes of the audit of the financial statements, the auditors would place significant reliance on internal audit work performed by the audit firm** (we will look at this situation more deeply in your Audit and Assurance paper); or

- **for the purposes of the internal audit services, the audit firm would undertake the role of management.**

The EU Audit Regulation (June 2016) also prohibited internal control or risk management services for auditors of public interest entities, where these are related to the accounting records or financial statements.

Worked example: Internal audit

Lee was recently seconded to the internal audit department of his accountancy firm. While on secondment, he carried out a month's internal audit service as part of a four man team at Whitecross plc, an audit client of the firm. He carried out routine controls testing while on this service. He helped to draft the final report to the board of directors at Whitecross, recommending several improvements to the system.

On return to the audit department six months later, Lee has been allocated to the audit team for Whitecross, for the year including the month when he carried out the internal audit service.

Lee should raise this with the training partner or the engagement partner for Whitecross, as it is likely to be a threat to independence if he takes part in this audit. He worked in the internal audit team and made reports to the directors in that capacity. This could form both self-interest (not wanting to discover any work he did was incorrect or inappropriate) and self-review (using work carried out by him to rely on for the audit opinion) threats.

2.2.6 Corporate finance services

Certain aspects of corporate finance services will create self-review threats that cannot be reduced to an acceptable level by safeguards. Therefore, **assurance firms are not allowed to promote, deal in or underwrite an assurance client's shares. They are also not allowed to commit an assurance client to the terms of a transaction or consummate a transaction on the client's behalf.**

Other corporate finance services, such as assisting a client in defining corporate strategies, assisting in identifying possible sources of capital and providing structuring advice may be acceptable, provided that safeguards, such as using different teams of staff, and ensuring no management decisions are taken on behalf of the client are in place.

Note that corporate finance services can also constitute an advocacy threat if the audit firm is representing the interests of the client.

The EU Audit Regulation (June 2016) **prohibited** – for **auditors of public interest entities** – services linked to the financing, capital structure and allocation of the audit client. This is unless these services have no consequential (material) effect on the financial statements.

2.2.7 Information technology services

The key threats in providing IT services, such as designing and implementing a new IT system, are self-review and management. The *Code of Ethics* states that in the case of **public interest entities**, the audit firm shall **not** design or implement IT services that:

- form a significant part of the internal control over financial reporting; or

- generate information that is significant to the financial statements on which the firm will express an opinion.

For **non-public interest entities**, these services may be provided if safeguards are put in place ensuring that:

- the client acknowledges its responsibility for establishing and monitoring a system of internal controls

- the client assigns the responsibility to make all management decisions with respect to the design and implementation of the hardware or software system to a competent employee, preferably within senior management

- the client makes all management decisions with respect to the design and implementation process

- the client evaluates the adequacy and results of the design and implementation of the system The client is responsible for operating the system (hardware or software) and for the data it uses or generates

Further safeguards would include using only personnel who are not on the audit team to provide the IT services, and having the audit or non-assurance work reviewed by a professional accountant.

2.2.8 Litigation support services

An example of a litigation support service is acting as an expert witness. Such services can cause self-review threats if they involve estimating damages or other amounts that affect the financial statements. In addition, management and/or advocacy threats may arise.

Hence the FRC *Ethical Standard* (section 5) forbids acceptance of litigation support services for listed audited entities that are listed or significant affiliates when the situation above exists. Litigation support services for non-listed entities that do not involve such subjective estimations are not prohibited, provided that appropriate safeguards have been implemented.

2.3 Advocacy threat

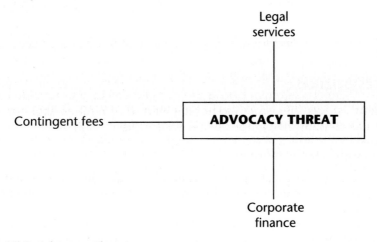

Figure 15.3: Advocacy threat

An advocacy threat arises in certain situations where the assurance firm is in a position of taking the client's part in a dispute or somehow acting as their advocate. The most obvious instances of this would be when a firm offered legal services to a client and, say, defended them in a legal case. The FRC *Ethical Standard* (section 5) forbids the provision of legal services to an audited entity where it would involve acting as the solicitor formally nominated to represent the audited entity in resolution of a dispute or litigation which is material to the financial statements. An advocacy threat might also arise if the firm carried out corporate finance work for the client; for example, if the audit firm were involved in advice on debt restructuring and negotiated with the bank on the client's behalf.

As with the other threats above, the firm has to appraise the risk and apply safeguards as necessary. Relevant safeguards might be using different departments in the firm to carry out the work and making disclosures to the audit committee. Remember, the ultimate option is always to withdraw from an engagement if the risk to independence is too high.

2.4 Familiarity threat

A familiarity threat is where independence is jeopardised by the audit firm and its staff becoming over familiar with the client and its staff. There is a substantial risk of loss of professional scepticism in such circumstances.

We have already discussed some examples of when this risk arises, because very often a familiarity threat arises in conjunction with a self-interest threat.

Figure 15.4: Familiarity threat

2.4.1 Long association of senior personnel with assurance clients

It can be a significant threat to independence if senior members of staff at an audit firm have a long association with a client. All firms should therefore monitor the relationship between staff and established clients and use safeguards to independence such as rotating senior staff off the assurance team and involving engagement quality control reviews. Where appropriate safeguards cannot be applied, the firm should resign.

The requirements of the FRC's *Ethical Standard* are stricter in this area that those of the *Code of Ethics*.

Worked example: Long association

Peter has been the audit engagement partner for Santa Ltd for a number of years. During that time, he has formed a friendly relationship with the finance director, to the point that on occasion, usually at client hospitality days organised by the firm, but sometimes not, he might play a round of golf with the FD or attend a dinner function with him and his wife.

There is a risk of a familiarity threat here, particularly if the relationship is growing closer and more personal as time evolves. Peter should monitor this situation and request a review of the audit file by an engagement quality control reviewer to ensure that the risk is not too significant for the audit firm. Alternatively, the audit firm might decide that it would be better to 'rest' Peter from this engagement for a period of time to ensure that independence was not affected, if the firm were confident that this would not affect the professional relationship between the firm and Santa Ltd.

The *Code of Ethics* sets out general provisions for **all audit engagements**. These state that when an audit engagement partner has held that role for a continuous period of 10 years in relation to a non-public interest client, careful consideration must be given as to whether a reasonable and informed third party would consider the firm's objectivity and independence to be impaired. If that individual is still not rotated, alternative safeguards should be put in place, the reason for lack of rotation should be documented, and the facts should be communicated with those charged with governance.

For **public interest entities**, the *Code of Ethics* has more stringent rules. The FRC *Ethical Standard* (section 3) states these as follows.

- **No one shall act as the audit engagement partner for more than five years.**

- **Anyone who has acted as the audit engagement partner for a period of five years, shall not subsequently participate in the audit engagement until a further period of five years has elapsed.**

However, there may be circumstances in which it is necessary to be flexible about rotation of the audit engagement partner or audit quality control reviewer in relation to the audit of a public interest entity. If the audit committee of the audited entity decides that flexibility is necessary to safeguard the quality of the audit (and the audit firm agrees), then the audit engagement partner may continue in the role for **two more years**. This might happen for example where:

- Substantial change has recently been made or will soon be made to the nature or structure of the audited entity's business

- There are unexpected changes in the senior management of the audited entity

In such situations, alternative safeguards should be applied such as an expanded review of the work by an engagement quality control reviewer.

The FRC *Ethical Standard* (section 3) then goes on to specify the following rules for engagement quality control reviewers:

- **No one should act as the engagement quality control reviewer for a continuous period longer than seven years.**

- **Where the engagement quality control reviewer becomes the audit engagement partner the combined service in these two positions should not exceed seven years.**

- **People who have held these positions for seven years (continuously or in aggregate) should not return to them for at least five years.**

Staff in senior positions and other partners who have been responsible for significant affiliates should be reviewed by the audit engagement partner where they have been involved in the audit of a public interest entity for a continuous period exceeding seven years. Safeguards should be applied such as the removal of members of staff from, or the rotation of roles within, the engagement team.

When an audited entity becomes a listed company, the length of time the audit engagement partner has been involved should be taken into consideration. The engagement partner should only continue in the position for another two years where four or more years have already been served by that individual.

2.4.2 Recruitment

Recruiting senior management for an assurance client, particularly those able to affect the subject matter of an assurance engagement creates management, familiarity, self-interest and intimidation threats.

Assurance providers must not make management decisions for the client. Their involvement could be limited to drawing up a shortlist of candidates, providing that the client has drawn up the criteria by which they are to be selected, and makes the final decision in respect of who to hire.

The FRC *Ethical Standard* (section 5) states that an audit firm should not undertake an engagement to provide recruitment services in relation to a key management position of the audited entity (or significant affiliate of such) for a **listed** entity.

2.5 Intimidation threat

An intimidation threat arises when members of the assurance team have reason to be intimidated by client staff.

Figure 15.5: Intimidation threat

These are also examples of self-interest threats discussed in section 2.1, largely because intimidation may only arise significantly when the assurance firm has something to lose.

2.5.1 Actual and threatened litigation

The most obvious example of an intimidation threat is when the client threatens to sue, or indeed sues, the assurance firm for work that has been done previously. The firm is then faced with the risk of losing the client, bad publicity and the possibility that they will be found to have been negligent, which will lead to further problems. This could lead to the firm being under pressure to produce an unqualified audit report when they have been qualified in the past, for example.

Generally, assurance firms should seek to avoid such situations arising. If they do arise, factors to consider are:

- the materiality of the litigation
- the nature of the assurance engagement
- whether the litigation relates to a prior assurance engagement

The following safeguards could be considered:

- Disclosing to the audit committee the nature and extent of the litigation
- Removing specific affected individuals from the engagement team
- Involving an additional professional accountant on the team to review work

However, if the litigation is at all serious, it may be necessary to resign from the engagement, as the threat to independence is so great. The FRC *Ethical Standard* (section 4) requires a firm to not continue with/accept an engagement where the threat of litigation is anything other than insignificant, however it is not required to resign immediately in circumstances where a reasonable and informed third party would not regard it in the interests of the shareholders for it to do so.

The EU Audit Regulation (June 2016) states that legal services are prohibited in the case of audits of public interest entities.

2.6 Management threat

The management threat is identified in the FRC *Ethical Standard* rather than in ICAEW Code. A management threat arises when the audit firm undertakes work involving making judgements and taking decisions that are the responsibility of management. There is a significant cross-over with self-review threat here, and, as we have already seen, assurance providers are forbidden to take decisions on behalf of management, therefore this risk should be removed by avoiding situations or not accepting engagements where the client is asking the assurance firm to take management decisions.

An important factor in whether a management threat exists is whether there is 'informed management' at the client.

Definition

Informed management is where the auditors believe that the member of management designated by the audit client to receive the results of a non-audit service provided by the auditor has the capability to make independent management judgements and decisions on the basis of the information provided.

If there is informed management, it is possible that safeguards can be effective to avoid a management threat or reduce it. If there is not, it is unlikely management threat can be avoided. For example, consultancy services are generally acceptable where there is informed management and the auditors do not take management decisions.

Interactive question 1: Type of threat

In each of the following cases, indicate the principal threat that the assurance firm is facing.

(a)　Peter Perkins recently resigned as finance director of Assiduous Limited. Peter joined the assurance firm that provides the audit to Assiduous after his notice period of six months.

(b)　Artifice Limited has suggested to the engagement partner that a qualified audit report would be unacceptable in the current year because the company is considering a flotation.

(c)　Anonymous Limited has requested that the audit team should not be changed from the previous year as they got on well with client staff.

See **Answer** at the end of this chapter.

2.7　Accepting new clients

We outlined the issues relating to accepting new clients in Chapter 2. We stated that auditors must consider any ethical issues that might be a bar to acceptance. Any of the ethical issues outlined above could constitute a barrier to acceptance. In addition, the assurance firm must consider whether there appear to be any factors at the client that could be a threat to the firm's integrity or professional behaviour. These are likely to arise from:

- illegal activities of the client
- apparent dishonesty of the client
- questionable accounting practices of the client

It may not be possible to reduce these risks, in which case, the assurance service should be declined. However, some safeguards, such as obtaining a commitment from those charged with governance to improving corporate governance, might be sufficient to make acceptance possible.

Interactive question 2: Engagement acceptance

Notable LLP is a small assurance firm that has been asked to take on the statutory audit of the following two companies. For each of the companies, indicate on what basis the audits could be accepted, if at all.

Notorious Limited is a small company that has had a number of HMRC investigations in recent years. The company has had to pay a number of back taxes where incorrect figures had been declared. Recently a director was banned from being a director for five years for wrongful trading. This person has left Notorious and a new managing director has been appointed, who has intimated to the firm that improved corporate governance is at the top of his agenda.

☐　Do not accept

☐　Accept with safeguards

☐　Accept with no safeguards

Pristine plc is a listed company that has good references from all parties whom the firm made enquiries of. It has requested that Notable LLP both prepare and audit the financial statements. It does not feel that these services are divisible.

☐ Do not accept

☐ Accept with safeguards

☐ Accept with no safeguards

See **Answer** at the end of this chapter.

3 Resolving ethical conflicts

Section overview

- The ICAEW Code sets out a framework for professional accountants to follow when faced with an ethical conflict.

- It is generally better to resolve conflicts 'in-house' than to refer to external bodies, although that option is always available and ICAEW has an ethical helpline.

The ICAEW Code sets out a framework that professional accountants can follow when seeking to resolve ethical problems. It states that the professional accountant should consider:

- the relevant facts
- the relevant parties
- the ethical issues involved
- the fundamental principles related to the matter in question
- established internal procedures
- alternative courses of action

The accountant should then consider which is the course of action that most aligns with the fundamental principles.

If the accountant cannot determine the best course of action himself, he should refer it to the relevant department within his firm for more advice.

It is generally better for firms to come to conclusions 'in-house', but if needs be, further advice can be sought from ICAEW.

This is a useful structure for you to use when considering ethical problems in the assessment. Think about the facts, parties, issues and fundamental principles involved and try and see the best course of action. Remember that as a trainee, referral to a more senior member of staff may be your most appropriate course of action.

Interactive question 3: Audit trainee issues

You are a trainee in the audit department of Harris Brothers LLP. You have recently started your training, have not attended any courses and have attended one audit, where you carried out some simple audit tests under the audit senior's supervision.

An audit manager has asked you to attend the inventory count of Brox Bros, which has a large amount of inventory, which is subject to an annual inventory count. There are very few other controls over the inventory at Brox Bros. Inventory is highly material to Brox Bros' financial statements. No other audit staff will be attending the inventory count.

Which of the following is the most appropriate course of action for you to take:

☐ Perform the work

☐ Refer to training partner

☐ Contact ICAEW

See **Answer** at the end of this chapter.

---

4 Conflicts of interest for the accountant

Section overview

- An accountant in industry may face more pressure to behave unethically at times.

- The accountant should evaluate the threats that such pressures bring.

- Safeguards might include:
    - obtaining advice
    - using a formal dispute resolution process at work
    - seeking legal advice

In this section we will consider the problem that an accountant employed by someone other than a practice of other accountants might face if the needs of his professional duty and his employer conflict. This is less likely to be a problem for accountants in practice, as their employers or partners will be bound by the same professional duties as them, but in industry, employers might not understand the importance and nature of an accountant's professional duty.

The *Code of Ethics* gives advice to accountants in such conflicting situations.

It is important to remember that accountants in a non-practice environment are subject to the same fundamental principles as accountants in practice. However, an accountant in business (as opposed to practice) may find that he is faced with implicit or explicit pressure to:

- act contrary to law or regulation

- act contrary to technical or professional standards

- facilitate unethical or illegal earnings management strategies

- lie to or mislead auditors or regulators

- issue or be associated with published reports (for example, financial statements, tax statements) that materially misrepresent the facts

The accountant in question should evaluate the threats that such situations bring (for example, the accountant may face severe intimidation and self-interest threats if he could lose his job by not complying). Available courses of action should be applied as follows:

- First, resolve internally (if possible) using a formal dispute resolution process or audit committee (if the employing organisation has one)

- Second, obtain advice from ICAEW

- Third, seek legal advice

- As a last resort, resign

Interactive question 4: Conflict of interest

Imo is a qualified accountant. She has recently moved out of practice and taken up the position of financial controller of a small, unlisted company, Lavender Lane Limited. The company has a short-term cash flow problem.

Imo was recently called into the board meeting and asked if she could defer some income from the previous financial year so as to influence when the tax (both VAT and corporation tax) would be due on those sales. The directors were insistent that such deferral was necessary and that she should consider this request more in the nature of an order.

Which **two** of the following possible courses of action are likely initially to be the most appropriate in this situation?

☐ Report her concerns to the audit committee of the board of directors

☐ Seek advice from ICAEW

☐ Take steps in line with the company's formal dispute resolution process

☐ Take advice from her legal advisors

☐ Resign her job

See **Answer** at the end of this chapter.

Summary and Self-test

Summary

Assurance providers are required to work with intergrity, objectivity and independence

Integrity is being straightforward and honest

Objectivity is the state of mind that has regard to all relevant considerations but no others

Independence is the outward circumstances that surround integrity and objectivity and could affect them, or appear to affect them – for example, the relationships between client and firm

Objectivity and independence may be threatened by various factors which fall into the following general categories of threat

Self-interest

Advocacy

Self-review

Intimidation

Familiarity

Management

The ICAEW Code of Ethics recommends a framework for resolving ethical conflicts, and recommends that such conflicts be dealt with 'in house' before reference is made ultimately to ICAEW

The same concept can be applied to resolving conflicts between an employer and employee's professional duties. The employee should consider:
- Raising concerns with senior staff members/audit committee
- Resolving the problem through company dispute resolution procedures
- If necessary, seeking legal advice or further advice from ICAEW

Self-test

Answer the following questions.

1   Match the ethical principle with the right description.

(a)   Integrity

(b)   Objectivity

(i)   Not allow bias, conflicts of interest or undue influence of others to override professional or business judgements.

(ii)   Be straightforward and honest in all business and professional relationships.

2   The IESBA *Code of Ethics* applies only to statutory audits.

☐   True

☐   False

3   Fill in the blanks.

In general, the recurring work paid by the client or group of connected clients should not regularly exceed .... % of the firm's annual fee income.

In the case of.. companies, the figure should be 10% of the firm's annual fee income.

4   Which of the following services would it be least appropriate for a firm to carry out for an audit client?

A   Preparation of tax computation
B   Provision of tax advice
C   Provision of internal audit services
D   Preparation of the financial statements for a public interest entity

5   Audit engagement partners of listed companies should be rotated away from the engagement:

A   After 2 years
B   After 5 years
C   After 7 years
D   After 10 years

6   Justine, who is audit senior on the in progress audit of Wedding Planner plc, has recently placed her CV with a recruitment agent. She has had no feedback from the agent, with whom she has a meeting on Friday. The agency is currently carrying an advert for financial controller at Wedding Planner plc, but the advert does not give the company's name.

This represents:

A   A self-interest threat
B   An intimidation threat
C   A management threat
D   No threat

7   An ethical conflict should never be referred outside of the assurance firm for advice in relation to resolving that conflict.

☐   True

☐   False

8   When an accountant is faced with a conflict between professional duty and duty to his employer, he should always seek legal advice.

☐   True

☐   False

Now, go back to the Learning Objectives in the Introduction. If you are satisfied you have achieved these objectives, please tick them off.

Answers to Interactive questions

Answer to Interactive question 1

(a) Self-review

(b) Intimidation

(c) Familiarity (however, unless any of the members of the team have been on the team for a significant period of time or have close personal relationships with any client staff, this risk is probably insignificant)

Answer to Interactive question 2

Notorious Limited could be accepted with safeguards. The key safeguard is that the managing director has expressed an intention of improving corporate governance. This safeguard would be strengthened if the audit firm obtained this intention from him in writing.

Pristine plc should not be accepted. This is because the self-review threat associated with preparing the accounts and then auditing them for a listed company is considered too great.

Answer to Interactive question 3

You should refer this matter to the training partner. You have no experience or training to undertake this work. The risks attaching to the audit tests being carried out are high. The person allocating the work must have allocated you in error.

Answer to Interactive question 4

It is unlikely to be appropriate to make disclosure to the audit committee in this case, as Lavender Lane Limited, a small, unlisted company, is unlikely to have one. Given the instructions have come from the board of directors, it will be fruitless to take steps in line with the company's formal dispute resolution process. Thus, resolving the situation internally is not possible in this situation.

Imo should seek advice from ICAEW and then take advice from her legal advisors. Resigning her job is not an initial option and should only take place if the other options have been unsuccessful.

CHAPTER

15

Integrity, objectivity and independence   283

1   (a)   (ii)

    (b)   (i)

2   False – it applies to all assurance services

3   15, listed/public interest

4   D   Preparation of financial statements for a listed company as this brings a significant self-review threat and is rarely acceptable

5   B   As laid down by the FRC Ethical Standard (section 3)

6   D   There is currently no threat. If Justine were aware that she was being put forward for a job at an audit client, then she would be faced with a self-interest threat, as she might want to impress client staff to the detriment of doing her job properly

7   False – however, external referral should be seen as a last option

8   False – it may not be necessary to seek legal advice unless failure to make a disclosure would constitute a criminal offence. The matter may be resolved internally.

CHAPTER 16

Confidentiality

Introduction
Examination context
Topic List
    1   Importance of confidentiality
    2   Safeguards to confidentiality
    3   Disclosure of confidential information
Summary and Self-test
Answer to Interactive question
Answers to Self-test

Introduction

Learning objectives

Tick off

- Understand the nature and importance of confidentiality

- Recognise risks to confidentiality

- Identify steps to prevent accidental disclosure of information

- Understand when information may be disclosed

- Understand when information must be disclosed

Specific syllabus references for this chapter are: 4i, j, k.

Syllabus links

These matters will all be considered again in Audit and Assurance, and in particular, the topical and practically challenging issue of money laundering regulations will be looked at in more detail at the higher level.

Examination context

Two of the ten ethics questions in the sample paper touched on confidentiality.

In the assessment, candidates may be required to:

- determine an appropriate course of action in a situation where confidentiality is a potential issue
- identify situations in which confidential information may be disclosed

1 Importance of confidentiality

Section overview

- Confidentiality is a fundamental ethical principle.

- Client information must be kept confidential unless there is a genuine exception to this requirement.

- Confidentiality is important as it is a key factor in the trust between client and accountant.

Confidentiality is a fundamental principle of both the IESBA and ICAEW *Codes of Ethics*, as set out in Chapter 14.

Accountants are required to keep client information confidential. This is an important aspect of the trust between client and accountant, as, to do their job, accountants require access to information about their business that clients would not want made public externally to the business, and, in some cases, such as where it relates to pay or future intentions of the directors, internally to the business either.

In practice this means that an accountant should not discuss client matters with anyone outside the firm of accountants, and, in cases where there is a conflict of interest with another audit client, with anyone outside of the team assigned to that client.

It is appropriate to discuss client matters, where necessary, with other members of staff from the firm; for example, an audit team member may have to *liaise* with a member of the tax department over client affairs, but in general it is better to keep discussions about client affairs to when they are professionally necessary, not merely as gossip.

This is because the greatest risk of breach of confidentiality is likely to be accidental disclosure rather than deliberate disclosure. It is unlikely that an accountant or a firm would make a deliberate disclosure of client information (under the exceptions to the duty of confidentiality noted below) without having taken legal advice and making very sure that it is appropriate to do so. A greater risk of breach of confidentiality is by accidental disclosure (talking about client affairs in the wrong place or leaving client information exposed accidentally).

2 Safeguards to confidentiality

Section overview

- There is probably a greater risk of accidental disclosure of information than of inappropriate deliberate disclosure.

- Accountants should follow a number of security procedures to prevent accidental disclosure.

- Accountants should always confer with senior staff members when they have a concern that a disclosure is required.

There is probably a greater risk of accidental disclosure of information that is confidential within the business than external to the business. Such risk arises where client staff members are exposed to confidential information by overhearing audit staff conversations or by seeing documents that would normally be kept away from them.

However, there is also a risk of information passing outside the business if assurance providers work on a different client's file at another client's premises, or by losing or leaving files unprotected (for example, in a car, which might be stolen) or through lack of electronic controls (for example, by computer hacking).

The following security procedures are probably wise to prevent accidental disclosure of information:

- Do not discuss client matters with any party outside of the accountancy firm (for example, friends and family, even in a general way).
- Do not discuss client matters with colleagues in a public place.
- Do not leave audit files unattended (at a client's premises or anywhere).
- Do not leave audit files in cars or in unsecured private residences.
- Do not remove working papers from the office unless strictly necessary.
- Do not work on electronic working papers on systems that do not have the requisite protection.

In addition, to prevent unauthorised deliberate disclosures of information:

- raise concerns with more senior staff in the firm (or the MLRO, see section 3.1)
- seek legal advice before making any disclosures of potentially confidential information

Worked example: Accidental disclosure of information

Kat is a trainee in the audit department of Fox Brothers & Co. She is working on the audit of Candleworks Limited. Kat is driving to work with two of the audit files in locked cases in the boot of her car. She stops at a petrol station to buy petrol and goes into the petrol station to pay for the petrol. During that time, her car is stolen. When it is found, the cases are missing.

Later that day, Kat arrives at Candleworks Limited and begins work on a different part of the audit file. She leaves the office unattended and unlocked and goes to the toilet. During that time, the purchase ledger clerk goes into the audit office and reviews the payroll. She later raises a complaint with the pay department that the sales ledger clerk earns more than she does.

Kat has breached two simple security measures in this scenario, which has resulted in confidentiality being breached twice.

3 Disclosure of confidential information

Section overview

- Accountants may be compelled by law or consider it desirable in the **public interest** to disclose details of clients' affairs to third parties.

Information acquired in the course of professional work should **only be disclosed** where:

- **consent has been obtained** from the client, employer or other proper source;
- there is a **public duty** to disclose; or
- there is a **legal** or **professional right or duty** to disclose.

The *Code of Ethics* identifies three circumstances where the professional accountant is or may be required to disclose confidential information:

- Where disclosure is permitted by law and is authorised by the client or the employer, for example where the auditor has uncovered a fraud and the client is in agreement that the matter should be referred to the police.

- Where disclosure is required by the law.

  Examples include:

  - Reporting clients involved in terrorist activities to the police
  - Reporting directly to regulators such as the Financial Services Authority on regulatory breaches in respect of financial service and investment businesses or the Charity Commission in respect of charities
  - The reporting of suspected money laundering (for example tax evasion) to the National Crime Agency

In making such a report, an auditor is not deemed to have broken the confidence of the client. It is normally addressed by setting out the auditor's right to disclose in the engagement letter.

- Where there is a professional duty or right to disclose, when not prohibited by law. An accountant may defend himself in a negligence claim, for example. The *Code of Ethics* states that a professional accountant may disclose confidential information to third parties if the disclosure can be justified in 'the public interest' and is not contrary to laws and regulations.

Difficult judgements are required by auditors as to whether the 'public interest' overrides the duty of confidentiality. Usually, the assurance providers should take legal advice on the matter.

A professional accountant acquiring or receiving confidential information in the course of his or her professional work should neither use, nor appear to use, that information for his or her personal advantage or for the advantage of a third party.

Examples of particular circumstances are:

- On a change in employment, professional accountants are entitled to use experience gained in their previous position, but not confidential information acquired there.

- A professional accountant should not deal in the shares of a company in which the member has had a professional association at such a time or in such a manner as might make it seem that information obtained in a professional capacity was being turned to personal advantage ('insider dealing').

- Where a professional accountant has confidential information from Client 1 that affects an assurance report on Client 2 he cannot provide an opinion on Client 2 that he already knows, from whatever source, to be untrue. If he is to continue as auditor to Client 2 the conflict must be resolved. In order to do so, normal audit procedures/enquiries should be followed to enable that same information to be obtained from another source. Under no circumstances, however, should there be any disclosure of confidential information outside the firm.

3.1 Money laundering

Accountants are subject to laws concerning money laundering, which make it a criminal offence not to disclose a suspicion of money laundering (the process by which criminals attempt to conceal the proceeds of crime). In addition, it is an offence to let a suspected money launderer know that an investigation may be taking place against him.

Therefore, accountants must report suspicions of money laundering to the appropriate authority, and this disclosure will not constitute a breach of confidentiality. In addition, they should not advise the client that they have done so.

Firms must have a Money Laundering Reporting Officer (MLRO), who will be responsible for making such disclosures. Therefore, trainees and staff carrying out assurance work must make a report to that MLRO when a suspicion of money laundering arises.

Each firm must have an MLRO, so an audit team member will never be required to make a report to the authorities personally. It will always be appropriate for him to make the report of the suspicion to the MLRO, and having made a report to the MLRO is a defence against the criminal offence of failing to report a suspicion of money laundering.

Examples of money laundering in this context could include (but are not limited to):

- keeping customer overpayments (theft?)

- offences under the Companies Act that are criminal (such as making a loan to a director – so that the director is in possession of the proceeds of the company's crime)

- offences that involve a saved cost (such as failure to meet environmental regulations about disposal and dumping waste instead)

The following issues therefore may give rise to suspicions of money laundering:

- Credits on the receivables ledger
- Unusual related party transactions
- Lack of expected costs in income statement

- The existence of a complicated group structure with no obvious business reason for the complexity
- High number of cash transactions without genuine business reason

Worked example: Money laundering

Jim is carrying out some assurance work in connection with sales at Trying Ltd. He discovers that the owner of the business, who is also the MD, regularly collects cash from customers in respect of sales. In such cases, neither the sale nor the receipt is included in the accounting records of Trying Ltd.

This allows him to bypass accounting for VAT or corporation tax on these sales, so it constitutes money laundering. Jim must therefore report this issue to the MLRO of his firm.

3.2 Conflicts of interest

Situations are frequently perceived by clients as 'conflicts of interest' where in reality they involve no more than concerns over keeping information confidential. Hence the issues of confidentiality covered in sections 1 and 2 and conflicts of interest are related.

The Code states that firms should have in place procedures to enable them to identify whether any conflicts of interest exist and to take all reasonable steps to determine whether any conflicts are likely to arise in relation to new assignments involving both new and existing clients.

If there is no conflict of interest, firms may accept the assignment. If there is a conflict of interest, the significance of any threat to compliance with the fundamental principles should be evaluated. If any threats are other than clearly insignificant, the safeguards must be applied to eliminate the threat or to reduce it to an acceptable level.

There is nothing improper in a firm having two clients whose interests are in conflict provided that the activities of the firm are managed so as to avoid the work of the firm on behalf of one client adversely affecting that on behalf of another.

Where a firm believes that a conflict can be managed, sufficient disclosure should be made to the clients or potential clients concerned, together with details of any proposed safeguards to preserve confidentiality and manage conflict. If consent is refused by the client then the firm must not continue to act for one of the parties.

Where a conflict cannot be managed even with safeguards, then the firm should not act.

A self-interest threat to the objectivity of a professional accountant or his firm will arise where there is or is likely to be a conflict of interest between them and the client or where confidential information received from the client could be used by them for the firm's or for a third party's benefit.

The test to apply is whether a reasonable and informed observer would perceive that the objectivity of the member or his firm is likely to be impaired. The member or his firm should be able to satisfy themselves and the client that any conflict can be managed with available safeguards.

Safeguards might include:

- disclosure of the circumstances of the conflict
- obtaining the informed consent of the client to act
- the use of confidentiality agreements signed by employees
- establishing information barriers ('Chinese walls', see below)
- regular review of the application of safeguards by a senior individual not involved with the relevant client engagement
- ceasing to act

Information barriers, traditionally known as Chinese walls, include:

- ensuring that there is no overlap between different teams
- physical separation of teams
- careful procedures for where information has to be disseminated beyond a barrier and for maintaining proper records where this occurs

Some commentators argue that the term 'Chinese walls' is culturally insensitive and disrespectful of the ability of the Great Wall of China to keep China's enemies at bay. However the term is in common use and likely to remain so for some time in the future.

Interactive question: Confidentiality

During the course of an assurance engagement, Aleem, a member of the assurance team from Goose Brothers & Co discovers that Dave Milton, the owner of D Manufacturing Limited, has told certain customers to write cheque payments out in favour of DM, rather than the full company name. Mr Milton has then been amending the cheques to read D Milton, and paying them into his personal account rather than the company's, reducing the company's overall tax liability.

Requirement

Which **one** of the following is the most appropriate action for Aleem to take in respect of this matter?

A   Discuss the matter with the client and advise him of the legal position
B   Report the matter to HM Revenue and Customs
C   Obtain the client's permission to report the matter to the MLRO within the firm
D   Report the matter to the MLRO within the firm

See **Answer** at the end of this chapter.

Summary and Self-test

Summary

Assurance providers must comply with the fundamental principle to keep client affairs confidential

They should take basic security precautions, such as:
- Not leaving assurance files unattended
- Not leaving assurance files in cars
- Not working on client files on unprotected computers
- Not talking about assurance clients to parties outside the assurance firm
- Not talking about assurance work in a public place

There are occassions when it is appropriate to make disclosures of client information:
- With client permission
- When required to by law (for example, when money laundering is suspected)
- In accordance with auditing standards, such as ISA 250A
- To protect a member's interests
- In the public interest
- When compelled by process of law

Assurance providers should generally seek legal advice when making disclosures to ensure that they are made appropriately

Self-test

Answer the following questions.

1   The principle of confidentiality is the duty to keep client affairs secret in all circumstances.

   ☐ True

   ☐ False

2   Which **one** of the following actions would not be recommended with regard to securing professional confidence?

   A   Keeping assurance files locked up
   B   Carrying out audit work at client premises
   C   Discussing client affairs on the telephone at a different client
   D   Discussing client affairs in the firm's office

3   If an ICAEW trainee is asked for information about a client by the police, which **four** of the following actions would be appropriate?

   ☐ Asking his training partner for advice

   ☐ Seeking legal advice

   ☐ Ringing the ICAEW ethics line for advice

   ☐ Answering the police without taking further action

   ☐ Asking the police what authority they have to ask him

   ☐ Asking the client if he may talk to the police

4   (a)   Which of the following are legitimate reasons for breach of client confidentiality?

   (i)   Auditor **suspects** client has committed treason
   (ii)   Disclosure **needed** to protect auditor's own interests
   (iii) Information is **required** for the auditor of another client
   (iv)   Auditor **knows** client has committed terrorist offence
   (v)   There is a **public duty** to disclose
   (vi)   Auditor **considers** there to be non-compliance with laws and regulations
   (vii) Auditor **suspects** client has committed fraud

   (b)   Of the above reasons, which are voluntary disclosures and which are obligatory disclosures?

5   Explain what is meant by the term 'Money Laundering Reporting Officer'.

Now, go back to the Learning Objectives in the Introduction. If you are satisfied you have achieved the objectives, please tick them off.

Answer to Interactive question

D   The appropriate thing is to make a report to the MLRO. C is inappropriate, because it could constitute a crime to warn Dave Milton that a report has been made about his money laundering. A is therefore also inappropriate. B might be an appropriate act, but it is better practice for assurance team members always to make reports to the MLRO and let them take responsibility for determining whether a report should be made.

1   False. There are recognised exceptions to the principle of confidentiality

2   C   This is potentially harmful to the client's confidentiality; the others are sensible security measures

3   Asking his training partner for advice, seeking legal advice, ringing the ICAEW ethics line for advice and seeking more information from the police about the nature of the enquiry would all be sensible approaches. The trainee should not talk to the police until he was certain that it would not breach his duty of confidentiality to do so, and although while in theory getting the client's permission would solve the problem, it is possible this could constitute a criminal offence, depending on the nature of the police enquiries, so it is better not to do this until more information has been obtained

4   (a)   Option (iii) is not a legitimate breach of confidentiality. All of the other options may be legitimate breaches in some situations.

    (b)   (i)   Obligatory
           (ii)   Voluntary
           (iv)   Obligatory
           (v)   Voluntary
           (vi)   Obligatory in some cases. The auditor must check/take legal advice about what his duties are.

    (Note: In the case of (vii), the auditor should not take action outside the company until he is certain. When he is certain, he should seek legal advice.)

5   The Money Laundering Reporting Officer is the nominated official in the audit firm through whom disclosures of money laundering suspicions should be made. There should not be a need for other individuals in the firm to make reports direct to the appropriate authority, as having made a report to the MLRO is a defence against the criminal offence of failure to report a suspicion of money laundering

Glossary of terms

Analytical procedures	Evaluations of financial information through analysis of plausible relationships among both financial and non-financial data. Analytical procedures also encompass such investigation as is necessary of identified fluctuations or relationships that are inconsistent with other relevant information or that differ from expected values by a significant amount.
	They include consideration of comparisons of the entity's financial information with other information, and the consideration of relationships among elements of financial information that would be expected to conform to a particular pattern or between financial information and relevant non-financial information.
Anomaly	A misstatement or deviation that is demonstrably not representative of misstatements or deviations in a population.
Application controls	Manual or automated procedures that typically operate at a business process level. Application controls can be preventative or detective in nature and are designed to ensure the integrity of the accounting records. Accordingly, application controls relate to procedures used to initiate, record, process and report transactions or other financial data.
Appropriateness	The measure of the quality or relevance and reliability of the audit evidence
Assurance engagement	An engagement in which a practitioner expresses a conclusion designed to enhance the degree of confidence of the intended users other than the responsible party about the outcome of the evaluation or measurement of a subject matter against criteria.
Assurance team	(a) All members of the engagement team for the assurance engagement.
	(b) All others within a firm who can directly influence the outcome of the assurance engagement.
Audit documentation (working papers)	The record of procedures performed, relevant evidence obtained and conclusions the auditor reached.
Audit evidence	Information used by the auditor in arriving at the conclusions on which the auditor's opinion is based.
Audit of financial statements	The objective is to enable the auditor to express an opinion whether the financial statements are prepared, in all material respects, in accordance with an applicable financial reporting framework.
Audit plan	An audit plan is more detailed than the strategy and sets out the nature, timing and extent of audit procedures (including risk assessment procedures) to be performed by engagement team members in order to obtain sufficient appropriate audit evidence.
Audit risk	The risk that the auditor expresses an inappropriate audit opinion when the financial statements are materially misstated. Audit risk is a function of the risks of material misstatement and detection risk.
Audit sampling	The application of audit procedures to less than 100% of items within a population of audit relevance such that all sampling units have a chance of selection in order to provide the auditor with a reasonable basis on which to draw conclusions about the entire population.
Audit strategy	The formulation of the general strategy for the audit, which sets the scope, timing and direction of the audit and guides the development of the audit plan.
Audit trail	A stream of evidence that permits the tracing of a transaction forward from its inception to the appropriate ledger accounts or to vouch from the ledger account to the inception of the transaction.

Business risk	A risk resulting from significant conditions, events, circumstances, actions or inactions that could adversely affect an entity's ability to achieve its objectives and execute its strategies, or from the setting of inappropriate objectives and strategies.
Close family	A parent, child or sibling who is not an immediate family member.
Contingent fee	A fee calculated on a predetermined basis relating to the outcome of a transaction or the result of the services performed by the firm. A fee that is established by a court or other public authority is not a contingent fee.
Control activities	The policies and procedures that help ensure that management directives are carried out.
Control environment	The control environment includes the governance and management functions and the attitudes, awareness and actions of those charged with governance and management concerning the entity's internal control and its importance in the entity. The control environment sets the tone of an organisation, influencing the control consciousness of its people.
Control risk	The risk that a misstatement that could occur in an assertion about a class of transaction, account balance or disclosure and that could be material, either individually or when aggregated with other misstatements, will not be prevented, or detected and corrected, on a timely basis by the entity's internal control.
Data analytics	When used to obtain audit evidence in a financial statement audit, data analytics is the science and art of discovering and analysing patterns, deviations and inconsistencies, and extracting other useful information in the data underlying or related to the subject matter of an audit through analysis, modelling and visualisation for the purpose of planning and performing the audit.
Detection risk	The risk that the procedures performed by the auditor to reduce audit risk to an acceptably low level will not detect a misstatement that exists and that could be material, either individually or when aggregated with other misstatements.
Direct financial interest	A financial interest: • Owned directly by and under the control of an individual or entity (including those managed on a discretionary basis by others); or • Beneficially owned through a collective investment vehicle, estate, trust or other intermediary over which the individual or entity has control, or the ability to influence investment decisions.
Entity's risk assessment process	A component of internal control that is the entity's process for identifying business risks relevant to financial reporting objectives and deciding about actions to address those risks, and the results thereof.
Error	An unintentional misstatement in financial statements, including the omission of an amount or a disclosure.
Fair	Information is free from discrimination and bias in compliance with expected standards and rules. The accounts should reflect the commercial substance of the company's underlying transactions.
Financial interest	An interest in equity or other security, debenture, loan or other debt instrument of an entity, including rights and obligations to acquire such an interest and derivatives directly related to such interest.
Financial statement assertions	Representations by management, explicit or otherwise, that are embodied in the financial statements, as used by the auditor to consider the different types of potential misstatements that may occur.

Fraud	An intentional act by one or more individuals among management, those charged with governance, employees, or third parties, involving the use of deception to obtain an unjust or illegal advantage.
General controls	Policies and procedures that relate to many applications and support the effective function of application controls by helping to ensure the continued proper operation of information systems.
Immediate family	A spouse (or equivalent) or a dependent.
Independence	Freedom from situations and relationships that make it probable that a reasonable and informed third party would conclude that objectivity either is impaired or could be impaired.
Independence in appearance	The avoidance of facts and circumstances that are so significant that a reasonable and informed third party would be likely to conclude, weighing all the specific facts and circumstances, that a firm's, or a member of the assurance team's, integrity, objectivity or professional scepticism has been compromised.
Independence of mind	The state of mind that permits the expression of a conclusion without being affected by influences that compromise professional judgement, allowing an individual to act with integrity, and exercise objectivity and professional scepticism.
Indirect financial interest	A financial interest beneficially owned through a collective investment vehicle, estate, trust or other intermediary over which the individual or entity has no control or ability to influence investment decisions.
Information system relevant to financial reporting	A component of internal control that includes the financial reporting system, and consists of the procedures and records established to initiate, record, process and report entity transactions (as well as events and conditions) and to maintain accountability for the related assets, liabilities and equity.
Informed management	Where the auditors believe that the member of management designated by the audit client to receive the results of a non-audit service provided by the auditor has the capability to make independent management judgements and decisions on the basis of the information provided.
Inherent risk	The susceptibility of an assertion about a class of transaction, account balance or disclosure to a misstatement that could be material, either individually or when aggregated with other misstatements, before consideration of any related controls.
Integrity	This means that an accountant must be straightforward and honest. It implies fair dealing and truthfulness.
Internal audit function	An appraisal activity established or provided as a service to the entity. Its functions include, amongst other things, examining, evaluating and monitoring the adequacy and effectiveness of internal control.
Internal control	The process designed, implemented and maintained by those charged with governance, management, and other personnel to provide reasonable assurance about the achievement of an entity's objectives with regard to reliability of financial reporting, effectiveness and efficiency of operations and compliance with applicable laws and regulations. The term "controls" refers to any aspects of one or more of the components of internal control.
Limited assurance	A meaningful level of assurance, that is more than inconsequential but is less than reasonable assurance, that engagement risk has been reduced to an acceptable level, which then allows a conclusion to be expressed negatively.

Management	The person(s) with executive responsibility for the conduct of the entity's operations. For some entities in some jurisdictions, management includes some or all of those charged with governance, for example, executive members of a governance board, or an owner-manager.
Materiality	An expression of the relative significance or importance of a particular matter in the context of financial statements as a whole. The IFRS *Conceptual Framework for Financial Reporting* states that a matter is material if its omission or misstatement could influence the economic decisions of users taken on the basis of the financial statements.
Misstatement	A difference between the amount, classification, presentation, or disclosure of a reported financial statement item and the amount, classification, presentation, or disclosure that is required for the item to be in accordance with the applicable financial reporting framework. Misstatements can arise from error or fraud.
Non-sampling risk	The risk that the auditor reaches an erroneous conclusion for any reason not related to sampling risk. For example, the use of inappropriate procedures, or misinterpretation of audit evidence and failure to recognise a misstatement or deviation.
Non-statistical sampling	A sampling approach that does not have the characteristics of statistical sampling (see entry for statistical sampling).
Objectivity	A state of mind that excludes bias, prejudice and compromise and that gives fair and impartial consideration to all matters that are relevant to the task in hand, disregarding those that are not.
Performance materiality	The amount or amounts set by the auditor at less than materiality for the financial statements as a whole to reduce to an appropriately low level the probability that the aggregate of uncorrected and undetected misstatements exceeds materiality for the financial statements as a whole.
Population	The entire set of data from which a sample is selected and about which an auditor wishes to draw conclusions.
Professional judgement	The application of relevant training, knowledge and experience in making informed decisions about the courses of action that are appropriate in the circumstances of the audit engagement.
Professional scepticism	An attitude that includes a questioning mind, being alert to conditions which may indicate possible misstatement due to error or fraud, and a critical assessment of audit evidence.
Public interest entity	A listed entity; and
	An entity (a) defined by regulation or legislation as a public interest entity or (b) for which the audit is required by regulation or legislation to be conducted in compliance with the same independence requirements that apply to the audit of listed entities. Such regulation may be promulgated by any relevant regulator, including an audit regulator.
Reasonable assurance	A high level of assurance, that is less than absolute assurance, that engagement risk has been reduced to an acceptably low level, which then allows a conclusion to be expressed positively.
Sampling risk	The risk that the auditor's conclusion based on a sample may be different from the conclusion if the entire population were subjected to the same audit procedure.
Sampling units	The individual items constituting a population.

Statistical sampling	An approach to sampling that has the following characteristics:
	(a) random selection of the sample items; and
	(b) the use of probability theory to evaluate sample results, including measurement of sampling risk.
Substantive procedures	Audit procedures designed to detect material misstatements at the assertion level. Substantive procedures comprise:
	• Tests of detail (of classes of transactions, account balances and disclosures)
	• Substantive analytical procedures
Sufficiency	The measure of the quantity of audit evidence.
Tests of controls	Audit procedures designed to evaluate the operating effectiveness of controls in preventing, or detecting and correcting material misstatements at the assertion level.
Tolerable misstatement	A monetary amount set by the auditor in respect of which the auditor seeks to obtain an appropriate level of assurance that the monetary amount set by the auditor is not exceeded by the actual misstatement in the population.
Tolerable rate of deviation	A rate of deviation from prescribed internal control procedures set by the auditor in respect of which the auditor seeks to obtain an appropriate level of assurance that the rate of deviation set by the auditor is not exceeded by the actual rate of deviation in the population.
True	Information is factual and conforms with reality, not false. In addition the information conforms with required standards and law. The accounts have been correctly extracted from the books and records.
Valuation	A combination of the making of assumptions with regard to future developments, the application of appropriate methodologies and techniques, and the combination of both to compute a certain value, or range of values, for an asset, a liability or for a business as a whole.
Vouching	Matching entries in the accounting records to supporting documentation.
Walk-through procedure	A procedure that involves tracing a few transactions through the financial reporting system.
	Walk-through procedures would normally be performed near the start of the field-work stage of the audit. They involve tracing transactions from the very beginning to the very end, in order to confirm that the auditor has correctly understood how the controls are supposed to operate. Walkthrough procedures aim to test the auditor's understanding, and are not tests of controls.

Index

Notes

Notes

Notes

Notes

Notes

Notes

Notes

REVIEW FORM – ASSURANCE STUDY MANUAL

Your ratings, comments and suggestions would be appreciated on the following areas of this Study Manual.

	Very useful	*Useful*	*Not useful*
Chapter Introductions	☐	☐	☐
Examination context	☐	☐	☐
Worked examples	☐	☐	☐
Interactive questions	☐	☐	☐
Quality of explanations	☐	☐	☐
Technical references (where relevant)	☐	☐	☐
Self-test questions	☐	☐	☐
Self-test answers	☐	☐	☐
Index	☐	☐	☐

	Excellent	*Good*	*Adequate*	*Poor*
Overall opinion of this Study Manual	☐	☐	☐	☐

Please add further comments below:

Please return completed form to:
The Learning Team
Learning and Professional Department
ICAEW
Metropolitan House
321 Avebury Boulevard
Milton Keynes
MK9 2FZ
E learning@icaew.com